What People Are Saying About David Parsons and *Floodgates*...

If you have ever wondered what Jesus meant by this saying, *"But as the days of Noah were, so also will the coming of the Son of Man be,"* then *Floodgates* is the book for you. David Parsons gives a masterful explanation, with in-depth review of Scripture, archeology and history. At the end of the book, you will have the answers you need to know if we are now living in the days of the coming of the Son of Man.

—*Gordon Robertson*
CEO, The Christian Broadcasting Network

Floodgates is a must-read for everyone who wants to understand the times in which we live. David Parsons combines his deep knowledge and balanced approach to Scripture with unique historical insights. The connection he draws between Hitler's Nazism and Social Darwinism should be studied in every school and university today. This book is an excellent tool that will help keep the Church from repeating the mistakes of the past and prepare for the trials ahead.

—*Dr. Jürgen Bühler*
President, International Christian Embassy Jerusalem

In a season of violent, cataclysmic change, we desperately need a God-perspective to maintain our bearings. David Parsons provides just such a perspective in his new book *Floodgates*. His message is a welcome and necessary reminder of the choices before us. David has provided a timely message, rooted in Scripture and filled with hope for those who can receive.

—*Allen Jackson*
Senior Pastor, World Outreach Church, Murfreesboro, TN

Floodgates is a gripping, face-slapping, wake-up call for all to reevaluate our global mind-set and spiritual downgrade. With the aid of Scripture and prophetic writings, we are amazed to observe that human behavior has little changed or improved through the passage of time. Sadly, a selfish and pridefully sin-tolerant generation now teaches in our schools, floods our universities and governs many nations. The floodgates are open! This new book by David Parsons proves, through illustrations and biblical applications, that abandonment of God's holiness and divine plan brings destruction—whether it be an ancient worldwide Flood or a modern genetic modification program threatened by egocentric madmen. Floodgates gives solid, informed answers to existential questions, and feeds a delectable flow of Scripture and words of wisdom from the world's great minds. Read it and share!

—*Dr. Michael Little*
President Emeritus, Christian Broadcasting Network
Chairman, National Religious Broadcasters

Floodgates provides a timely, refreshing and welcome contribution to the end-times debate. With a redemptive theme throughout, sterling scholarship and a penetrating analysis of the days in which we live, David Parsons gives this current generation the tools to understand our times and be like the biblical Sons of Issachar who "knew what to do." With his legal background, he chronicles the moral slide of our age, yet his biblical perspective shows the way of escape. I highly recommend this excellent, easy-to-read and first in a series of books which Parsons is writing to recognize the prophetic signs of the times.

—*Chris Mitchell*
Middle East Bureau Chief, CBN News, Jerusalem, Israel

Convinced! Over a span of forty-two years, I have read differing views about the biblical "giants" of Genesis 6 and numerous other passages, but I have never read anything as well researched and convincing as the material put forth in this book by David Parsons. He delves into this puzzling antediluvian question and gives thoroughly biblical answers that are theologically sound and prophetically relevant. I read *Floodgates* in one sitting and then read it again. It is a must-read for every serious Bible student!

—*Tony Crisp, PhD*
Lead Pastor, Eastanallee Church, Riceville, TN
Director, Strategic Initiatives, International Christian Embassy
Jerusalem–USA

David Parsons is uniquely qualified to understand major historical trends in relation to the present-day unfolding of biblical prophecy. From Jerusalem, at the crossroads of the world's spiritual and political currents, he tracks the development of humanistic understanding in alignment with God's warnings of judgment. David writes with the ease of a gifted communicator. His book, *Floodgates*, is a wake-up call for those who are watching the signs of the times, and a ray of hope to those who are waiting for the Lord's redemption.

—*Peter Tsukahira*
Author and international speaker
Cofounder, Carmel Congregation, Israel

Seldom will you read an author who can communicate such a combination of insights as is found in *Floodgates*. David Parsons shows us why the story of Noah's Flood is becoming increasingly relevant to our generation and how it parallels our modern world. But, as usual, he also snaps into place many prophetic puzzle pieces about Israel, the Jewish people and the end of the age. Get ready for numerous "aha moments"!

—*Jerry Dirmann*
Senior Pastor, The Rock, Anaheim California

DAVID R. PARSONS

FLOOD GATES

Recognize the End-Time Signs to Survive the Coming Wrath

WHITAKER
HOUSE

FLOODGATES:
Recognize the End-Time Signs to Survive the Coming Wrath

David R. Parsons
P.O. Box 1192
Jerusalem 9101002, Israel
david.parsons@icej.org

ISBN: 978-1-64123-032-2
eBook ISBN: 978-1-64123-034-6
Printed in the United States of America
© 2018 by David R. Parsons

Whitaker House
1030 Hunt Valley Circle
New Kensington, PA 15068
www.whitakerhouse.com

Library of Congress Cataloging-in-Publication Data (Pending)

1 2 3 4 5 6 7 8 9 10 11 ⨈ 25 24 23 22 21 20 19 18

For my mother,
Loretta JoAnn Parsons,
who contended for my calling.

"In the six hundredth year of Noah's life,…all the fountains of the great deep burst open, and the floodgates of the sky were opened."
—Genesis 7:11 (NASB)

*"But as the days of Noah were,
so also will the coming of the Son of Man be."*
—Matthew 24:37

CONTENTS

FOREWORD

The saga of Noah has gripped our imaginations for centuries, especially children. The story has everything a fairytale should. There is a big boat that rescues animals and people, a mysterious hero who claims to speak for God, a world that laughs at his warning of a coming flood, and a global deluge, followed by a happy ending framed with a rainbow. What more could you ask for? It is not surprising that many seemingly wise people have discounted the story as mere legend. Even Bible scholars have joined this bandwagon. Unbelief is always camouflaged in "clever speak." But when it comes to the Bible, history—coupled with archaeology—has taught us to be careful about what we dismiss as fable. There is indeed compelling evidence that the ark of Noah did exist, and has been seen by many reliable witnesses over the centuries on Mount Ararat!

Still, the most important testimony to the reality of the Flood comes from Jesus, who spoke of it as a real historic event and warned of a similar cataclysm in the last days, saying:

> And as it was in the days of Noah, so it will be also in the days of the Son of Man: they ate, they drank, they married wives, they were given in marriage, until the day that Noah entered the ark, and the flood came and destroyed them all.   (Luke 17:26–27)

For Jesus, the story of Noah is no myth but absolute fact, and we would do well to heed its warning.

This remarkable book, *Floodgates*, by my dear friend David Parsons, unravels the events of the *"days of Noah"* so we can better understand our modern world and the perils to come. Based on careful research and keen biblical insights, Parsons draws the curtain on Noah's day and exposes all the ungodly and even demonic influences that led that generation to destruction. God will not allow evil to triumph, and when it becomes epidemic, He will carry it away in divine judgment—not a popular theme today, but a necessary one for us to pay attention to.

Jesus asserted that the days before His return would descend into depravity, just as took place in Noah's day. Parsons exposes how this "parallel plunge" is already occurring today—and one of the great catalysts for it has been Darwin's theory of evolution, because it has rejected God as Creator and glorified man as the center of all things. The fruit of this ungodly theory is rotten to the core! This development, coupled with the restoration of Israel in her ancient homeland, is a sure sign that we must heed Jesus's warning about Noah's generation.

Floodgates is timely, persuasive, and worthy of study. I have worked closely with the author for many years, and I know that this book has been on his heart for a long time. It is with much admiration for him that I commend this very important volume to you. It will open your eyes to biblical truth, strengthen your faith, and inspire you to draw close to God through Jesus Christ.

—*Malcolm Hedding*
Executive Director Emeritus
International Christian Embassy Jerusalem

INTRODUCTION: A TALE OF TWO SHIPS

"It was the best of times, it was the worst of times, it was the
age of wisdom, it was the age of foolishness, it was the epoch of
belief, it was the epoch of incredulity, it was the season of Light, it
was the season of Darkness, it was the spring of hope, it was the
winter of despair,…we were all going direct to Heaven, we were
all going direct the other way."
—Charles Dickens, *A Tale of Two Cities*[1]

"*He changes the times and the seasons;*
He removes kings and raises up kings."
—Daniel 2:21

A s time marches on, we like to divide history into distinct periods. The setting for Charles Dickens's novel *A Tale of Two Cities* was a time of transition from one era to another. A relative calm prevailed over

Europe in the early nineteenth century, following the bloody French Revolution, while the Industrial Revolution was just getting underway. It was a moment marked by boundless optimism and yet also deep foreboding about the future.

Giving voice to the optimism of that day, Georg Wilhelm Friedrich Hegel boldly declared the "end of history"—by which he meant that societies were irreversibly moving toward universal adoption of the liberal ideals of liberty, equality, and fraternity.[2] The age of kings and clerics ruling by divine right would soon end, giving way to democracy and secularism. Yet, in Britain, Dickens also saw the harsh toll of industrialization on the masses, especially hapless women and children. Thus, the tense paradox of his novel's opening lines.

In 1989, Princeton philosopher Francis Fukuyama also declared the "end of history" in an attention-grabbing essay in the *National Interest*. He contended that the Soviet Union's imminent collapse meant the competing ideologies that had dominated human history were now converging in the triumph of liberal democracy and market-oriented economies. Hopefully, the end of the Cold War spelled the end of major conflicts worldwide.[3]

However, in another *National Interest* essay ten years later, Fukuyama confessed to having spoken prematurely, saying that we have not reached the end of history because we have not reached the end of science.[4] With an even more buoyant outlook, he assessed that we are just starting to tap into the amazing potential that modern technologies and biomedical advances hold for humanity. He expanded on this theme in his book *Our Posthuman Future*, which explores the intriguing world of biotechnology and the transformation it will soon bring to mortal man.[5]

No doubt, we now live in a time of extreme paradoxes. There is immense hope and yet great trepidation about the future. Decades ago, President John F. Kennedy noted a similar stark contrast in his memorable inaugural address, cautioning that "man holds in his mortal hands the power to abolish all forms of human poverty and all forms of human life."[6] Today, the Cold War may be over, but the daily news remains filled with stories of violence and terror worldwide, especially with the rise of radical Islam. Besides the fear that jihadists might resort to using weapons of mass destruction, there also are growing concerns about global warming, pandemics, and other serious threats. Much of this foreboding centers on the same march of science and technology that gives us such bright hope for the future. Indeed, climate change and viral epidemics are widely considered man-made threats. So, can we survive our own harmful devices long enough to reach that beckoning age in which technology and biomedical advances bring us unimagined ease, unlimited knowledge, unassailable health, unprecedented longevity, and universal bliss? Or will we fall prey to some global catastrophe of our own making?

The Bible actually has much to say about the ages of man. It claims that there are indeed distinct times and seasons (see Daniel 2:21), that God governs these epochs and has even predetermined them (see Acts 17:26), and that there truly will be an "end of history"—in the sense that we will soon reach the end of *"this present evil age"* (Galatians 1:4; see also 1 Corinthians 10:11). It also speaks of the paradox of hope and despair that will mark the end of this current age. We are assured that an eternal paradise awaits those who put their trust in God, but only after a time of sudden darkness and wrath upon those in rebellion against Him. (See, for example, Isaiah 60:1–2.)

Many people are fascinated by these biblical prophecies about the coming end of the age, also referred to as *the apocalypse*, or the unveiling of the messianic age. Hollywood jumped on the bandwagon long ago and has produced an endless stream of movies with Armageddon themes and dark, post-apocalyptic worlds. The studios and production companies know these themes sell! Meanwhile, there is a whole cottage industry of Christian books about the end times. Most of them tend to cram every bad thing predicted in the Bible into the seven-year period at the very end of the age known as the Great Tribulation, while shedding little new light on events leading up to that turbulent time.

In this book, I set out to break new ground in our understanding of the prophetic Scriptures. In particular, *Floodgates* widens the lens to reveal what will transpire before we reach those last seven years. The moment the world enters the Tribulation will be self-evident, but what about the period leading up to it? What can be gleaned from Scripture about the signs indicating we are edging closer to that day? Again, it turns out the Bible has much to say in this regard.

God is sovereign, and He still decides when kingdoms rise and fall. He appoints the times and epochs of man, and knows their end from their start. Further, God has an "end game"—a precise strategy for how He wants to bring this age to a close. And the Bible provides a very clear picture of this end game by reference to two major events in the past, both of which serve as analogies or models for the end of days. One is the "days of Noah," and the other is the Exodus from Egypt. These paradigms from biblical history actually roll back the curtain on our times in amazing ways. Thus, this book deals with the Flood of Genesis as a full analogy for the end of days—and the analogy is more complete than most people realize. A follow-up book will reveal how the Exodus also serves as a profound parallel for the end of the age.

We are dealing here with typology, in which Bible passages cite past episodes as precedents for future events. Sometimes the biblical writers drew clear analogies, such as Paul describing Adam as a *"type"* of Christ (see Romans 5:14), or the festivals and Sabbaths of Israel as *"a shadow of things to come"* (see Colossians 2:16–17). Another common typology involves prophetic passages that say a future day will be "like" a certain past day or event. (See, for example, Zechariah 12:11.)

A third typology uses subtle allusions to past events to anticipate things to come. Accordingly, the Hebrew prophets employed a number of Flood allusions to portend the close of this age. Several New Testament figures—including Jesus—also point directly to the Flood as a paradigm for the end of days. Jesus is recorded on two separate occasions as saying that *"as the days of Noah were, so also will the coming of the Son of Man be"* (Matthew 24:37; see also Luke 17:26). The apostles Peter, John, Paul, and Jude also draw upon the Flood analogy, making it one of the most prevalent typologies for the end times in Scripture.

In the chapters that follow, we will explore the various passages of Scripture that shed light on the pre-Flood world and why God chose to destroy all life on earth, save for a small remnant of humans and animals. And we will apply those insights to our contemporary world to answer the critical question of whether a countdown to destruction is happening all over again. Ultimately, we will find that the parallels between that dramatic historical episode and our contemporary times are inescapable. The moral slide of Noah's day is being repeated in nearly every respect. We may think we are on the brink of transforming our world and our own mortal bodies through science and technology, but we are actually regressing and in serious peril of God's wrath.

I certainly am not the first to cite the Flood analogy as a dire warning for our day if we do not repent. But I go beyond that. Instead, I make the case that the grave moral slide happening all around us today is a sign that God has already decided to judge the world. That is, we are already living in the "days of Noah"—meaning the divine waiting period between God's decree that man's days are numbered and His actual execution of that divine judgment. (See, for example, Genesis 6:3; 1 Peter 3:20.) This point is a core aspect of the Flood analogy. God has reached a verdict and is now simply letting the rebellion that is bound in man's heart ripen to His just judgment. For some time now, He has been storing up His wrath for a wayward and unsuspecting world. Repentance might temporarily postpone this inevitable judgment, but we will never cancel it. In the legal profession, we call that *res judicata*—a matter adjudicated with no further avenue of appeal.

It is my contention that the broad acceptance of Darwinian evolutionary thought—and particularly its refutation of the divine origins of man—was a major turning point in human history, and its dire consequences for our world have yet to play out in full. To start with, it provided a scientific veneer for Nazi eugenics and the atrocities of the Holocaust. On-demand abortion, the growing acceptance of homosexuality, and the rise of militant atheism are all fruits of this profound moral and intellectual blunder. Additionally, it is now driving biomedical advances that are tampering with our very nature as human beings. Above all, Darwinism has provided mankind with an excuse, a scientific pretext, for walking away from God, thereby producing a mounting rebellion against our Creator that will soon draw His extreme wrath.

There are many remarkably close similarities between today's moral descent and that of the ancient world destroyed by the Flood. In addition, there is an incredible parallel today, seen in the phenomenal growth of the Evangelical movement worldwide (including Pentecostal and charismatic believers), to Noah and his family, the righteous remnant that God brought through the Deluge and used to make a fresh start upon the earth. Finally, just as the building of the ark served as the most visible, unmistakable sign to the pre-Flood world that they were about to be judged, there is a similar unavoidable sign in the earth today that the end of the age is near—that sign is the building up of Zion, meaning the modern-day restoration of Israel.

What makes all this even more astounding is that each of these three developments has been running parallel to the others over the past century or so. The mainstream acceptance of Darwinian evolution, the explosive growth in Evangelical ranks, and the movement to restore Israel all date to around the year 1900, and they have been marching in lockstep ever since. Further, these historic trends are amazingly interconnected. And they are all foretold in Scripture.

Floodgates aims to set a new paradigm for determining where we are on the prophetic timetable. There is great need today, as well as great hunger, for solid prophetic truths. This is especially true among millennials, who are not buying into the standard old prophecy charts, as their parents once did. Here, we have another framework for approaching the end times that sheds much-needed light on our current world, while standing on the firm ground of the actual teachings of Jesus and the apostles. An objective look at this material will allow you to see, as never before, the reality and nature of God, His dealings with mankind, and the fate that soon awaits the world.

I hope this book serves as an effective warning, to as many as will heed it, that the "floodgates" of God's wrath will soon open—though in a different form this time. This is a fearsome but unavoidable truth. Yet those who refuse to join the rebellion against God, and instead remain faithful to Him, will be preserved as a righteous remnant in the earth and enter together into that glorious age to come.

Truly, it is the best of times and the worst of times. But unlike the setting in the famous Dickens novel, not all of us are going directly to heaven, nor are we all going directly the other way. Each of us has a clear choice to make about which one will be our ultimate destiny. And rather than a tale of two cities, this book is more of a "tale of two ships." One was a primitive ark, built and captained by a humble man who feared and obeyed God and thus was able to save his family and all the animal world from destruction, to serve as the genesis for a new age. The other was a sailing ship named the HMS *Beagle*, which carried a young naturalist named Charles Darwin around the globe on a voyage of discovery that gave birth to his atheistic theory of evolution. The irony of Darwin is that although he cared for humans, animals, and nature, the godless ideologies he inspired have actually helped consign the world to destruction. By the end of this book, you will need to decide which ship you would rather be on, as it could determine your eternal destiny.

PART ONE
THE FLOOD OF NOAH

1

THE DIVINE NATURE

"God is the only comfort, He is also the supreme terror: the thing
we most need and the thing we most want to hide from."
—C. S. Lewis, *Mere Christianity*[1]

"*The* Lord *has made all for Himself, yes,*
even the wicked for the day of doom."
—Proverbs 16:4

Growing up on the Outer Banks of North Carolina, I lived through many a hurricane. Some scored direct hits on our fragile barrier islands—wreaking havoc, cutting new inlets, and scattering the summer tourists. Others bounced harmlessly off Cape Hatteras and headed for the open Atlantic, leaving behind epic swells for us local surfers. The strongest hurricanes felt like freight trains rushing right over my head for hours. Yet the temporary calm at the eye of the storm also gave me butterflies due to the extremely low pressure. So I developed a real love/hate relationship with these tropical monsters.

Hurricanes were not the only storms we faced, and many years, they were not even the worst ones. That distinction belonged to northeasters—powerful winter storms that can pound the whole Eastern seaboard for days at a time. Because their winds have such a broad fetch over an extended period of time, northeasters produce massive waves that erode the shoreline through several high tides, causing extensive damage right along the beachfront. Still, these storms have a good side, as well; for example, we would go beachcombing afterward and find many interesting items washed ashore by the sea. Once, we came upon a formerly buried shipwreck, now exposed by the pounding surf.

My earliest childhood memory is of one such gale—the "Ash Wednesday Storm" of March 7, 1962. My family lived right on the ocean at my grandfather's fishing pier in Nags Head. My grandfather was awakened early that morning by huge breakers crashing over his house. The bone-chilling winds were gusting over a hundred miles per hour, blasting us with snow and sand as we huddled into several cars trying to flee the tempest. But our vehicles stalled out as the onslaught of ocean waves broke through the dune line and flooded the beach road—our only route of escape.

Still a small child, I can remember holding myself up to the car window and looking out to sea. There in the darkness was one rolling wall of whitewater after another, lined up like steps and marching relentlessly toward us. Thanks to a brave local man with an all-terrain truck, we were rescued from the swirling waters. But my grandfather's home and pier were completely lost. By the next day, an Associated Press wire photo of him had gone nationwide—a grim-faced Irishman, with tears in his eyes, standing in the empty space where his house once stood. But my granddad rebuilt his fishing pier—just as he always had. In the eight years he owned that pier, it was severely damaged by hurricanes or northeasters six times. Yet he always rebuilt.

Because of such childhood memories, I tend to bristle whenever someone says a certain storm or natural disaster is a divine judgment on some community or nation for their sins. The truth is that hurricanes are natural phenomena that lash out at both the just and the unjust. So I am always cautious about assigning God credit or blame for the tragedies caused by nature. That just gets too personal for me. As a young attorney, I even balked at drafting *force majeure* clauses into business contracts, which let a party off the hook for "acts of God."

Yet some people are quick to link natural disasters to particular sins they think have riled the Almighty. And the occasions for doing so are strangely on the rise lately. In 2010, for instance, an Icelandic volcano shrouded Europe in ash and temporarily grounded all flights over the continent; at the same time, apocalyptic floods drowned large swaths of Australia, and bizarre wildfires choked Moscow for weeks, killing an estimated fifteen thousand people. The next year, Hurricane Sandy slammed into New York City, while Japan was staggered by a massive earthquake and tsunami. Such rumblings have everyone wondering about the bizarre behavior of nature. It is global warming? El Niño? What about solar flares? Or is God really upset? And are these natural disasters signs of the end times?

Among Christians today, there seem to be two extremes on such questions. One camp is heavily into a God of judgment and insists that His wrath is being poured out, a little here and a little there, due to our growing immorality. This includes many of my fellow Christian Zionists[2] who see these things as divine punishment for the way the nations are bullying Israel. Some cite Hurricane Katrina in August 2005 as an example, claiming it was a chastisement on America for forcing Israel out of Gaza that summer. Yet, within two years, the city of New Orleans had rebuilt and returned to its old sinful ways. When God truly judges a city, it does not recover so quickly. In fact, we are still looking for the remains of Sodom and Gomorrah!

At the other extreme are Christians who counter that they serve a God of love who would never do such things. To me, their message is one of "sloppy agape"—the idea that because of the cross, we should no longer expect any dire punishment of humanity. It is a gospel of hyper-grace in which God ends up looking like a pushover and there are no longer any consequences for sin.

The apostle Paul actually stood squarely in between these two camps when he proclaimed, *"Therefore consider the goodness and severity of God"*

(Romans 11:22). Paul understood the balance between those two seemingly polar opposites within the character of God—he recognized that God is, indeed, a God of love and compassion, but He is also a holy God who cannot tolerate sin. And Paul knew that these paradoxical attributes of God meet together in His righteous character. This means He never judges unjustly; His judgments are *"true and righteous"* (Revelation 19:2), and He always gives fair warning beforehand.

Paul also spoke of how creation itself travails as a woman in birth pangs for the consummation of the age and the revealing of the sons of God. (See Romans 8:18–22.) Thus, I believe that as we inch ever closer to the end of the age, sin is increasing around us and nature itself can sense mankind's growing rebellion against the Creator and is going a little haywire. That, more than anything else, explains all the strange weather and natural catastrophes of late.

Jesus also shed some light on the rampant natural disasters of our day. In Matthew 24:7, He foretold of *"famines, pestilences, and earthquakes in various places."* Most Christians are familiar with this Scripture and thus rightly see the current upheavals in nature as signs of the end times. But Jesus did not directly ascribe these calamities to God, suggesting instead they would be random. Further, He said the message of such disasters is always "Repent!" For example, Jesus once spoke of how a tower had just toppled and crushed eighteen people. He asked, *"Do you think that they were worse sinners than all other men who dwelt in Jerusalem? I tell you, no; but unless you repent you will all likewise perish"* (Luke 13:4–5). In other words, such misfortunes could happen to anyone at any moment, so get your life clean and keep it clean before God!

Yet Jesus also warned in very clear terms that a severe divine judgment would indeed come upon the earth one day, when He finally would be ready to return. The warning came in His Mount Olivet Discourse, in which Jesus set out for His disciples His eschatology concerning the end of days:

> But of that day and hour no one knows, not even the angels of heaven, but My Father only. But as the days of Noah were, so also will the coming of the Son of Man be. For as in the days before the flood, they

were eating and drinking, marrying and giving in marriage, until the day that Noah entered the ark, and did not know until the flood came and took them all away, so also will the coming of the Son of Man be.
(Matthew 24:36–39)

In a separate setting, in a conversation with some Pharisees, Jesus again gave a specific warning about the *"days of Noah."* Here, it is paired with a reference to another episode of severe judgment from heaven—the destruction of Sodom and Gomorrah:

And as it was in the days of Noah, so it will be also in the days of the Son of Man: they ate, they drank, they married wives, they were given in marriage, until the day that Noah entered the ark, and the flood came and destroyed them all. Likewise as it was also in the days of Lot: they ate, they drank, they bought, they sold, they planted, they built; but on the day that Lot went out of Sodom it rained fire and brimstone from heaven and destroyed them all. Even so will it be in the day when the Son of Man is revealed. (Luke 17:26–30)

Two times, Jesus gave a very stark warning—once to His followers and once to the Pharisees—about an end-time cataclysmic judgment on a global scale. Consequently, any Christian has to take it seriously, and even nonbelievers should as well. If something like that is going to happen again, we would do well to understand exactly what transpired in Noah's day for the world to deserve such a fate. The Bible has much to say on this subject.

A World at Ease

What is most striking about these warnings by Jesus is His emphasis on how carefree and optimistic people were in the days of the Flood. In the passage from Matthew 24, He said they were *"eating and drinking"* (verse 38)—today we call it "partying" or enjoying leisure time. They also were *"marrying and giving in marriage"* (verse 38). This does not necessarily refer to a high divorce rate, but to the fact that people were looking forward to starting families. That is, they were upbeat about the future, despite the increase in sin around them. There was an ease to life, but this sense of normalcy and optimism was deceptive, as disaster lay just around the corner.

The same attitude toward life was prevalent in Sodom and Gomorrah. The people were buying and selling, planting and building, until the moment fire and brimstone rained down from heaven. They carried on with business as usual, totally unaware that the stench of their wickedness had aroused the judgment of a holy God.

Such a casual attitude seems out of place when we consider how Genesis describes both the pre-Flood world and Sodom prior to its destruction. For instance, there was wanton violence and unbridled sexual perversion in the pre-Flood world—so much so, that a loving God decided to wipe out everyone on earth except Noah and his family and start over. And yet the people of that day acted as if the good times would never end.

Many Christians today sense we are living in similar times; the world is far too upbeat about the future in light of the serious global threats we face and our steady moral decay. Thanks to militant secularism, multiculturalism, and other factors, many people no longer believe there are moral absolutes. Even worse, right is called wrong, and wrong is deemed right, just as the prophet Isaiah warned. (See Isaiah 5:20.)

No doubt, in many ways the world is becoming a better place. There are still conflicts raging worldwide, but fewer people are dying in them. Even in poor, developing nations, we are starting to win the war on poverty. Fewer people are going hungry, education is more universal, literacy rates are up, and infant mortality rates are down. The Internet has accelerated the move toward globalism—with its promise of political, economic and social progress—and technological advances are seemingly driving us forward into an exciting future.

Yet evil is advancing, too, and no one appears to be able to stop it. For many Christians, at least, it seems as if a dark genie has escaped the bottle, and no one can put it back inside. We have stood against abortion-on-demand to little avail, our schools teach godless evolution, same-sex marriages are being legalized worldwide—with some churches even ordaining gay priests—and both radical Islam and militant atheism are on the ascent. We call for urgent intercession for our nations, and rightly so. We lobby and preach and put up billboards. Yet the current moral slide continues unabated.

In one measure of this moral decline, an annual "Values and Beliefs" survey by Gallup has found that over the past fifteen years, behaviors once considered taboo have gradually became trendy and now enjoy majority acceptance. For example, American acceptance of gay and lesbian relations has climbed from 38 percent in 2002 to 58 percent in 2015—the year the US Supreme Court legalized same-sex marriages nationwide. The same trend is now starting to occur with transgenderism. Yet Gallup also found that a substantial 74 percent of Americans think the state of morality in their country is getting worse. In other words, most Americans are becoming more tolerant of controversial behaviors, yet at the same time, they are troubled by our overall moral decline.[3]

These trends have many Christians alarmed by the constant erosion of our values. It is as if evil is mysteriously allowed to prosper, and something irreversible is taking place. I share this sense, as well, but I am no longer frustrated by it because I have come to realize God may actually be in it. That may sound strange, but the Bible counsels that sometimes God can be so upset with mankind's rebellion that He allows people to destroy themselves. The Flood of Genesis involves such an exercise of divine justice—when God decided to allow an irredeemable generation to become so wicked that He had no choice but to destroy almost the entire population and start over. This theological concept requires fuller explanation before we start unpacking the specifics of the Flood.

The Parameters of Divine Justice

Many of us have taken personality tests or had job interviews in which we were asked to describe ourselves and list our strengths and weaknesses. What if we were able to sit down with God and ask Him to describe His personality, or to identify His particular qualities? In the Bible, God is very honest regarding His own persona. And He provided the most succinct self-description of His divine nature when He formally introduced Himself to Moses on Mount Sinai:

> And the Lord passed before him and proclaimed, "The Lord, the Lord God, merciful and gracious, longsuffering, and abounding in goodness and truth, keeping mercy for thousands, forgiving iniquity and transgression and sin, by no means clearing the guilty, visiting the

iniquity of the fathers upon the children and the children's children to
the third and the fourth generation."   (Exodus 34:6–7)

In Moses's day, most of the gods of the surrounding peoples were viewed as very demanding and unpredictable. If something were to upset them, you never knew when they might fly off the handle and throw a lightning bolt at you. In other words, they were a lot like us humans. But in Exodus 34, the God of the Bible describes His personality as quite different from that. First, He says He is loving and kind, slow to anger, and ready to forgive. In fact, the Bible says God actually delights in showing mercy. (See Micah 7:18; Jeremiah 9:24.) Second, God identifies another side of His personality—His holiness. This is the aspect of His nature that many people fail to respect, and thus they lose their fear and reverence toward God. As mentioned earlier, Paul concisely captured the breadth of the divine nature in this statement: *"Therefore consider the goodness and severity of God"* (Romans 11:22). Unlike the false gods, however, God's wrath is not arbitrary or demanding, but fully righteous.

Since God is love, by definition there needs to be an object of that love, and this is where mankind comes in. Scripture presents God as a loving, faithful Father over all His creation. He is not some aloof, grand watchmaker who set the planets in motion and then stepped back to let the universe run on its own. Rather, He cares about all that He has made and is fully engaged with it. His fatherly love is immeasurable and unchanging, and He created humans to be a central object of that love. The Bible is clear on this point, repeatedly expressing God's desire to come "dwell" among us. And He still wants to fellowship with human beings and enjoy our company as the part of His creation that is most like Him, just as He walked with Adam in the garden of Eden. (See, for example, Genesis 3:8; Exodus 25:8; Exodus 29:45–46; Psalm 132:13; 2 Corinthians 6:16; Revelation 21:3.)

Having been made in God's image, human beings possess a free will. Robotic beings are incapable of returning true love and worship to their Maker. Yet because we are free to make our own choices, we have the capacity for making either right or wrong decisions. Indeed, humans are capable of great good as well as great evil. And the first man—Adam—made a terribly wrong decision to disobey God, which has cost us all dearly.

Because of mankind's disobedience, a problem emerged. God is indeed loving and kind, but He is also holy and cannot abide sin. Disobedience within His creation is an affront to Him, as if it were an attack on His character. Thus, the two aspects of God's nature—His love and His holiness—had to be reconciled in His relationship with mankind. Yet in His infinite wisdom and foreknowledge, before the universe was ever made, God already had a plan in place for redeeming humanity back to Himself following its disobedience. (See, for example, Micah 5:2; Ephesians 1:3–6; 1 Peter 1:20; Revelation 13:8.) This foreordained plan began to play out some four thousand years ago with the calling of Abraham. It is the story of a loving God who came looking for a wayward humanity and initiated a means by which He could finally come to dwell among us, despite our inclination to disobedience.

This redemptive plan is progressively revealed in Scripture and culminates in the gospel message—that God inflicted on His own Son, Jesus, His righteous anger and judgment over the sins of all human beings. Through His death on the cross, Jesus took the punishment that we deserved for our rebellion against God. This act was foretold by Isaiah when he said of the Messiah, *"He was wounded for our transgressions, He was bruised for our iniquities…. All we like sheep have gone astray; we have turned, every one, to his own way; and the LORD has laid on Him the iniquity of us all"* (Isaiah 53:5–6). Likewise, the New Testament refers to Christ's suffering as a "propitiation" for our sins, so God could satisfy that part of His character which demands righteousness. (See, for example, Romans 3:25; Hebrews 2:17; 1 John 2:2; 1 John 4:10.)

The Bible records how, as mankind waited for the cross, a holy God loved us yet also dealt with our waywardness—on both an individual and a collective scale. If we read through the Old Testament, we indeed find that *"every transgression and disobedience received a just reward"* (Hebrews 2:2). God's relationship with Israel serves as a prime example of this. Sometimes the people of Israel were obedient and enjoyed His blessing, while at other times they were rebellious and suffered the consequences. God was patient and forgiving, but sometimes they forced His hand of correction. The apostle Paul makes an important point about how a righteous God often dealt severely with His own people: *"But if our [Israel's] unrighteousness demonstrates the righteousness of God, what shall we say? Is God unjust who inflicts wrath? (I speak as a man.) Certainly not! For then how will God judge the world?"* (Romans 3:5–6). That is, if God ever did anything unjust to Israel, then He has no right to judge the rest of humanity. Indeed, God will never judge anyone who does not deserve it. (See, for example, Isaiah 3:11; Ezekiel 7:27; Romans 1:32; Revelation 16:6.)

Again, God always gives fair warning of His coming judgments. (See, for example, 2 Chronicles 36:15; Psalm 19:11; Ezekiel 3:17–21; Jonah 1:1–2; 3:1–4.) He is longsuffering and ever ready to hear the prayers of the contrite. (See, for example, Psalm 34:18; Isaiah 66:2.) He gave us all a conscience and an ability to hear His pleas to turn back to Him. (See, for example, Romans 2:15; 2 Corinthians 4:2; 1 Timothy 1:5–6.) Finally, in the midst of judgment, He always remembers His mercy. (See, for example, 2 Samuel 24:14; Habakkuk 3:2; James 2:13.) The apostle Peter expressed the heart of God in all such matters: *"The Lord is not slack concerning His promise, as some count slackness, but is longsuffering toward us, not willing that any should perish but that all should come to repentance"* (2 Peter 3:9).

But what if a nation or a people absolutely refuses to repent? What if they are no longer responding to God's voice or their own consciences? At such times, God takes a certain drastic path that is knowable beforehand. When we have moved beyond repentance, something in God's righteous character demands that He judge us in a certain way, by allowing our sin and rebellion to ripen to His just judgment. If we are stubborn, persist in our sins, and even take pleasure in them, His Spirit stops striving with us, and He frees us up so that the rebellion bound in our hearts can run its course. He turns us over to our lusts and desires, all the while storing up His wrath against us. And when He finally does show up to deal with our rebellion, we are without excuse and always get what we deserve. Whatever form it may take, God is fully justified in chastening any part of His creation that is in such open rebellion against Him.

This process is explained in detail by the apostle Paul in Romans 1:18 and following. Yet, even in such times, when God withdraws in order to bring divine judgment, He is always longsuffering and waits for those who would turn back to Him. Likewise, He always preserves a righteous remnant amid the judgment; and He always remembers His mercy and brings about a fresh start.

We can see these principles of divine justice played out repeatedly in Scripture. For instance, God told Abraham that the Hebrew children would have to remain in bondage in Egypt because *the iniquity of the Amorites is not yet complete.*" (See Genesis 15:13–16.) This meant that Israel's deliverance from Pharaoh's hard taskmasters was delayed until the corruption of those living in the land of Canaan had reached a point where God was finally ready to judge them. Additionally, the Exodus itself is a textbook example of a patient God giving clear and timely warnings of each coming plague against Egypt, and dealing fairly with Pharaoh based on his own stubborn response.

We can find many more biblical examples of divine justice at work, but the clearest is that of Noah and the Flood. It follows a distinct pattern of humanity's irreversible moral slide, leading to divine warning, patience, and judgment, and it bears a closer look if Jesus Himself has warned that this pattern will play itself out again at the end of the age. In examining the Flood story, we will find it holds the key to understanding God's real end game for our world today.

As we begin this review, it is only natural to first ask some basic questions, which will serve as the framework for the next few chapters. These inquiries are:

1. Did the Flood really happen?
2. Exactly what happened in the Flood?
3. Why did the Flood occur?
4. Why should we believe a similar judgment will happen again?

2

PROOF OF THE FLOOD

"If the ark of Noah is discovered,
it will be the greatest archaeological find in human history,
the greatest event since the resurrection of Christ,
and it would alter all the currents of scientific thought."
—Dr. Melville Bell Grosvenor,
former president, National Geographic Society[1]

"Then the ark rested…on the mountains of Ararat."
—Genesis 8:4

The Search for the Ark

Did the Flood described in the book of Genesis really happen?

The easiest way to prove the Flood took place would be to find the ark of Noah. Surely, if we can put a man on the moon, we ought to be able to find the ark here on earth. Such a quest has consumed many people down through the ages, including one man who actually did walk on the moon. American astronaut James Irwin stepped on the lunar surface in the early 1970s, and later joined two expeditions to find Noah's ark on Mount Ararat, its traditional resting place. On his first trek in 1982, he reached the summit at 16,900 feet but fell on the glacier, suffering severe injuries, and was taken down on horseback. "It's easier to walk on the moon," he later quipped.[2]

Indeed, Noah's ark has proven an elusive treasure. So far, no definitive proof of it has been found, but there have been enough past sightings of a large wooden ship high on Mount Ararat to keep fueling the search. For instance, James Bryce, a respected Oxford professor and British ambassador to Washington, climbed above the tree line on Ararat in 1876 and found a slab of hand-hewn timber that he speculated was from the ark—a claim that is still considered reputable.[3]

During World War II, an American serviceman named Ed Davis was stationed near Mount Ararat when a local villager led him on a three-day journey along winding mountain roads and steep trails in foggy conditions, and showed him a large vessel of wooden timbers that was sticking out from the mountain's ice cap. It had different levels, rooms, and cages for animals inside.[4]

In 1970, an Armenian named Georgie Hagopian claimed that when he was a young boy, his uncle took him twice onto Mount Ararat to visit Noah's ark, sometime around 1908–1910. Hagopian even said he climbed onto the ark and walked along the roof. His description of the ship and the terrain around it was fairly identical to that provided by Ed Davis.[5]

The quest to locate Noah's ark has continued in recent decades, with some of the latest ventures capturing sensational headlines. No doubt, the credibility of those honestly searching for Noah's ark has not been helped by certain hoaxes and attempts to manufacture evidence for its existence.[6] However, in 2015, a team led by Dr. Norman Geisler of Southern Evangelical Seminary and ark researcher Philip Williams revealed they had visited the remains of a massive wooden ship buried beneath volcanic rock and ice at about four thousand meters on Mount Ararat. It had several levels and chambers, as described by so many other eyewitnesses.[7] The wooden remains dated to the time of Noah, Geisler told Fox News.[8]

Whether this latest claim turns out to be true, there have been far too many sightings of a large wooden ship stuck in the grip of a glacier on Mount Ararat to ignore. This includes numerous aerial sightings reported by people flying over Ararat.[9] Additionally, there have been multiple sightings on foot by Kurds, Armenians, and other local villagers, including one in 1948 by a local farmer that was reported by the Associated Press.[10] Meanwhile, recent commercial satellite imagery has also shown what is purportedly a large wooden vessel in an ice field on Ararat.[11]

Even *National Geographic* concedes that something very interesting is located in a certain gorge high on Mount Ararat, although nothing is verified yet:

> Reports of ark sightings have been common. Witnesses have described an old wooden structure sticking out of the snow and ice near the summit of Mount Ararat….

> …[S]cores of climbers have scaled the mountain but failed to substantiate what the object is.

> In 1997 the U.S. government released images taken by its Air Force in 1949 that were believed by some to show a structure covered by ice on Mount Ararat. These photographs had reportedly been kept in a government file labeled "Ararat Anomaly."[12]

Any further expeditions will continue to face obstacles. Mount Ararat has a year-round snow-and-ice field from above thirteen hundred feet, and moving ice flows could bury or sweep away any wooden structure. Earth tremors also are common to the region. In addition, Turkish authorities can be uncooperative, since most of the mountain is in a closed military zone near the border with Iran and Armenia. Any evidence also needs to be solid enough to overcome the skepticism caused by recent false alarms. But there undoubtedly will be additional anxious trekkers hoping to scale Mount Ararat in the warmer months each year in the continuing search for Noah's ark. And should it be found, this ancient relic will reemerge onto the stage of world history not only to affirm a major episode from the past, but also to serve again as a warning sign that the people of the earth are about to be judged.[13]

Meanwhile, there is ample proof for the Flood itself, which we turn to next.

The Flood in the Bible

The case for the historicity of a global Deluge that wiped out the ancient world begins with the Bible itself. As an historical document, it has yet to be proven irretrievably wrong, despite many determined efforts to refute it. Rather, the archeological record so far has tended to verify various biblical accounts, with any related controversies focused more on the correct dating of events. In both the Old and New Testaments, the Bible consistently presents the Flood as a literal event. For Christians, there can be no doubt about the fact of an actual worldwide flood, since Jesus Himself considered it to be a real occurrence. The same was true of the apostle Peter and the writer of Hebrews. In an unbroken continuum through both the Hebrew and Christian Scriptures, the Flood story is depicted as a real, historic, global disaster. Beyond that, there are many similar stories corroborating the Genesis narrative in the written histories and collective memories of various other peoples.

Ancient Corroborative Accounts

Many of the mysteries of the ancient world were lost in the fire that razed the legendary library of Alexandria in Egypt some two thousand years ago. Today, the Vatican in Rome and the British Museum in London are home to the richest collections of books, tablets, scrolls, artwork, and other rare items still left from antiquity. In 1872, a lowly assistant in the British Museum named George Smith shot to fame when he discovered an Assyrian version of a worldwide deluge story similar to the one in Genesis. Inscribed on a clay tablet excavated in Nineveh (in modern-day Iraq), the *Epic of Gilgamesh* told a legend of how human failings prompted the Babylonian gods to wipe out mankind by water, yet one single man saved a remnant of all living things. When Smith realized the significance of what he had just deciphered, he reportedly ran in circles and stripped off his clothes in excitement. The discovery instantly propelled him into the Victorian limelight, since the Bible was under assault from science, and dramatic corroboration of one of its oldest stories was exhilarating news.[14]

More than a century later, another curator at the British Museum made a similar breathtaking find on another cuneiform tablet. In 2009, Irving Finkel deciphered a Babylonian tablet with a virtual instruction manual for building a huge ark intended to preserve man and animals. The Ark Tablet dates to about 1900 BC and called on a Noah-like figure to build a large circular vessel with several levels and waterproofing inside and out. Finkel also discovered the text spoke of "wild animal[s]…two each, two by two." This was a rare expression in the Akkadian language, and its use is considered a strong affirmation of the Genesis account.[15]

There are at least nine such Mesopotamian accounts of the Flood story, while hundreds of similar flood legends are found all over the world, from such diverse peoples and places as the Maasai tribes in Kenya, the Aztecs in Mexico, the Maori of New Zealand, and the Incas of Peru.[16] In *Moons, Myths and Man*, researcher H. S. Bellamy estimated there are over five hundred such flood legends worldwide.[17] Meanwhile, James Perloff studied over two hundred flood stories and found that a global deluge was mentioned in 95 percent of them, people were saved in a boat in 70 percent, and survivors found respite on a mountain in 57 percent.[18]

In another study of thirty-five flood legends worldwide, all thirty-five claimed the world was destroyed by a massive flood that covered the mountaintops, and that the human race was spared by a family—usually by a man, his three sons, and their wives—with thirty-two crediting this to a great boat.[19] Another common element among these far-flung stories is the release of birds to determine if the waters had subsided. Such consistency indicates these stories all describe the same event, but oral transmission has altered some details with time.[20]

The Chinese classic *Hihking* tells the story of a man and his family (his wife, three sons, and three daughters) who are spared in a boat from a great flood that covered all the land. The Chinese consider this man the father of their civilization, and his family repopulated the whole world. Elements of this story are even embedded in the ancient pictographs that became the Chinese language.[21] For instance, the Chinese pictorial word for "boat" consists of characters for container, mouth and eight—that is, a vessel for eight people to enter.[22]

Still, the most important flood legends are from the ancient Near East, due to the similar details and the unique worldview they shared with the Semitic Hebrew tribes. Of these Mesopotamian accounts, the most important remains the *Epic of Gilgamesh*, which, again, is so similar to Genesis it leaves no doubt these stories tell of the same event.

In it, the storyteller (Gilgamesh) meets an old man (Utnapishtim), who told about how the gods once warned him of a coming flood. He was instructed to build a large ship covered with pitch, and to take on board male and female animals of all kinds, plus his wife and family. With the ship completed, intense rains fell for six days and nights. The ship eventually settled on a mountaintop, and Utnapishtim waited seven days before releasing a dove, which soon returned. He then released a swallow, and finally a raven, which never returned because the ground had dried.[23]

What is noteworthy is that both Genesis and the *Epic of Gilgamesh* divide the world into three tiers: the heavens above, the earth itself, and the underworld. In fact, this three-tiered cosmology can be found throughout both the Old and New Testaments. (See, for example, Exodus 20:4; Philippians 2:10; Revelation 5:13.) According to the *Epic of Gilgamesh*, not only did it rain from the heavens above, but the hero also warned that the waters of the Abyss (or underworld) would soon fill the land. This matches the biblical version, which states in Genesis 7:11 that the floodwaters came from springs in the great depths below, as well as rain from the *"windows of heaven"* above.[24]

This still leaves us with a nagging question: which story came first—the Babylonian version or the Hebrew version? And did one just borrow from the other? Some Bible detractors insist the writer of Genesis simply took the *Epic of Gilgamesh* and other existing flood stories, changed some names and details, and propagated a fable. The traditional view among Bible scholars has been that Genesis, like the other four books of Moses, was compiled by the patriarch Moses himself under divine inspiration. Over recent centuries, practitioners of "higher criticism" developed an alternate theory that later redactors composed these books from various, often conflicting, sources—the so-called Documentary Hypothesis.[25] Yet modern scholarship is moving back toward the traditional view.[26]

A core reason for viewing the Genesis record of the Flood as a unique, original account by a single author is based on the recent introduction of literary and form criticism into biblical scholarship. From this perspective, the story is told with such genius of composition that it virtually defies any effort to tie it to outside sources. For example, Genesis scholar Gordon Wenham has noted the complex poetic form known as *chiasmus* used in the original Hebrew. Chiasmus poetry adopts a mirroring literary effect that builds the plot to a crescendo in the middle of the story, where the thematic message is highlighted, only to wind down the second half of the story in a reflective reversal of the first half.[27] So the view that the Genesis narrative of the Flood is a mere spinoff of the Mesopotamian renditions is now thoroughly discredited, even though they have such striking similarities.[28]

My own view is that Moses was granted unique access to knowledge of past events, including Creation and the Flood, and wrote them down under divine direction. In Exodus 33:7–11, Moses set up the Tent of Meeting, away from the camp of the Israelites at Mount Sinai, in which he spent time alone speaking to God "*face to face, as a man speaks to his friend*" (verse 11). At the end of Exodus 33, Moses is also given the awesome opportunity to see the "*goodness*" of God pass by while he is hidden in the cleft of a rock. (See verses 19–22.) Verse 23 says that God allowed Moses to see His "*back*"—using the Hebrew word *achowr*, which can mean "backward" or "back in time."[29]

The bottom line is that the Genesis account of the Flood stands on its own two feet as a unique and accurate telling of a literal event, and is corroborated by hundreds of similar stories from that era with amazing parallels to the Bible. The fact that these other legends can be found all over the globe confirms that the Flood was indeed a universal event. So many diverse peoples know about it because we all came from the same family of Noah.

Yet the notion of a global flood some 4,350 years ago has come under increasing challenge in modern times from geologists studying the earth's crust.

Geological Proof

At the heart of the scientific challenge to the Genesis Flood are the earth's sedimentary layers and whether they were quickly reshaped by a global deluge less than five millennia ago, or by slow changes over eons of time, including by colliding tectonic plates, the Ice Age, and other forces.

Like most fields of modern science, geology was pioneered by Christians who believed the Bible. Yet as geologists have studied the earth's strata and developed methods for estimating the ages of various rock layers, they have concluded that the earth is much older than six thousand years, as the standard literal interpretation of the Bible holds. In the face of this challenge, creation scientists today attribute many of the major changes in the earth's geological column to the biblical Deluge. As a result, evolutionists and creationists disagree about nearly everything found embedded in the earth.

For instance, fossil remains of fish, mollusks, and other sea life have been found high atop every mountain range on earth—even the Himalayas! This includes entire whale skeletons and even pods of whales.[30] The evolutionists explain this as evidence that these areas were once below sea level but were pushed upward over millions of years by colliding tectonic plates. But creationists point to these remains as proof that floodwaters once covered the entire planet, including every mountaintop, just as Genesis states. They also contend that fossilization can occur only when the organism is buried quickly, protecting the remains from scavengers or decomposition. Thus, the fossil record is proof of a single cataclysmic flood and not slow changes over millions of years, since fossils do not ordinarily form on the sea bottom.[31]

The Genesis text states that *"all the fountains of the great deep"* (Genesis 7:11) were broken up and water gushed forth from inside the earth in a constant burst for *"one hundred and fifty days"* (verse 24). This could account for much of the rapid alteration in the earth's geological landscape. In addition, the *"floodgates"* (verse 11 NASB) were opened from above, producing torrential rains worldwide for forty days and nights. (See Genesis 7:11–12.) All this would have left billions of dead plants and animals buried and fossilized in rock layers all over the earth—as happens to be the case.[32]

More recently, marine archeologists working around the Black Sea have rekindled scientific interest in the Genesis Flood. In 1993, oceanographers

Bill Ryan and Walter Pitman of Columbia University used sonar to survey the floor of the Black Sea and found proof of a massive flood. On the bottom were ancient streambeds, river canyons, and shorelines. The sea's outer edges were once dry land, indicating it had been only two-thirds its current size. The entire sea bottom was a thin, uniform layer of sediment that could have been deposited only during a great flood.[33]

In their book *Noah's Flood*, Ryan and Pitman connected the Black Sea flood to the end of the Ice Age, when ice fields as far south as central Europe began melting, causing sea levels to rise. They estimate that, just over seven thousand years ago, the rising waters of the Atlantic filled up the Mediterranean via the straits of Gibraltar, and then, like cascading fountains, spilled over into the Black Sea. For those living in the area, the breach of water triggered a catastrophic flood of biblical proportions. The volume of water was equal to two hundred Niagara Falls, and the roar would have been audible a hundred miles away.[34]

Robert Ballard, the oceanographer who discovered the wreck of the *Titanic*, was intrigued by the Black Sea discoveries and used underwater robots to verify the submerged river valleys and ancient shorelines, as well as stone, wood, and mud houses, and polished tools, beneath the Black Sea.[35]

Following this find, similar evidence surfaced of late Ice Age floods in such far-off places as the Columbia River Valley, the English Channel, and a deep gorge in China.[36] In his recent book *The Rocks Don't Lie*, geologist David Montgomery surveyed some of those areas hit by catastrophic floods around five thousand years ago.[37] But he concluded there is not enough water on earth to account for sea levels topping the highest mountains, as Genesis claims.[38]

Yet it turns out there is, indeed, enough water on earth to cover the mountains. In 2014, scientists discovered a vast reservoir of water trapped deep beneath our planet's surface, capable of filling our oceans three times over. Located some three hundred and fifty miles down, this water is locked in a blue mineral called *ringwoodite* that lies in the transition zone of hot rock between the earth's surface and core. Geophysicist Steven Jacobsen suggests it means that the earth's surface waters came from deep below the ground.[39] His team of experts also explained in *Science* magazine that this vast reservoir of water is connected to the surface waters by subterranean cracks in the tectonic plates.[40] Jacobsen added: "If [the stored water] wasn't there, it would be on the surface of the Earth, and mountaintops would be the only land poking out."[41]

Therefore, not only is there enough water inside the earth to cause a global flood that could reach past the mountaintops, but those waters would also probably leave a lot of scars and other fingerprints in the geological surface map if they were ever to gush forth in abundance and then rapidly recede, as the Bible states. The geological record indicates such massive flooding did occur around the globe roughly five thousand years ago. Once again, the Genesis account of a global Deluge still stands upright, despite all the scientific attempts to discredit it.[42]

Interestingly, all this happened about the same time mankind suddenly transitioned from being mainly hunters and gatherers to being farmers and shepherds—the dawn of civilization. And this leads us to our next proof of the Flood—the spread of languages and peoples in the post-Flood era.

Dispersion of Languages and Nations

The study of language origins is another field of science that is verifying the Flood. The two Columbia University professors who discovered the Black Sea deluge followed the accepted theory that some forty-four hundred years ago (about the time of the Flood), a number of new peoples suddenly appeared in places as far apart as Egypt, the Himalayas, and France. Many spoke derivatives of the Indo-European mother tongue, which is now thought to have originated around the Black Sea. Thus, Ryan and Pitman suggest their Black Sea flood might have triggered the scattering in all directions of these earliest farmers, who carried civilization with them.[43]

Ian Wilson researched the Ryan-Pitman findings and other accumulating evidence of a catastrophic flood occurring around five thousand years ago, and wrote *Before the Flood*, in which he concludes that civilization started out not in Mesopotamia or Egypt but rather in northern

Turkey, and was dispersed from there after a great flood, much as the Bible describes.[44]

Genesis 11 tells the story of the Tower of Babel, the division of languages, and the dispersion of Noah's offspring. After the Flood, Noah and his family left Mount Ararat and moved near the Black Sea, where they could farm and keep livestock. There were eventually seventy "sons of Noah"—meaning his seventy great-grandsons. They still had "one speech" and moved to the land of Shinar (Iraq), where they built a huge tower to "make a name for themselves." This displeased God, so He confused their languages and dispersed them throughout the earth. Hence, all nations descend from the sons of Noah.

It is remarkable that linguists, archeologists, and anthropologists—many of them not friends of the Bible—all now agree that around four thousand years ago, the family of Indo-European languages originated near the Black Sea, spread to Mesopotamia, and then moved to the entire Eurasian land mass, bringing civilization with them. How could that not be more in tune with Genesis?

In addition, Genesis 10 names Noah's three sons, sixteen grandsons, and seventy great-grandsons from whom all nations sprang. These named individuals and their lineages can be found in numerous secular histories, proving that Noah's sons and their offspring were real historical figures whose names were indelibly carved on much of the ancient world.[45]

In conclusion, proof of the global Flood described in Genesis has held up despite the relentless assault by scientists and Bible detractors. The ark is still waiting to be found in a frozen, petrified state atop Mount Ararat; the Flood was a universal event that has been spoken of universally; the earth's geological record exhibits telltale signs of a global deluge in about the right time period, with a massive reservoir of possible floodwaters now locked deep inside the earth; finally, the spread of languages and peoples and the birth of civilization all date to the time the Bible says the survivors of the Flood repopulated the entire world.

With this background, we can now turn with confidence to the pages of Scripture to determine exactly what happened during those fateful days.

3

WHY THE DELUGE?

"The time was fulfilled, the evening came, the rider of the storm
sent down the rain."
—*Epic of Gilgamesh*[1]

*"Will you keep to the old way which wicked men have trod,
who were cut down before their time,
whose foundations were swept away by a flood?"*
—Job 22:15–16

What happened in the Flood? And, more importantly, why did it happen? Why would God decide to wipe out all living creatures, save for a small remnant of people and animals?

In *The Annals of the World*, first published in 1650, Anglican archbishop James Ussher arrived at the year 2,348 BC as a date for the Flood. His dating is still taken to be fairly accurate. In Genesis 6–9, the Flood story is recounted in chronological fashion. Other portions of Scripture—such as Matthew 24, Luke 17, Romans 1, Hebrews 11, and the books of 1 and 2

Peter and Jude—also provide insight into the days of Noah. The first thing to note in Genesis 6 is that humanity was continuing to fall away from its Creator. The focus of the Flood story, both in that chapter and throughout the Bible, is not so much on the details of what happened in the physical sense, but on the moral descent of humanity and how it pained the heart of God. It is good to know about the natural forces involved, but the greater lessons are found in understanding why it took place:

> Now it came to pass, when men began to multiply on the face of the earth, and daughters were born to them, that the sons of God saw the daughters of men, that they were beautiful; and they took wives for themselves of all whom they chose. And the LORD said, "My Spirit shall not strive with man forever, for he is indeed flesh; yet his days shall be one hundred and twenty years." There were giants on the earth in those days, and also afterward, when the sons of God came in to the daughters of men and they bore children to them. Those were the mighty men who were of old, men of renown. Then the LORD saw that the wickedness of man was great in the earth, and that every intent of the thoughts of his heart was only evil continually. And the LORD was sorry that He had made man on the earth, and He was grieved in His heart. So the LORD said, "I will destroy man whom I have created from the face of the earth, both man and beast, creeping thing and birds of the air, for I am sorry that I have made them." But Noah found grace in the eyes of the LORD. This is the genealogy of Noah. Noah was a just man, perfect in his generations. Noah walked with God. And Noah begot three sons: Shem, Ham, and Japheth. The earth also was corrupt before God, and the earth was filled with violence. So God looked upon the earth, and indeed it was corrupt; for all flesh had corrupted their way on the earth. And God said to Noah, "The end of all flesh has come before Me, for the earth is filled with violence through them; and behold, I will destroy them with the earth. Make yourself an ark....
>
> (Genesis 6:1–14)

Some scholars suggest that the opening lines of the Flood story in Genesis might be a condensed version of a much longer account, since the description jumps so abruptly between scenes and characters. Yet there is actually a chiasmus poetic rhythm in the original Hebrew, as explained in the last chapter.

To provide a simple framework for handling the material, my approach will be to sort out the various sins taking place by going from bad to worse, and in the process try to ascertain why God finally gave up on humanity.

The Jewish Sages on Humanity's Plunge

For Christians, one of the moments in Scripture that is most difficult to explain is when God *"was sorry that He had made man on the earth"* (Genesis 6:6). Apparently, something had gone awry with the way He had placed man in this world. (See Genesis 2:7–25.) The Jewish sages, also, were uneasy with the Creator's regrets over mankind and His decision to destroy the world. They always searched for the real reason to justify God's dialing up a global Flood. Rabbinic Judaism has identified three major sins that afflicted the antediluvian world. These are cardinal sins—meaning it would be better to die than be forced to commit one of them! They are, in ascending order of depravity: idolatry, murder, and sexual immorality.[2]

According to Talmudic tradition, the moment that mankind first lapsed into idolatry—the worship of a false god—appears subtly in Scripture. Genesis 4:26 says that after Seth fathered Enosh, *"men began to call on the name of the LORD."* Most Christians take that as a positive statement which means people started to seek God. But the rabbis give it a less noble spin: people began to give names to God, and these terms gradually became names for other gods.[3]

In this view, the Hebrew word for *"began"* (*chalal*) in Genesis 4:26 can also mean "pollute, defile, profane, or desecrate."[4] The same word also appears in Genesis 6:1 at the start of the Flood story, and in Genesis 10:8 with the introduction of Nimrod, who built the Tower of Babel. Both the story of the Flood and the story of the Tower of Babel are tales of rebellion against God. Thus, idolatry was viewed as the first step downward in the grave moral slide of humanity before the Deluge. People began to turn away from their Maker and seek after new deities, a course that always leads to even worse troubles.

A surge in murder was the next stage of man's downward spiral. Two murders had already occurred, as recorded in Genesis: Cain slew his brother Abel in a fit of jealousy (see Genesis 4:1–15), and Lamech, a descendant of Cain, killed another man (see Genesis 4:23–24). In both instances, the assailants appear to have had some reservations over their actions, largely out of fear of revenge attacks. But it seems that humanity eventually discarded such fears, and people became very violent toward each other; concerns over payback or punishment were no longer a deterrent. Thus, both verse 11 and verse 13 of Genesis 6 state that the earth was *"filled with violence."* The Hebrew word translated *"violence"* in these verses is *hamas*, which can have several connotations—all of which refer to something unconscionable.

The *Midrashim* (rabbinic commentaries) on Genesis 6:13 first describe *hamas* as robbery, but the word was later expanded to cover other acts of wickedness. Throughout the Hebrew Scriptures, it usually carried the sense of a great injustice, typically an act of physical violence.[5] In Joel 3:19, the word *hamas* refers to the shedding of innocent blood. But Psalm 11:5 may get to the heart of the matter when it declares that the Lord's soul hates *"the one who loves violence [hamas]."* It seems that a spirit of lawlessness permeated the earth. There was no longer any reason behind the violence; people merely took pleasure in harming others, and no one worried about ever paying a price. They completely lost their fear of God and respect for their fellow humans.

If that were not enough, the Jewish sages viewed sexual immorality as by far the most crippling sin of the pre-Flood era. Sexual activity lost its sanctity and was taken frivolously. The *Midrashim* say Noah's generation was not judged until people started writing songs about their sexual perversions, which meant that such perversions were no longer kept discreet but were flaunted openly.[6]

Thus, Genesis 6 says that *"every intent of the thoughts of* [man's] *heart was only evil continually"* (verse 5), and that *"all flesh had corrupted their way on the earth"* (verse 12). The rabbis said it was the combination of unbridled sexual immorality and wanton violence that produced an all-encompassing wickedness which had to be arrested. People's sinfulness was getting progressively worse. They took pleasure in it and even came to consider what they were doing as right. Such an ideological commitment to evil meant they were beyond repentance. This is what left God full of sadness, *"grieved in His heart*" (Genesis 6:6), because He knew that human beings needed to be blotted out.[7]

Therefore, God said to Noah, "*The end of all flesh has come before Me...*" (Genesis 6:13). Here, the Hebrew word translated *"end"* is not the usual *sof*, but rather *ketz*, which refers to plant debris, such as thorns and dead branches, which are good only for burning. The rabbinic commentaries often use parables equating the pre-Flood world with a withered, fruitless vineyard in need of drastic pruning. In the allegory, even though most of a vineyard needed to be uprooted and burned, if a vinedresser could find even a few live, healthy vines, those could be preserved to revive the whole vineyard. Thus, the purpose of the Flood was not so much divine revenge on the wicked as renewal of the earth through a righteous remnant. From this principle flows the Jewish concept of *tikkun olam*, which means to renew or repair the world. It originates in the divine commands, or laws, that Noah received immediately after the Flood, which were intended to preclude a repeat of the very breakdown of morality that had triggered the Deluge.[8]

According to the *Talmud*, there are seven traditional Noahide laws. These include bans on idolatry, blasphemy, incest (sexual perversion), murder, stealing, and eating live flesh, as well as a positive command to set up civil courts to enforce these laws. These moral guidelines afford us a further window into the failings of the antediluvian world. And Judaism continues to stress the concept of *tikkun olam*, with the aim of preventing another catastrophic judgment like the Flood from ever occurring again.[9]

The New Testament View

The main figures of the New Testament take a similar approach to the Flood as the Jewish sages. This should come as no surprise, since they studied the same writings and teachings. For instance, Jesus taught similar parables about the vineyard of the Lord, the pruning and burning of lifeless branches, and the harvest at the end of the age. (See, for example, Matthew 13:24–30; Luke 13:6–8; John 15:5–6.) Yet He also stressed the complacency and optimism that marked the "days of Noah." (See Matthew 24:37–39; Luke 17:26–27.) Despite the violence and moral bankruptcy of the time, people were carefree and totally unaware of the disaster just ahead.

The writer of Hebrews applauds the faith and character of Noah for being obedient and upright in a wicked and perverse generation, thereby condemning everyone else to God's judgment. (See Hebrews 11:7.) That is, if one man was able to walk humbly and reverently before God, even in a woefully lost world, it meant anyone could do it, and His standards are not too high. Thus, righteous Noah passed a sentence of guilt on the rest of humanity.

But it is the apostle Paul who supplies the most comprehensive New Testament commentary on the moral slide that doomed the pre-Flood world. His insights bear careful examination.

The Pauline Approach

In Romans 1, Paul begins tracing the ancient world's moral slide in much the same way as the mainstream rabbis of his day, which makes sense, because he studied under the respected Pharisaic teacher Gamaliel. (See Acts 22:3.) Like those rabbis, he singles out idolatry as the first step in the downward spiral, followed by violence and sexual perversion, and ends up with a laundry list of other vile behaviors. But Paul also emphasizes the longsuffering of God in the days of Noah. Even later, in Romans 9, he is still extolling the patience of God with rebellious man: *"What if God, wanting to show His wrath and to make His power known, endured with much longsuffering the vessels of wrath prepared for destruction..."* (Romans 9:22).

For Paul, the Flood story hits a key moment when God first pronounces judgment over mankind, but then does a strange thing. He decides to wait a hundred and twenty long years before bringing it to pass. Why? Because the righteous character of God demands that He judge humanity in a certain way. He first takes His hands off mankind to allow the rebellion bound in people's hearts to run its course, so that it ripens to His just judgment. It is by this withholding of divine judgment in hopes that some people may turn and repent that *"the wrath of God is revealed from heaven..."* (Romans 1:18).

Paul writes that even though the ancient world had knowledge of the incorruptible Creator God, *"they did not glorify Him as God, nor were* [they] *thankful"* (Romans 1:21). They lost their awe and appreciation for God, and were no longer grateful to Him for all they had. They began to lower their concept of the Divine Being to their level, making idols of Him in the form of *"corruptible man"* and even of beasts and *"creeping things."* (See Romans 1:22–23.) Indeed, idols in the shape of scarabs (dung beetles) were popular in ancient Egypt, and many people worshipped phallic symbols and other human forms. This mirrors the rabbinic view that idolatry was the first misstep in the pre-Flood rebellion. In the face of this apostasy, the Spirit of the Lord stopped dealing with men's consciences and left them to their own devices. *"Therefore God also gave them up to uncleanness, in the lusts of their hearts, to dishonor their bodies among themselves"* (Romans 1:24); *"God gave them up to vile passions"* (verse 26); *"God gave them over to a debased mind"* (verse 28).

Where did this newfound freedom take humanity? Men left natural relations with woman and turned to homosexuality. Women also left the natural order (we will explore how shortly). Additionally, Paul teaches, they removed God from their knowledge, so He gave them over to their own degenerate minds. (See verses 26–30.) This is a fearful thought: God can come to a point where He actually wants human beings to be deceived by their own wild imaginations. His standards were being completely ignored, so He freed up mankind to decide right from wrong for themselves. The result was a people who believed that the evil they were committing was right, which meant their fall was beyond repair.

Thus, God determined to wipe out almost the entire population and start over, but He first waited a hundred and twenty years before unleashing the Flood, during which time He instructed Noah to build an ark and thereby warn the world of impending judgment. Again, we note the divine patience and fair warning given by the Lord in the days of Noah. When God finally did show up in judgment, the generation of the Flood was without excuse and thoroughly deserved what befell them.

Once more we see it is in God's forbearance and longsuffering that His wrath is revealed from heaven. And this haunting question posed by Paul still rings true today: *"Do you despise the riches of His goodness, forbearance, and longsuffering, not knowing that the goodness of God leads you to repentance?"* (Romans 2:4). That is, when mankind crosses a line with God in its moral descent, and there is no immediate lightning from heaven, or the earth does not swallow people up, we should not misread this as a stamp of divine approval of mankind's actions. He is letting us go our own way, and we actually are storing up for ourselves the just punishment we deserve. (See Romans 2:5.)

The apostle Peter joins Paul in highlighting the patience and fairness of God, writing, "...*when once the Divine longsuffering waited in the days of Noah*" (1 Peter 3:20). He also commends Noah for his role as "*a preacher of righteousness*" who withstood the lure of evil in his generation and earned the special honor of restoring the human race. (See 2 Peter 2:5.)

But Peter, along with Jude, addresses one more aspect of the Flood story that has baffled Bible readers for centuries: who exactly are the "*sons of God*" (*ben Elohim*) and the giants (*Nephilim*) mentioned in Genesis 6:2–4? And how did they contribute to the moral decay that brought on the Deluge? This intriguing subject will now command our attention.

4

THE FORBIDDEN UNION

"We came to see these your sorrows, Prometheus,
and this agony of your chains...."
—*Prometheus Unbound*, by the Greek poet Aeschylus[1]

*"And the angels who did not keep their proper domain, but left their
own abode, He has reserved in everlasting chains under darkness for
the judgment of the great day."*
—Jude 6

On a man-made island in Berlin stands a museum containing some of the most treasured relics of the ancient Near East. The most prized piece is the reconstructed Pergamon Altar, a large edifice transported to Germany in the late nineteenth century from the historic city of Pergamos, on Turkey's western coast. This massive altar is considered the apex of Hellenistic art. The three-sided structure is adorned with exquisitely carved marble statues and friezes depicting the main gods of classical Greek mythology, with a focus on the battle of the Olympians, led by Zeus, against the Gigantes, the superhuman offspring of the earth goddess Gaia. In Greek lore, this was the second victory of the greater gods over the children of the lesser gods, the first one being the defeat of the legendary Titans.

I visited the Pergamon Museum a few years back, and it was easy to be taken in by the beauty of this ancient Greek masterpiece. But it also was chilling to stand amid this grand tribute to Hellenism's pantheon of gods and their breeding with humans. My sense of revulsion was compounded by knowing that the Nazis were enthralled with this altar, due to their mysticism about the superior origins of the Aryan race. Additionally, the site of the huge Nuremburg rallies was built by Albert Speer, Hitler's chief architect, to resemble the altar of Pergamon. Add to this the fact that the book of Revelation identifies Pergamos as the place *"where Satan's throne is"* and *"where Satan dwells"* (Revelation 2:13). No wonder I was relieved to exit the museum.

Greek mythology has always seemed strange to me, with its tales of the gods coming down and mating with humans to produce mutant offspring. Yet I have come to realize the Bible contains a similar story related to the Flood. And for those looking for a deeper reason why God destroyed the world by water, here it is. After all, many of the sins of the antediluvian world—idolatry, violence, sexual perversion—have occurred in other ages. Why were the people of those times not destroyed? The difference was due to the illicit union between rebellious angels and humans that accelerated the moral collapse of pre-Flood times—so much so, that God decided to bring things to a complete end. This is how the Genesis account was understood for centuries, until Rabbinic Judaism and some early church fathers felt it sounded too much like Greek mythology. But the New Testament affirms this scenario to be the case, so we must face it head-on.

In Genesis 6:2, the Flood story actually opens with the *"sons of God"* being drawn to the *"daughters of men"* due to their beauty. *"And they took wives for themselves of all whom they chose"* (verse 2). Two verses later, we are told, *"There were giants [Nephilim] on the earth in those days, and also afterward, when the sons of God came in to the daughters of men and they bore children to them. Those were the mighty men [gibborim] who were of old, men of renown"* (verse 4).

Thus, these *"sons of God"* who conceived giant offspring with women are central to the Flood story. But who exactly were they?

The Sons of God

In Genesis 6, the Hebrew term for *"sons of God"* is *ben Elohim*. This phrase occurs often in the Hebrew Scriptures and was traditionally understood to mean angelic beings. Such beings usually show up in the context of a heavenly council of angels who make decisions along with the Most High God.[2] Besides Genesis 6:2–4, we find the *ben Elohim* in Job 1:6 and 2:1, where they are meeting in heaven, and Satan also stands among them. Here, Satan appears for the first time in Scripture as a sort of prosecutor or "accuser of the brethren"—a role that carries over all the way into Revelation. (See Revelation 12:10.) Job 38:4–7 adds that these *"sons of God"* were present at the creation of the world. We see them again in an odd story recorded in 1 Kings 22:19–23, while a similar divine court proceeding is found in Zechariah 3. In Psalm 89:5–7, the *ben Elohim* again appear in the *"assembly of the saints"* (*kadoshim*, or "holy ones"), referring to an angelic court. In Psalm 82:6, the *"children of the Most High"* (*ben Elohim*) once more serve as heavenly judges. Finally, Daniel 4 makes three references to these angelic beings, using the term *"watcher*[s]." (See verses 13, 17, 23.)

Those of us with faith in Christ can look forward to one day becoming *"sons of God"* ourselves (see Matthew 5:9; Romans 8:19; Galatians 3:26), yet only after we receive our new glorified bodies at the end of the age, so that we are then *"like the angels."* (See Luke 20:36 NIV.) But in the context of Genesis 6:2–4, the *"sons of God"* were originally identified as angelic beings, both by Judaism and early Christianity.[3] This accepted view held that they belonged to the heavenly host, but some of these "watchers" rebelled by coming to earth to mate with humans, thus violating the heavenly/earthly division established by God. The hybrid offspring of this illicit union were giants, called *Nephilim* in Hebrew. Even the Jewish historian Josephus, in his work *Antiquities of the Jews* (Book 1, chapter III), adopts this view, and equates their hybrid offspring with "those whom the Grecians call giants."[4]

However, in the second century AD, Jewish commentaries began interpreting "sons of God" to mean human dynastic rulers or judges over society who disobediently mated with the common daughters of Cain. This was largely a theological reaction to the dual challenges of Christianity and Hellenism; the former centered on the worship of a distinctive God-man, while the latter featured a pantheon of gods and their human-hybrid offspring. Some early church fathers developed a similar theory, that the sons of God were human descendants from the "righteous" lineage of Seth who violated the commands of holiness and married women from the un-righteous line of Cain. In these later views, the *Nephilim* were merely the mighty warriors of an ancient era.[5]

Yet no place in Scripture are Seth and his descendants identified as being righteous, elect, or sons of God. In fact, Luke 3:38 describes Seth as *"the son of Adam,"* who in turn is called *"the son of God."* Jesus, also, is referred to as *"the Son of God"* (see, for example, Matthew 14:33) and *"the only begotten of the Father"* (John 1:14). But again, every other biblical reference to the "sons of God" (*ben Elohim*) is speaking of angelic beings.

Some may still be squeamish at the notion that angels can take human form. But in the Bible, not all angels have wings. We read about many obedient angels who took on the appearance of men as they carried out divine assignments. This includes the two angels sent to deliver Lot from Sodom (see Genesis 19:5, 10); the angel who wrestled with Jacob (see Genesis 32:24); and even the angel sitting in the empty tomb of Jesus, who is described as *"a young man clothed in a long white robe"* (Mark 16:5). Thus, we are told to be hospitable to strangers, since we might be *"entertain*[ing] *angels unawares"* (Hebrews 13:2 KJV). Meanwhile, disobedient angels apparently have a similar ability to assume different forms. Paul even warns that *"Satan himself transforms himself into an angel of light. Therefore it is no great thing if his ministers also transform themselves into ministers of righteousness"* (2 Corinthians 11:14–15).

In the end, the contrast between the sons of God and the daughters of men in Genesis 6 makes sense only if the passage is referring to angelic-human unions, not royalty with commoners or one family line with another. By merging the earthly with the heavenly and producing hybrid giants, both the offending angels and the rebellious humans crossed a line with God, and this unholy union was a major factor in His decision to judge the ancient world.

In the New Testament, Peter and Jude followed this traditional view that the sons of God in the Flood story were disobedient angels. In so doing, both writers relied on the book of Enoch, an intertestamental work that did not make the canon of Scripture but was highly regarded by both Jews and Christians in the Second Temple era.

The Book of Enoch

There are over fifty references in the Bible to some two dozen noncanonical writings utilized by biblical authors. For instance, the book of Jasher is mentioned twice, in Joshua 10:13 and 2 Samuel 1:18. But all these original sources have been lost, except for one: the book of Enoch.

The book of Enoch is part of the Apocrypha, a group of works viewed as containing "hidden truths" useful for the church, though not necessarily divinely inspired. Additionally, Enoch is written in an apocalyptic style, like Daniel and Revelation. Finally, it is a pseudepigrapha work, meaning the author assumed the name of a revered biblical figure. As the term suggests, these works were often seen as "false writings." But scholar James Charlesworth has defended them as treasured writings, in honor of Old Testament heroes, that hold sacred truths.[6]

The book of Enoch is named for an ancient patriarch who walked uprightly in the days before the Flood—so much so, Genesis 5:24 says that one day he could not be found, *"for God took him."* That is, Enoch was taken up to heaven alive, much like Elijah, but not before warning that God would soon punish mankind for its ungodliness. The New Testament confirms Enoch's translation to heaven in verse 5 of Hebrews 11, while his stern warnings are found in verses 14–15 of Jude.

The book of Enoch is actually a compilation of five books and a few loose chapters that claim to be based on visions and events experienced by Enoch. The most respected and influential of these books is 1 Enoch, which contains the first thirty-six chapters and dates to the third century BC.[7] First Enoch describes in detail a conspiracy among two hundred heavenly watchers, led by the high-ranking angels Semjaza and Azazel, who rebel against God and come down to earth on Mount Hermon, located on the Golan. Jewish and Christian scholars agree that the opening lines of Enoch's Flood account are an elaboration of Genesis 6:1–4.[8]

First Enoch tells how these watchers mated with women to produce mutant giants, a great sin that led to the Flood. These disobedient angels also began teaching mankind secrets of the occult, enchantments, and astrology, as well as the arts of weapon-making and warfare. Their gigantic children are described as bloodthirsty gluttons who became violent toward ordinary humans, even engaging in fits of cannibalism. Perhaps this is why God instructed Noah after the Flood never to eat live flesh—whether man or animal. (See Genesis 9:4.) The book also recounts Enoch's heavenly journeys and his prophetic calling to proclaim judgment upon the watchers and their hybrid offspring.[9]

This expanded version of pre-Flood events is not considered part of Holy Scripture, but neither can it be dismissed as fable. Both Peter and Jude treated 1 Enoch as trustworthy enough to quote from, and scholars agree the entire book of Enoch had great influence on other New Testament figures and writers, including Jesus Himself.[10] Among New Testament passages, verses 14–15 of Jude are the most explicit in plainly quoting from 1 Enoch 1:9.[11]

The Gates of Hades

Jude not only quotes verbatim from 1 Enoch, but his letter also mirrors its pattern and phrases in undeniable ways. Enoch tells how the watchers "abandoned the high holy and eternal heaven and slept with women and defiled [themselves] with the daughters of the people, taking wives…and begetting giant sons" (1 Enoch 15:3). Additionally, he says that these rebellious angels were bound "underneath the rocks of the ground until the day of their judgment" (1 Enoch 10:12). The sixth verse of Jude reads in this way: *"And the angels who did not keep their proper domain, but left their own abode, He has reserved in everlasting chains under darkness for the judgment of the great day."* Peter also insists these mutinous angels were chained in the underworld for breaching the heavenly/earthly divide. (See 2 Peter 2:4–5.)

According to 1 Enoch, the disobedient *ben Elohim* who sired the giant *Nephilim* were locked away in a special section of the deepest part of *Sheol*—the Hebrew term for hell, or *Hades* in Greek. The entryway to this underworld was believed to be located at the base of Mount Hermon—where the whole rebellious enterprise began.

At the foot of Hermon's western slope, the Banias spring emerges from under the mountain to form one of the main tributaries of the Jordan River. *Banias* derives from the Arabic name for "Pan," since Arabs pronounce the letter *p* as a *b*. Pan, of course, is the name of the half man/half goat demigod of Greek mythology who is driven by sexual lust—a mutant hybrid formed by the union of two different species. So the Romans built an altar to the god Pan at the very spot in northern Israel where the traditional gateway to hell was located in Hebraic thinking. It was also at that place that Jesus said He would build His church, *"and the gates of Hades shall not prevail against it"* (Matthew 16:18), thereby alluding to this Jewish tradition.

In Greek mythology, *Tartarus* refers to the lowest part of Hades, where the Titans were bound due to their rebellion against the gods. Peter uses a derivative of that Greek word in describing the fate of the rebellious angels from the time of Noah. *"For if God did not spare the angels who sinned, but cast them down to hell [tartaroo] and delivered them into chains of darkness, to be reserved for judgment…"* (2 Peter 2:4). Peter relies here on 1 Enoch, which uses the same term *tartaroo* to describe the lowest part of hell where the fallen angels were chained.[12]

Other peoples in the Near East also have a long tradition connecting the *Rephaim*—descendants of the *Nephilim*—with Sheol and Bashan (today's Golan). The Bible itself describes Bashan as *"the land of the giants [Rephaim]"* (Deuteronomy 3:13), whose inhabitants were described as being as tall as the *Anakim*. (See Deuteronomy 2:11, 20.)

Indeed, the ancient world had many stories about the mating of lesser gods and humans, and the punishments meted out by the greater gods for these illicit unions. This aspect features prominently, for instance, in the flood passages in the *Epic of Gilgamesh*. My own response to all these legends is to be extremely grateful once again that the Bible has preserved the most accurate and trustworthy version of these events, and uses them to ever call us to fear and reverence toward the one true Creator God.

The Double Warning of Enoch

Another notable link between the book of Enoch and the epistles of Jude and Peter is the way they all pair the sins of the pre-Flood world with the destruction of Sodom and Gomorrah. Jesus Himself adopts this dual warning in Luke 17:26–32 when speaking of *"the days of Noah"* and *"the days of Lot."* A closer look at this linkage further clarifies the nature of the pre-Deluge rebellion, while also altering our biblical definition of *sodomy*.

First Enoch is the earliest Jewish religious literature to twin the judgments of the Flood and Sodom as involving the same transgression of having sexual relations outside the human species. A mention of this pairing does not occur anywhere in the Old Testament, but it can be found in Luke 17:26–29, 2 Peter 2:4–11, and Jude 6–7. It also appears in other Jewish writings from the Second Temple period that speak of the sin of leaving the natural order.[13]

After Jude recalls the punishment of the angels who mated with women, he immediately states, *"...as Sodom and Gomorrah, and the cities around them in a similar manner to these, having given themselves over to sexual immorality and gone after strange flesh, are set forth as an example, suffering the vengeance of eternal fire"* (Jude 7). Here, the Greek expression for *"strange flesh"* (*heteros sarx*) indicates the pursuit of something outside our human race, and thus it cannot refer to homosexuality. When the New Testament refers to homosexual acts, it uses the Greek phrase *para physin*, which means "contrary to nature." (See Romans 1:26.) But going after *heteros sarx*, or "strange flesh," involves going outside the human species to couple with other beings—in this case, angels. From God's perspective, the sin of Sodom was not that they were going after other men, but after angels. Certainly, the Bible condemns homosexuality, but again the sin of Sodom condemned by Jude and Peter was humans trying to mate with angels.[14]

Once again, we find the same linkage between the days of Noah and Lot in 2 Peter 2 and in Luke 17. The reason for these dual warnings becomes even clearer when we look more closely at the nature of the *Nephilim*, not only in the pre-Flood world but for generations afterward.

Tracking Down the Nephilim

Only two places in Scripture—Genesis 6:4 and Numbers 13:32–33—use the Hebrew word *Nephilim*, a term usually translated as "giants." Yet there are many other biblical references to *Nephilim* by other names or in relation to their own progeny, such as the *Rephaim*, *Anakim* and *Gibborim*.

Some prophecy teachers today confuse the *Nephilim* with the *ben Elohim*, as though they both refer to rebellious angels. But like the majority of ancient biblical translations, including the Greek Septuagint and Latin Vulgate, the Brown-Driver-Briggs Lexicon gives the meaning of *Nephilim* as "giants."[15] This is the plural form of the Hebrew root *nephil*,[16] which is associated with the word "fall." Thus, most scholars consider the *Nephilim* to be extremely large "bullies," like Goliath, who violently fell upon or preyed upon ordinary humans.[17]

In Genesis 6, the emphasis is on the breach of the heavenly/earthly divide, which led to the births of the giants of old. This violation is also stressed in Jude 6–7 and 2 Peter 2, immediately followed by references to Sodom as having committed the same sin. The two are easily connected.

Before the destruction of Sodom and Gomorrah in Genesis 19, we read in chapter 14 about the great battle of the four kings against the five kings—essentially, the first world war. It took place soon after Abraham had arrived in the land of Canaan, and his nephew Lot had settled in Sodom. When the battle began, the invading kings first went through the land and killed off the *Rephaim*, *Zuzim* and *Emim*—all giants descended from the *Nephilim*. With their mightiest warriors now dead, the Canaanite cities—including Sodom—were easy prey for the invaders. Lot was taken prisoner with the other Sodomites, forcing Abraham and his private army to pursue and rescue them. Then, in Genesis 19, two angels arrived to extract Lot from Sodom before it was destroyed by God. But verse 4 says that *"all the people from every quarter"* (not just the men of the city) surrounded Lot's house and demanded to have sexual relations with the angels. Traditionally, this crowd has been viewed as a mob of homosexuals, but I believe something else was occurring here. The people of Sodom thought that if they could mate their wives with these two angels, it would produce new warrior giants to help defend a city still recovering from a crushing defeat. So they brought every able-bodied person in town to help subdue the two angels. Yet from God's perspective, they were again trying to cross the line, to have humans mate with angels, which gives a whole new meaning to the term *sodomy*. Thus, Jude, Peter, and Jesus Himself give double warnings about the similar sins related to the Flood and Sodom—in line with the book of Enoch.

The Lord stopped the Sodomites from mating with the angels, but there were still giant offspring of the *Nephilim* around until the time of King David. In Numbers 13:32–33, for instance, the Israelite spies reported that *Nephilim*—the descendants of Anak—were still in the land of Canaan, such that they said, "*We were like grasshoppers in our own sight.*" During Israel's conquest of the land, Joshua launched a special campaign to eliminate these *Anakim*, leaving only a remnant among the Philistines. (See Joshua 11:21–22.) One of these notable giants was King Og of Bashan, who is described as sleeping on a huge iron bed measuring approximately six by thirteen feet. (See Deuteronomy 3:11.) Finally defeated by Joshua (see Joshua 12:1–4), Og's kingdom was located on the Golan near Mount Hermon, where the rebellious angels had first appeared before the Flood.

Interestingly, on the Golan today are many mysterious stone ruins likely connected to these giants of old. They include a Stonehenge-type structure, dating to around 2700 BC, called *Gilgal Rephaim* ("Circle of Giants"). Some believe this circular megalithic site was originally ground zero for the rebellious mating of angels and humans, which produced the giant *Nephilim*. Their progeny were still around until David and his mighty men slew Goliath and his four giant brothers. (See 1 Samuel 17; 2 Samuel 21:15–22; 1 Chronicles 20:4–8.)

One might ask, "How did the giants survive the Flood and get into the new world?" This is a good question. Genesis 6:4 itself affirms that there *"were giants [Nephilim] on the earth in those days, and also afterward"*— meaning both before and after the Flood. Exactly how this happened we are not told. But the *Nephilim* and their offspring were finally vanquished by King David, a forerunner of the Messiah, while the rebellious angels remain chained in the deepest pit of Sheol.

Rivalry of the Seeds

Thus, there was more going on before the Flood than just idolatry, violence, and sexual immorality. Rebellious angels were crossbreeding with humans, and fueling the violence and perversion. I actually believe this was a demonic plot to so alter the nature of mankind that we would no longer be like Adam. And for mankind to be redeemed from his fall, the Redeemer to come had to be like Adam. (See, for example, Romans 5:12–18; 1 Corinthians 15:42–49; Hebrews 2:17.) We already see a hint of this plot in the punishments meted out by God after Adam and Eve's sin in the garden of Eden. God first turns to the serpent, which the New Testament identifies as Satan (see Revelation 12:9; 20:2), and proclaims, "*And I will put enmity between you and the woman, and between your seed and her Seed; He shall bruise your head, and you shall bruise His heel*" (Genesis 3:15).

This tells us there is a bitter rivalry between humanity as the offspring of Eve, and Satan and his fallen comrades. These cohorts happen to be angelic beings who rebelled against God, even though they could see Him, and thus have been sentenced to eternal punishment. Mankind, on the other hand, was made "*a little lower than the angels*" (Psalm 8:5; Hebrews 2:7); and even though we are unable to look upon God in this current world, many of us still love, worship, and obey Him and believe in His Son, Jesus. As noted earlier, if we continue to do so, we will one day have glorified new bodies and be like the good angels in heaven. (See Matthew 22:30.) And every human who is able to walk through this life in faith and devotion toward God heaps coals of fire on the devil and his minions, justifying their eternal punishment. Realizing this, the rebellious angels are simply trying to take down with them as many humans as they can by luring us into sin, thereby separating us from God.

This demonic plot also aimed to produce a counterfeit of the one true union of the human and the divine that God intended from the start—the Immaculate Conception. God foreordained just one joining of the heavenly and the earthly in order to produce the God-man, Jesus. But when fallen angels arrived on earth beforehand and interbred with women, it twisted the concept of God coming in human form in order to finally "dwell among us." (See John 1:14.) The ancient Greeks and Romans developed their own distorted legends about this celestial intrusion, so that by the time the real thing came along in Jesus, the false had made it a repugnant idea to His own Jewish people.

Likely unaware of this dark scheme, most of mankind started going along with the insurrection. Perhaps they saw mating with these angelic beings as a path to self-deification, like that falsely promised by the serpent in the garden when he told Eve, "*You will be like God…*" (Genesis 3:5). In any event, the human race stood in jeopardy of losing its Adamic nature. That is why God was forced to wipe it out and start over. And for that new beginning, He chose a unique human vessel named Noah.

5

A NEW BEGINNING

Father, who teacheth the bird to fly
Builder of rainbows up in the sky
—Bob Dylan, "Father of Night"[1]

"Then He who sat on the throne said,
'Behold, I make all things new.'"
—Revelation 21:5

The Flood story has a happy ending, thanks to the mercies of God and a humble man named Noah. The recent Hollywood movie *Noah* had many flaws, but none greater than the way the lead character, played by Russell Crowe, was presented as stubborn and cold-hearted. That is far from his portrayal in the Bible. Noah first appears in Genesis 5:29, where his name is said to mean "comfort" or "rest." When Noah is reintroduced in chapter 6, his name appears twice in a row in Hebrew, with no punctuation mark in between. Whenever someone's name is repeated like that in the Hebrew Scriptures, it is usually a sign they are beloved by God. Abraham,

Moses, and Samuel share this distinction with Noah. Genesis 6:8–9 says, *"But Noah found grace in the eyes of the* LORD. *This is the genealogy of Noah. Noah was a just man, perfect in his generations. Noah walked with God."*

A Tribute to Noah

Several interesting words are used in Genesis 6 that are intended to draw a sharp distinction between the pure and the impure. First, Noah is described as *"perfect in his generations"* (verse 9). The Hebrew word translated *"perfect"* is *tamim*, which means "spotless" or "unblemished." The same word is repeatedly found in the Torah's commands to sacrifice only spotless or unblemished animals to the Lord. (See, for example, Leviticus 1:3, 10; 3:1, 6; 4:3, 23.) The purity of Noah's lineage is then contrasted with those who had "corrupted" their "flesh." (See Genesis 6:9, 12.) The Hebrew word translated "corrupt" and "corrupted" in Genesis 6:12 is *shachath*, which means perverted, ruined, or marred. The original text says all *"flesh,"* or *basar*, had become tainted and corrupted; this term pointedly refers to the physical body. So there was a corruption or ruining of flesh due to the illicit union of humans and angels, and God was not pleased. Yet Noah is described as still pure *"in his generations."*

What this really means is that Noah retained a pure gene pool; his DNA or bloodline had not been tainted by the alien seed. Noah was still fully human, like Adam! Thus, he qualified as someone God could use to repopulate the world, and thereby sustain His plan for a "second Adam" (Christ) to redeem the descendants of the "first Adam." (See, for example, 1 Corinthians 15:45–49.)

Noah also is described as *"a just man"* (Genesis 6:9)—*ish tsaddik* in Hebrew—the only man so described in the entire Bible. As we look closer at the character and actions of Noah, we better understand why he was chosen to survive the Flood and become the new father of all the living.

Besides his genetic purity, Noah is depicted as a man of great faith and reverence toward God. Twice in the Flood story, he is commended for his total obedience—first in completing the ark (see Genesis 6:13–22), and then in caring for all the animals (see Genesis 7:1–5). In Romans 1:21, Paul says mankind in those days was no longer thankful to God, yet the first thing Noah did upon leaving the ark was to build an altar and offer a sacrifice to God in thanks for preserving his family. (See Genesis 8:20.)

The text also notes that "Noah found grace in the eyes of the LORD" (Genesis 6:8). The word for "grace" here is *chen*, which also means "favor." It appears often in the Hebrew Scriptures, but one passage that the Talmudic rabbis connected to Noah is Zechariah 12:10, where the Lord promises to pour out on Israel "*the Spirit of grace [ruach chen] and supplication.*" This was taken to mean that God's favor comes in the form of a sharpened conscience, a full awareness of sin, and a capacity to repent of all wrongs. It was Noah's alert conscience and his ability to walk in reconciled relationship with God that kept him from partaking in the rebellion of his day.[2]

In the New Testament, Noah again is praised for his faith and obedience. In Hebrews 11, we find Noah described as a man who walked uprightly before God in the midst of a wicked generation—and Noah's righteous conduct condemned everyone else to divine judgment! (See verse 7.)

Noah was six hundred years old when he entered the ark, and many people have wondered how such an aged man could have gathered and cared for so many animals. But animals seem to have a certain connection to God and to nature that we humans lack. For example, when the devastating tsunami swept across the Indian Ocean in 2004, many locals said the animals in low-lying areas all fled to the hills ahead of time. They instinctively knew a disaster was coming and ran for safety. Similarly, when I was growing up on the Outer Banks, every time we experienced a bad storm, the ghost crabs, which live in holes right on the beach, always fled over the dunes about a day before it hit. This happened without fail! Those small crabs have a better internal forecasting mechanism than the weatherman has using sophisticated instruments. So, I have no doubt that God could have summoned all the animals He needed to the ark, and they probably already sensed something was brewing.

The Waters Recede

God preserved Noah, his family, and pairs of all animals on earth (see Genesis 7:23), in order to make a fresh start for humanity, the animal kingdom, and the earth itself. But this fresh start necessitated the elimination of the rest of mankind and the animals. Recall that Genesis 6:13 said the earth was to share in man's punishment. When man sins, the earth also suffers. Paul speaks of how nature itself is subject to the corrupting influence of man in this present age, but one day it will be freed from the curse of sin and death, and released into the glorious liberty of the messianic age. (See Romans 8:20–22; see also, for example, Isaiah 11:6–9.)

After the Flood, God made a covenant not only with Noah but also with every living creature, as well as with the earth itself, never to destroy them again by water. (See Genesis 9:8–17.) All three elements—humanity, the animals, and the earth—were given a fresh start, like the pruning, burning, and replanting of a vineyard in the parables of the Talmud and the Gospels. In many respects, this part of the Flood story reads like the Creation account at the start of Genesis. Indeed, Bible scholars have noted many parallels between the Creation story and the new beginning post-Deluge. And that new beginning starts in Genesis 8:1, where it says, "*Then God remembered Noah, and every living thing, and all the animals that were with him in the ark.*"

After a hundred and fifty days of flooding, the Lord rolled back the floodwaters, and they receded to the places from whence they came. (Compare Genesis 7:11 and 8:2.) Here, we already see parallels to the Creation story. The Bible speaks once more of the three tiers to the world: the earth, the heavens above, and the deep beneath, with the waters separated again by the firmament above and below. The fountains of the deep (*tehom*), first mentioned in Genesis 1:2, were closed, as were the "*windows of heaven*" (*arubbah shamayim*), what the NASB and NIV translate as "*floodgates.*" (See, for example, Genesis 7:11.) These act as gateways to the firmaments created in Genesis 1:6–8.[3]

These passages incorporate the three-tiered universe of the ancient Hebrews: a flat disc earth at the center, resting on immovable pillars and surrounded by waters and firmaments above and below. There are numerous biblical references to this three-tiered world. (See, for example, Exodus 20:4; Job 11:8; Psalm 139:8; Isaiah 7:11; Amos 9:2; Matthew 11:23; Luke 16:19–31; Philippians 2:10; Revelation 5:3.) This biblical cosmology may not fit our modern scientific concepts of the universe, but it served the ancient world well by emphasizing the function and purpose of the various tiers of creation, and the clear division between the earthly and the heavenly.[4] It also helps us answer the question, "Where did all the waters of the Flood come from, and where did they go?" There are gateways in the firmament that let the waters in from above and beneath, and they received them back afterward. Proverbs 8:27–30 actually explains how the waters of the Flood were first created and stored by God, and how they always obey His command. This idea is also the thrust of Psalm 104:

> He set the earth on its foundations; it can never be moved. You covered it with the deep as with a garment; the waters stood above the mountains. But at your rebuke the waters fled, at the sound of your thunder they took to flight; they flowed over the mountains, they went down into the valleys, to the place you assigned for them. You set a boundary they cannot cross; never again will they cover the earth.
>
> (Psalm 104:5–9 NIV)

After the waters covered all the mountains during the Flood, God rebuked them, and they fled either upwards through the "floodgates," or back down inside the earth, to a place where they now are impounded so as never to flood the earth again. The book of Job even states, "*The waters harden like stone, and the surface of the deep is frozen*" (Job 38:30). The *New American Standard Bible* renders the Hebrew word for "*frozen*" as "*imprisoned*." In other words, the waters of the Flood are divinely trapped deep inside the earth. How interesting, then, the recent discovery of three times the amount of the earth's surface waters currently trapped some three hundred and fifty miles down inside our planet, locked up in a unique rock layer in a form that is neither solid, liquid, nor gas.[5] That is the power and promise of God at work.

A New Creation

There are many more parallels between the Flood story and the Creation story. The Flood acted as the undoing of the original creation with Adam, and initiated a new beginning with Noah. In Genesis 1, as God separated the land from the waters and made the animals, fish, birds, and finally man, He looked down on the earth and saw that it was all "*very good [tov meod]*" (Genesis 1:31). But by the time of the Flood story, God looked down on the earth and saw wickedness and corruption. (See Genesis 6:5, 12.) Therefore, He sent the floodwaters to wash everything away, leaving a clean slate for a new world.[6]

We see these parallels even from the very first verse in Genesis, where the Hebrew term for the earth (*eretz*) created by God is found again in Genesis 6:13 to describe what is to be destroyed and made anew. The watery chaos of Genesis 1:2 is mirrored by the waters of the Flood. Genesis 1:2 says the Spirit of God hovered over the face of the waters (*panim mayim*), while in Genesis 8:8–11, a dove—a type of the Holy Spirit—hovers over the waters (*mayim*) covering the face (*panim*) of the earth. Soon, dry land emerged from the waters (see verse 13), just as in Genesis 1:9–10.

There are even parallels between Adam and Noah. For instance, Adam was made to till the ground (see Genesis 3:23), and Noah planted a vineyard after the Flood (see Genesis 9:20). Adam could eat of all the trees in the garden except one (see Genesis 1:29; 2:16–17); Noah could eat of all animal flesh except for live flesh (see Genesis 9:3–5). Adam and Eve realized their own nakedness after they sinned (see Genesis 3:7), and Noah was discovered naked by one of his sons (see Genesis 9:22); both incidents were accompanied by curses (see Genesis 3:14–19; 9:24–27). Both Adam and Noah were commanded to be fruitful, multiply, and fill the earth. (See Genesis 1:28; 9:7.) Last, Adam was told to take "*dominion*" over the earth (see Genesis 1:26–28), while Noah was told that "*the fear of you and the dread of you*" would be over all the animals (see Genesis 9:2).[7]

One more parallel between the Creation and Flood stories is the stress both put on the value of humanity in God's sight. In Genesis 1:26–27, we are told that man was made in the very image of God, and is thus most like Him of all His creation. This vital truth was lost in the generations before the Flood, as humans became rebellious toward their Maker, full of wickedness within, and outwardly violent toward each other. In the new world, God made a special point to stress to Noah and his family that human beings are made *imago Dei*. The murder of a human being by a fellow human is especially abhorrent to Him, so He put particular emphasis on that fact for those in the post-Flood world. They needed to understand this principle and to have respect for every human life. (See Genesis 9:6.)

So the Genesis accounts of Creation and the Flood parallel each other in many obvious ways. However, something new was introduced at the end of the Flood story that has no real equivalent in the Creation story—the covenant God made with humanity and the whole earth, and the sign of the rainbow that sealed it.

A Promise Kept

The rainbow is a natural phenomenon formed as light is refracted through water droplets. For a rainbow to appear, it needs the medium of air, plus sunlight and water, all of which are necessary to sustain life. The presence of all three elements on earth is not by chance; God placed them here to sustain the life He created. The fact that, in the universe, our planet has the combination of these essential yet rare elements, plus earth's specific position in relation to the sun, as well as other factors, have given rise recently to the "Goldilocks" theory.

In the new field of astrobiology, the Goldilocks zone refers to the habitable region around a star where complex life forms can develop and be sustained. For example, the earth is not too hot, and not too cold, but "just right" for life to exist. The Rare Earth Hypothesis, first proposed by Peter Ward and Donald E. Brownlee, explains why a planet must be neither too far away from, nor too close to, a star to support life.[8] Some scientists have countered that there are likely many such planets in temperate zones in the universe, though they would still need water, air, and all the others elements needed for life. To calculate the probabilities of all these factors coming together elsewhere, scientists have had to invent new abstract mathematical formulas. And the chances that the earth is randomly located in the "just right" zone and possesses all the necessary ingredients to support life are, well, astronomical! Consequently, the rainbow may be a simple act of nature, but it also is a powerful testimony to just how precious our earthly home is.

When that first rainbow appeared in the sky after the Flood, God said, *"I set My rainbow in the cloud"* (Genesis 9:13). Here, the biblical text does not use the plain Hebrew word for rainbow, *keshet*, but the personal possessive form *kashti*—"My rainbow." It was God's rainbow because it was His air, sunlight, and water that formed it, and He provided these for our benefit. It is a reminder that God loves this world and is fully invested in it.

God also called it *"My rainbow"* because it was a reflection of the rainbow around His throne in heaven. The Bible speaks of a glorious rainbow encircling the throne of God. (See, for example, Ezekiel 1:28; Revelation 4:3.) Whenever God executes His judgments, the rainbow is always there to remind Him of His mercies. (See, for example, Proverbs 20:28; Isaiah 16:5; Hebrews 4:16; James 2:13.) Thus, the prophet pleads, "*O LORD,…in wrath remember mercy*" (Habakkuk 3:2). Indeed, at the height of the Flood, "*God remembered Noah*" (Genesis 8:1). That is, He remembered that Noah and his family and all those animals were still in that tempest-tossed boat, huddled and afraid. God also remembered His promise to bring them through the Flood; in Genesis 6:18, He had said, "*I will establish My covenant with you.*" So the rainbow is also a reminder of His covenant promises to Noah and to all mankind, and indeed to the whole earth, delivered in two closing passages of the Flood story—Genesis 8:21–22 and Genesis 9:12–17.

The great covenants of the Bible are binding agreements whereby God firmly commits Himself to do certain things or to act in certain ways. Hebrews 6:13 explains, "*For when God made a promise to Abraham, because He could swear by no one greater, He swore by Himself.*" It does not even depend on the person whom God chose as the repository of His divine promises; they might be long dead, but His promises remain.

We see this principle in operation when God made a covenant *with Himself* after the Flood, promising never to destroy every living thing by water again. In Genesis 8:21, we are told, "*The LORD said in His heart,….*" He did not speak to a man or an angel or any other created being; He had a talk with Himself. Only afterward did He deliver the promise to Noah that He would never destroy the earth again by water, and He set the rainbow in the sky as an outward sign of this inward pledge. Noah died three hundred and fifty years after the Flood, but God's promises to him are still steadfast today. Even the regular turning of the seasons is built on His eternal faithfulness! (See Genesis 8:22.)

This is not always an easy concept for people to grasp. Many base their view of God on their understanding of our own human nature and therefore end up thinking He is like us. This is a mistake even many Christians have made over the centuries when insisting that God's covenants with Israel are no longer valid. But God is not flawed and fallen like us! He is absolutely trustworthy, and it is impossible for Him to lie or change His mind. (See, for example, Hebrews 6:18.) Thus, the Noahide covenant will continue to endure as long as heaven and earth endure. But it will come to an end one day. I add that cautionary note here because Isaiah 51:6 indeed says that one day *"the heavens will vanish away like smoke,* [and] *the earth will grow old like a garment...."* But we will save that discussion for the next chapter.

For now, we will end with the thought that the legacy of the Flood in the Bible is one of God's mercy. Here is the psalmist's remembrance of the Deluge of old.

> *Your mercy, O* LORD, *is in the heavens; Your faithfulness reaches to the clouds. Your righteousness is like the great mountains; Your judgments are a great deep; O* LORD, *You preserve man and beast.*
>
> (Psalm 36:5–6)

6

WHY AGAIN?

"Those who cannot remember the past are condemned to repeat it."
—George Santayana[1]

"I came to send fire on the earth,
and how I wish it were already kindled!"
—Jesus of Nazareth (Luke 12:49)

Having now covered the Flood—its background, causes, outworking, and aftermath—why should we believe such a worldwide judgment will happen once more? After all, God promised never to flood the earth again, did He not? Well, we just answered that question with an emphatic, "Yes!" But that promise referred only to never again drowning out all life. There are other means of destruction at God's disposal, and the Bible is clear that this age will end amid another catastrophic judgment similar in scope to the Flood, just not by water.

To begin with, Jesus says it will happen! We have seen in Matthew 24:36–39 and Luke 17:26–30 how Jesus not only treats the Flood as an historic event, but also says a global judgment such as in the days of Noah will occur again just before His return. Peter reaches the same conclusion. (See 2 Peter 2:4–9; 3:5–13.) Paul warns about a coming torrent of divine wrath, just as in the Flood. (See Romans 1:18–2:16.) And finally, the apostle John, in the book of Revelation, provides vivid descriptions of how this judgment will transpire in the last days. All these New Testament figures relied on Old Testament passages to reach their conclusions.

The Warning of Jesus

In His two prophetic warnings about the days of Noah, Jesus's emphasis is on the sudden surprise of the watery judgment. Yet the ease and complacency of that time is not as apparent in the record from Genesis. Thus, Jesus was likely relying on other passages to construct His Flood analogy. I believe one such source is the only place in the Old Testament where the phrase *"days of Noah"* appears in a prophetic sense: *"For this is like the days of Noah to Me, when I swore that the waters of Noah would not flood the earth again"* (Isaiah 54:9 NASB).

The setting here is God affirming His covenant to restore Israel in the last days, which He likens to His sworn covenant with Noah. There is so much meaning in this particular verse concerning Israel's restoration that it deserves its own chapter, which appears near the end of this book. But for now, we will focus on the unique wording of Isaiah 54:9.

Some English Bibles translate this verse as having the phrase *"waters of Noah"* twice: "this is like the waters of Noah to Me, when I swore that the waters of Noah…." But the *New American Standard Bible* translates the first reference as *"days of Noah."* In the traditional Masoretic text, the original Hebrew root word used here is מי (mem, yod), or *mi*, which is a derivative of *mayim* (water). However, the Great Isaiah Scroll, found at Qumran and dating back two thousand years, reads ימי (yod, mem, yod)—which could be read as *yomi* ("days"). So "like the days of Noah" is a valid translation for the first part of Isaiah 54:9.[2]

Genesis 6:3 says of mankind, *"Yet his days [yowm] shall be one hundred and twenty years."* In the Bible, a "day" can refer to a twenty-four-hour period, a distinct event, or a specific season. In this instance, it seems to refer to a peak season or a required period of limited duration, such as days of harvest. God decided to judge the world, but then He waited one hundred and twenty years before carrying out the sentence—giving humanity only a limited season left on earth.

In the two times He uses the phrase *"days of Noah,"* Jesus appears to be referring to this divine waiting period. Peter adopts it as well, saying, *"...when the patience of God kept waiting in the days of Noah, during the construction of the ark"* (1 Peter 3:20 NASB). So the expression *"days of Noah"* is used three times in the New Testament to refer to this prolonged waiting period between God's decision to judge the world and the actual Flood. This waiting period had a twofold purpose: perhaps some people would repent as the world grew more wicked; but for everyone else, God actually wanted to lure them into a false sense of ease.

For Jesus to say the end of this age will be *"as the days of Noah were"* (Matthew 24:37), He must expect a replay of that whole scenario. It may not play out in exactly the same way, that is, with fallen angels and giant *Nephilim* and floodwaters. But something similar will happen, involving a moral rebellion that God will allow to worsen until He has no choice but to judge it. In the meantime, He will patiently store up His wrath in the heavens above and the earth beneath. The verdict is in, but we are awaiting the sentence. And again, this scenario is based on the notion that God is just and fair. He gives warning, and He acts only when our rebellion is so full that we must be brought to account.

The Warning of Peter

Peter also speaks of the Flood, as well as the destruction of Sodom, and then warns of a similar sudden judgment linked to the Lord's return, when *"the heavens and the earth which are now preserved by the same word, are reserved for fire until the day of judgment and perdition of ungodly men"* (2 Peter 3:7). Speaking of the suddenness of this day, Peter uses the same *"thief in the night"* (verse 10) motif employed by Jesus in Matthew 24:42–44, just after His own warning about the Flood.

> But the day of the Lord will come as a thief in the night, in which the heavens will pass away with a great noise, and the elements will melt with fervent heat; both the earth and the works that are in it will be burned up. Therefore, since all these things will be dissolved, what

manner of persons ought you to be in holy conduct and godliness, look-
ing for and hastening the coming of the day of God, because of which
the heavens will be dissolved, being on fire, and the elements will melt
with fervent heat? Nevertheless we, according to His promise, look for
new heavens and a new earth in which righteousness dwells.

(2 Peter 3:10–13)

Thus, both Jesus and Peter clearly say another sudden, catastrophic judgment is coming upon the earth just before the Lord's return. Besides the words of Jesus Himself, Peter seems to be relying on Old Testament passages warning of an end-time judgment similar to the Flood. In fact, Bible scholars have concluded that Flood analogies linked to the end of days can be found throughout the Hebrew prophets, and that chapters 24 to 27 of Isaiah, in particular, serve as one continuous prophetic warning packed with Flood allusions.[3] It is just that these passages warn that the judgment to come will not be by water this time, but by fire!

In the clearest example, Isaiah 24 says the floodgates above and the foundations below will open once again to release God's judgment, causing the earth to stagger like a drunkard and even split open. (See verses 18–20.) Throughout the Bible, references to the windows of heaven above and the fountains below are often paired together, and these gateways usually open up to be sources of divine blessing. (See for instance, Genesis 49:25; Deuteronomy 28:12; Psalm 85:11; Malachi 3:10.) Based on such positive verses, we often hear songs and prayers in Evangelical circles calling on God to open the "windows of heaven" and pour out His blessings. Yet the same portals also function as the "floodgates" of His wrath. This reality is borne out in the very ominous prophetic warning of Isaiah 24:18 that these gateways will open up again one day to let through God's fiery judgment.

From the start, this chapter in Isaiah contains numerous phrases and concepts taken from the Genesis account of the Deluge. *"Behold, the* LORD *makes the earth empty and makes it waste, distorts its surface and scatters abroad its inhabitants. …Therefore the inhabitants of the earth are burned, and few men are left"* (Isaiah 24:1, 6). We are told that mankind has *"broken the everlasting covenant"* (verse 5), or *brit olam*, a direct reference to God's covenant with Noah taken from Genesis 9:16. The Lord promised never to destroy the world again by water, but He also insisted that human beings must respect each other as being made in the image of God. (See Genesis 9:4–7.) The clear implication is that mankind will one day be in serious breach of this condition, and Isaiah declares that a day of global reckoning is coming. He again alludes to the Flood in proclaiming that *"the host of exalted ones"*—meaning additional disobedient angels—will be chained in the pit for a season. (See Isaiah 24:21–22.) There are also ark-like references to God preserving Israel and the righteous during this cataclysmic judgment. (See, for example, Isaiah 26:20–21.)

A few chapters later, Isaiah adds that *"all the host of heaven shall be dissolved, and the heavens shall be rolled up like a scroll; all their host shall fall down as the leaf falls from the vine, and as fruit falling from a fig tree"* (Isaiah 34:4). Elsewhere, he prophesies that *"the heavens will vanish away like smoke, [and] the earth will grow old like a garment"* (Isaiah 51:6). Peter picks up on these themes, saying that *"the heavens will pass away with a great noise, and the elements will melt with fervent heat; both the earth and the works that are in it will be burned up"* (2 Peter 3:10). We also see a reference to global judgment in Revelation 21:1, where it says a new heaven and earth are created because the first heaven and earth have *"passed away."*

All this needs further explanation. In the Bible, there are multiple references to the *"day of the LORD"*—meaning the day of judgment. Everywhere, it is said to come suddenly. Many passages also say it is a day of great darkness (see Joel 2:1–2; Amos 5:18–20; Zephaniah 1:14–15), as well as of great judgment by fire and brimstone, like in Sodom (see, for example, Isaiah 13:9–19; 34:8–10; Joel 2:1–11; Zephaniah 1:18, 3:8). This last aspect is especially apparent as we read the book of Revelation.

The Warning of John

In Revelation, John divides the fiery judgment of the Lord into two phases. The first phase comes when God pours out a measure of His wrath during the last seven years of this age—what is known as the Great Tribulation. This time of judgment is described in Revelation 6–19, and the recurring theme there is fire, fire, and more fire! But then the Lord Jesus will return to set up His reign for a thousand years, during which time Satan and his angels will be bound, and peace and rest will finally come to a restored earth (see Revelation 20:1–6), with even the animal kingdom wonderfully changed to its Edenic state (see Isaiah 11:6–9). This binding of Satan and his angels is similar to how the rebellious angels before the Flood were chained in darkness to await judgment day, and we saw above how Isaiah 24:21–22 alludes to this binding, as well. Then as the millennium of peace concludes, Satan will be released for a short season to lead a final rebellion against God, after which he will be cast into the lake of fire forever, along with the other fallen angels. (See Revelation 20:7–10.) Those humans who join this final rebellion will be consumed by fire coming down from heaven. (See Revelation 20:9; see also Ezekiel 38:22.) God will then show up to create a whole new heaven and earth for the saints to dwell in forever. (See Revelation 21.)

Concerning God's judgment at the end of this present age, the Scriptures are clear that the judgment will be by fire, coming from both above and beneath the earth, just as the floodwaters did. This threat goes well beyond our current worries about global warming. It could easily take the form of molten lava erupting from the fountains of the deep. We all know the earth's thin crust is broken into moving tectonic plates, so that our planet resembles an eggshell that is already cracked all around. And what currently lies just beneath the earth's crust is molten hot rock, which makes it to the surface via superhot lava flows, volcanic eruptions, and earthquakes.

Meanwhile, the fiery-hot judgment from the windows of heaven above could take the form of flaming meteorites, which no doubt have struck the earth in times past. Scientists now maintain that the massive gravity of Jupiter actually shields the Earth from most asteroids and other space debris, or else our planet would be full of craters, like the moon.[4] If that protective shield were to shift even slightly, we could be doomed. There also are growing concerns about the destructive impact of powerful solar flares striking the earth. So whether meteors or solar flares from above or volcanic eruptions and earthquakes from below, these are just a few of the threats to life on earth that already exist in nature, in some cases on a daily basis, and thus it is fully conceivable they could one day be unleashed to fulfill ominous biblical prophesies.

We are warned to be ready in our hearts for this first phase of fiery judgment, which comes just before Christ's return, because if we are not in right relationship with Him, it will be too late! Even if you survive into the millennium, you will perish at some point, as mortal humans normally do, and rise again only at the end of that time to stand before the *"great white throne"* of God's judgment. (See Revelation 20:11–15.) We are always cautioned that the day of the Lord will come suddenly, like a thief in the night. However, if you are walking uprightly with God at the return of Jesus, you will instantly receive a new body—immortal and incorruptible—and enjoy eternal life with God forever. (See Romans 8:18–25; 1 Corinthians 15:50–53; Philippians 3:20–21; 1 Thessalonians 4:15–18; Titus 2:13.) That is an incredible promise that no one should ever turn down!

The wrath to be poured out just before the return of Jesus will come in the great seal, trumpet, and bowl judgments of Revelation. In Revelation 6:12–17, John uses some of the same imagery as in Isaiah 24 and 34. For instance, he describes a great earthquake, the sun and moon being darkened, the stars of heaven falling like ripe fruit dropping from a fig tree, and the sky receding like a scroll. He says every mountain and island will be moved out of its place, just as Isaiah says the Lord will "distort" the surface of the earth (see Isaiah 24:1), and it will be *"violently broken"* (verse 19). This is just the start of the fierce wrath to be unleashed in those days, and it parallels the way the surface of the earth was scarred and disfigured in the great Flood.

What is notable about these Tribulation judgments is the repeated theme of fire, smoke, and brimstone, either being cast down from heaven, rising up from within the earth, or being inflicted by man upon man. For example, fire repeatedly falls from heaven to earth in Revelation 8:5, 7–8, and 10. The two witnesses of Revelation 11 have the power to call forth fire on anyone who tries to harm them or to stop their ministry. (See verse 5.) The smoke of a great furnace rises from the abyss in Revelation 9:2. Anyone who worships the Beast and bears his mark *"shall be tormented with fire and brimstone"* (Revelation 14:10). Instead of being drowned by water, this time, the earth will become severely scorched by the sun. (See Revelation 16:8–9.) Instead of a deluge, water will become extremely scarce. What little water there is will become contaminated by *"a great star...from heaven, burning like a torch"* (see Revelation 8:10–11), or by water turning to blood (see Revelation 8:8–9; 16:3–4). Moreover, there will be numerous earthquakes, such as those mentioned in Revelation 8:5, 11:13, and 16:18, the last being the strongest earthquake ever known.

Thus, God's wrath was poured out in a watery chaos in the days of Noah, but it will manifest as a fiery furnace at the second coming of the Lord. This fact is consistently confirmed in such wide-ranging passages as Psalm 21:8–10, Isaiah 66:15–16, Joel 2:1–11, Zephaniah 3:8, and 2 Thessalonians 1:6–10. It appears that Sodom received just a foretaste of what is being stored up for the last days. In fact, Jude 7 says that Sodom and Gomorrah *"are set forth as an example, suffering the vengeance of eternal fire."* This same thought appears in 2 Peter 2:6, where it says *"the cities of Sodom and Gomorrah* [were turned] *into ashes,…making them an example to those who afterward would live ungodly."* Genesis actually says fire and brimstone *"rained"* on Sodom and Gomorrah *"from the* Lord *out of the heavens"* (Genesis 19:24; also see Psalm 11:6; Luke 17:29). Again, Scripture clearly warns this was just a foretaste of what lies ahead for the whole earth.

Many of these flaming judgments will likely be man-made. Revelation 6 speaks of four horsemen being loosed at the start of the Tribulation to take peace from the earth and cause widespread conflict and war, with multitudes killed by murder, famine, and the thirst for conquest. This means nations will be in heated wars with each other. Fire, smoke, and brimstone also come forth from an army of horsemen in Revelation 9:17–18, killing one third of mankind. Moreover, the great Beast eventually burns the harlot with fire (see Revelation 17:16–17), a second Beast has the power to call down fire from heaven (see Revelation 13:13), and the mystery city of Babylon is *"utterly burned with fire"* (Revelation 18:8; see also verse 18). Again, much of this seems to be man inflicting his own fiery anger upon man. Furthermore, many of the worst fears about global warming appear to happen in Revelation. In fact, Revelation 11:18 actually says God is coming to *"destroy those who destroy the earth."* Yet only toward the end, in Revelation 16, is God's full wrath finally poured out on the earth. So much of what happens before then will likely be by our own doing! Even Jesus said that in the last days, *"nation will rise against nation, and kingdom against kingdom"* (Matthew 24:7). All this would flow with the biblical principle that the rebellious are destroyed by their own vices. Such is the teaching of Paul.

The Warning of Paul

In chapter three of this book, we looked at how the apostle Paul began his letter to the Romans with a review of man's moral descent after slipping into idolatry. It seems conclusive that Paul is writing there specifically about the pre-Flood rebellion, because he speaks of how, "*since the creation of the world*," mankind had knowledge of the one true God but turned from Him and started worshipping idols. (See Romans 1:18–23.) The earliest example that Paul could have used to make this point would have been the days before the Flood, beginning in Genesis 4:26.

In addition, Paul mentions how women "*exchanged the natural use for what is against nature*" (Romans 1:26), before he talks about the men "*leaving the natural use of the woman*" (verse 27). In the pre-Flood world, we are told that women engaged in unnatural sex with fallen angels, which apparently left many men in those days to sleep with each other.[5]

Yet Paul is not just reviewing past events; he also begins to warn about the same moral slide happening again. We see this in how he starts out by speaking of "*they,*" meaning those in the past who sinned, but in chapter 2 ends up with a stern message to "*you,*" meaning those from Greco-Roman culture, with its pantheon of gods, notorious sexual license, and ruthless violence. Thus, he warns Roman believers that the society around them was "*treasuring up for* [themselves] *wrath,*" to be poured out "*in the day of wrath*" (Romans 2:5).

Paul explains how this wrath of God is revealed "*from heaven*" (Romans 1:18), where it is stored up unseen until the moment it is finally poured out on unsuspecting sinners. His warning focuses on the dire consequences of worshipping other gods, which is a slippery slope of sexual immorality, violence, wickedness, twisted knowledge, and so forth. But his original and primary model is the generation of the Flood, which involved a rebellion against God by disobedient angels that was actually viewed with nostalgia in the Rome of Paul's day.

This was not a case of people being ignorant of God—it was that they *did* have knowledge of Him but suppressed it and opted instead for false gods and perverse knowledge. Paul insists that God is knowable by all the evidence provided in nature, a truth captured in Psalm 19:1: *"The heavens declare the glory of God; and the firmament shows His handiwork."*

Thus, idolaters are without excuse; they become ungrateful to God for life and creation; they have vain imaginations and foolish, darkened hearts; they are full of unclean lusts and vile passions, which have led to corruption and sexual immorality. The result is that they have left the natural order and engaged in homosexual behavior and other ungodly acts. This all sounds like the people in the generation of the Flood, described in Genesis 6, whose thoughts were *"evil continually"* (verse 5) and whose flesh became *"corrupted"* (verse 12).

By the mid-first century, the Roman realm had become similarly decadent, especially the capital of Rome itself. As the empire expanded, many Roman citizens were scattered throughout its vast domain and rarely saw the monarch. So they began making images of the emperors and revering them as one would an idol. Julius Caesar and his successors fed into this practice by declaring themselves to be semi-deities. At the same time, the Romans were increasingly giving in to perverted sexual passions. Out of the first fifteen Roman emperors, fourteen were practicing homosexuals. The city of Rome itself became a hotbed of homosexuality. Paul calls out this sin and also decries many other immoral behaviors.[6]

It is clear Paul is not just referring to a process of "wrath" upon individuals in the present, but also to a future day of judgment for all mankind. There already existed a biblical tradition that the promised Messiah would preside over a future judgment of the world. (See, for example, Psalm 98:9; Isaiah 11:3–4.) Indeed, Paul says in Romans 2:16 that such a concept is part of *"my gospel."* In 1 Thessalonians 1:9–10, he describes Jesus as the One who will return from heaven and rescue believers from *"the wrath to come."* In 2 Thessalonians 1:6–10, Jesus is described as coming in *"flaming fire"* to take vengeance on those still lost in idol worship, even while Christ will be *"glorified in His saints and…admired among all those who believe."*[7]

There is one remaining point from this section of Romans that merits fuller explanation, as it is central to my entire thesis. In Romans 2:4, we are told not to *"despise"* the longsuffering, goodness, and patience of the Lord.

One despises God's forbearance by failing to appreciate the opportunity He gives to repent. When we cross a moral line with God, and the ground does not immediately open up and swallow us, we should never misread this delay of judgment as divine approval of our behavior. God's patience with the Flood generation over its gross immorality was not a sign that their conduct was acceptable. Rather, His silence was a function of His longsuffering, even while He was storing up the wrath due for such sin.

Bible teacher R. C. Sproul calls this verse "a scary passage, because what Paul is describing here is a hoarder. The idea behind hoarding is to amass a reserve supply of something against a rainy day…. Paul is talking about hoarding judgment, amassing wrath, heaping it up, piling it up."[8]

In the case of Roman society, a closer look at their moral decay will help us better understand why Paul warned that wrath was being stockpiled for them if they did not repent. As we open wider the pages of Roman history, we will encounter some unpleasant behaviors, yet it will help us grasp the truths the apostle was preaching. It will also provide us with another model for gauging where our own societies are today.

7

THE DECADENCE OF ROME

"Alas and alack! What a nothing is man! We all shall be bones at
the end of life's span, so let us be jolly for as long as we can."
—The character Gaius Pompeius Trimalchio, in Petronius's
Satyricon[1]

"If the dead do not rise, 'Let us eat and drink, for tomorrow we die!'"
—The apostle Paul (1 Corinthians 15:32)

The Roman Empire and its Greek antecedent are seen by many today as the pillars of Western civilization. Yet it is fair to say that
the Rome of Paul's day was so decadent it could never serve as a model for
emulation. But was it succumbing to a moral rebellion on a scale of the
pre-Flood world? And did Paul think it was about to incur God's wrath? A
brief look at the sin and self-indulgence of Rome does reveal the pre-Flood
pattern unfolding once again—idolatry leading to violence and sexual immorality.

Idol Worship

Rome was heavily influenced by Greek mythology, and the city housed many pagan temples and shrines. Idol worship often had a sexual component, and sex with a temple prostitute was even considered a purifying ritual that pleased the gods and brought their favor.[2] This was especially so when it involved the most popular goddess in town—Venus.

Venus (called Aphrodite in Greek lore) was one of the most highly revered deities in Roman society. She was even considered the mother and protector of the Roman people. Julius Caesar claimed her as his divine patron and the ancestral goddess of the Julian clan, insisting it was her personal favor that had brought his bloodline to power and granted it semi-divine status. His heir, Augustus, adopted both claims as proof of his inherent fitness for office.[3] Thus, Venus worship also birthed the imperial cult of the deified Roman emperor.

Venus was seen as the embodiment of love, beauty, and seduction, so Roman brides offered sacrifices and gifts to her before their weddings. She actually symbolized the beauty of the earthly women that had once allured the immortal gods to come down and mate with them. This meant the Roman cult surrounding Venus paid tribute to a heavenly/earthly union that the biblical, Hebraic mind-set deemed iniquitous. By worshipping Venus and other mythical gods, the Romans were romanticizing the very sin that had led to the Flood.

Sexual Immorality

Roman society was all about male domination for self-pleasure—what Augustine would later deride as the animalistic urge to satisfy "belly and loin."[4] Rome exalted masculinity to the point that male citizens were allowed to pursue sexual pleasure with few limitations. A Roman man could freely engage in sex acts outside marriage with either males or females of inferior status, as long as he remained the dominant partner.[5] Slaves were treated as property under Roman law, so using them as sex objects was not considered illegal or immoral. Rape was a pervasive theme in Roman mythology; thus, it became routine for Roman men to force themselves on anyone of lower status. Prostitution and brothels could also be found throughout the Roman Empire in all periods.[6]

Homosexuality in ancient Rome was slightly different from our contemporary view of an equal relationship between two consenting adults. Rather, it involved an inherently unequal setting of a dominant male and his submitted prey.[7] The male partners could be slaves, lower-class freedmen, or *infames*, but teenage boys seemed to be preferred by most.[8]

Infanticide

Another disturbing aspect of Roman culture was its attitude toward children, especially infants, which is a good moral gauge for any society. Rather than pre-birth abortions, the Romans largely followed the Greek precedent of exposing newborns to the elements if they were unhealthy, deformed, illegitimate, the "wrong" gender, or a financial burden. The Greek tradition called for the father to examine a child for defects at birth and leave it to die if it was flawed in any way. In Sparta, a circle of elders made this decision over each newborn child.[9] This method of disposal was not considered murder, since the infant theoretically could be rescued by the gods or a passerby.[10]

The widespread practice of infanticide was rooted in Greek mythology, where it was a recurring motif. The legendary founders of Rome, the twins Romulus and Remus, survived such an infanticide attempt after being tossed into the Tiber River, only to be rescued and raised by wolves. The Romans resorted to infanticide often, with letters from that day indicating it was treated quite casually.[11] A recent study of burial sites in ancient Roman towns ranging from Britain to Israel concluded that infanticide occurred widely in the Roman world, including by suffocation.[12] Once Rome became Christianized, infanticide was finally banned as a capital offense.

Rome's Craving for Violence

Rome was a very macho society in which people took pleasure in watching the infliction of pain and suffering, even in their sports. The Roman Empire lasted for a thousand years, largely due to its advanced weaponry, superior military tactics, and use of brutal force. Rome ruled the Iron Age because it mastered the use of iron. The metal was incorporated into all the equipment of ordinary soldiers, including their double-edged swords, daggers, shields, helmets, body armor, javelins, and spears. It was used to make the best battering rams, siege towers, catapults, crossbows, and other assault weapons. And Rome's ruthless application of superior might earned it a well-deserved reputation for cruelty.

We could recount any number of battles to demonstrate the sheer brutality of the Roman legions. But for present purposes, it will suffice to focus on how Rome put down the Judean revolt of 66–72 AD. At the time, the Jews were one of the largest minority groups within the Roman Empire, comprising around 10 percent of the overall population. Therefore, if Jews ever started resisting Rome, it could prove troublesome. The viciousness of Rome can be seen in the three main sieges imposed upon the Jewish rebels during the six-year Judean uprising. At Gamla, located on the Golan, some five thousand Jewish men, women, and children chose to jump off a cliff to their deaths rather than surrender. During the siege of Jerusalem, Jewish defenders trapped inside the walled city actually fought and killed each other over whether to resist to the last man or surrender and become Roman slaves. Finally, at the siege of Masada, the last remnant of some one thousand Zealots committed communal suicide to avoid capture. Their actions alone should tell us something about Rome's brutal fist.

Gospel Hour

We can certainly see why Paul thought the Romans were storing up divine wrath for themselves. There were indeed the tell-tale signs of a downward spiral of idolatry, violence, and sexual immorality. On the other hand, there were no fallen angels mating with humans at that time, just a lot of idol worship inspired by that rebellious episode. In addition, there was no flood-like judgment on the horizon because it was actually time for the preaching of the gospel, which was going forth throughout the Roman Empire. Jesus had only recently died for sinful mankind, and the world needed to hear about it. So Paul correctly discerned his times and sought to reach Rome and proclaim the good news, even to Caesar himself, if possible. (See, for example, Acts 19:21; 23:11; Romans 1:15.)

This is all about knowing the season in which you live and correctly discerning the purposes and judgments of God. There are times for building His kingdom, and then there is the time for ushering in the King who will judge all. Jesus urged His disciples to preach the gospel to all nations, after which the end would come. (See Matthew 24:14.) In his letter to

Roman believers, Paul wanted to make sure they were free of all the cultural baggage of Roman paganism and decadence that would hinder their walk with God—but make no mistake, the apostle also clearly warned that a day of wrath and reckoning before God was coming to the world.

As we move on to part two of this book, we will take what we have learned thus far and apply it to our world today. We will quickly find there is a growing rebellion against God—similar to the days of the Flood and to the decadence of Rome. But there is a big difference! Today, the gospel has been preached in nearly all nations, so the world has even less excuse for its rebellion. The West is quickly becoming post-Christian. We have turned our backs on God and denied the power of the cross. And the Bible is clear that this makes us worse off than those in ancient Rome, and even those in Sodom or before the Flood. We once embraced a great saving truth and are now rejecting it, and there is no recovery from that. The consequences are going to be dire!

> But I say to you that it shall be more tolerable for the land of Sodom in the day of judgment than for you.   (Matthew 11:24)

PART TWO
THE MODERN REBELLION

8

THE PARALLEL PLUNGE

"I questioned God's silence…. I don't have an answer for that.
Does it mean that I stopped having faith?
No. I have faith, but I question it."
—Eli Wiesel[1]

*"For nation will rise against nation, and kingdom against kingdom.
And there will be famines, pestilences, and earthquakes in various
places. All these are the beginning of sorrows."*
—Jesus of Nazareth (Matthew 24:7–8)

Looking around our modern world, it is hard to escape the fact that we have become very decadent, as in the days of Noah. Many people may think we are progressing and on an upward trajectory—intellectually, technologically and morally as well. Yet humanity is actually regressing in so many ways. And to begin exposing this stark reality, we return to Berlin.

Berlin not only hosts that chilling symbol of the pre-Flood rebellion, the Altar of Pergamon, but it is also home to one of the most notorious emblems of our present-day moral slide—the Wannsee Villa museum. At this exclusive lakeside mansion, Nazi leaders met in January 1942 to co-ordinate the extermination of European Jewry. The Nazi genocide against the Jews is considered the greatest atrocity ever committed by man—yet it occurred not in the days of the Romans or Mongols, but in modern times. For this reason alone, contemporary mankind has little reason to consider itself superior to any previous generation, including that of the Flood.

The Dark Legacy of Wannsee

On January 20, 1942, fifteen senior Nazi officials met at the party's plush estate on Lake Wannsee, just outside Berlin, to discuss the "final solution to the Jewish question." The gathering was convened by senior Nazi officer Reinhard Heydrich, who presented a plan for deporting Jews from across Europe to the east, where those fit for labor would be used on road-building projects and eventually worked to death. According to the recorded minutes of the meeting, any surviving remnant would be annihilated. This initial plan was soon altered due to unfolding events in World War II. Once Soviet and Allied forces began pushing back the German lines on the eastern and western fronts, most of the Jews of Nazi-occupied Europe were sent to extermination camps, or were shot dead by roving death squads. Thus, the Wannsee Conference stands out as the clearest evidence on which to indict the entire Nazi leadership for a collective geno-cidal plot to eradicate European Jewry.[2]

In the weeks leading up to Wannsee, the tide of the war was changing. Once America joined the fray after Pearl Harbor, the Nazi hierarchy realized the war would last longer than expected. There would not be enough food for everyone, so discussions turned from evacuating Jews to their elimination. On December 18, 1941, Heinrich Himmler met with Hitler and noted in his appointment book, "Jewish question—to be exterminated as partisans."[3]

A few weeks later, Heydrich summoned senior government officials to the Wannsee Villa to explain his plan for disposing of European Jewry, which his assistant Adolf Eichmann numbered at eleven million. Heydrich noted the new policy of evacuating Jews to the east was only "provisional," as "practical experience" was already being collected for the "final solution of the Jewish question."[4] He made clear their ultimate fate: "The possible final remnant will, since it will undoubtedly consist of the most resistant portion, have to be treated accordingly, because it is the product of natural selection and would, if released, act as the seed of a new Jewish revival."[5]

Heydrich's meaning would have been obvious to those present, as they were all well-versed in Nazi racial theory, including his references to resistant strains and natural selection. No one raised any moral objections. Heydrich anticipated at least some opposition based on arguments of putting the war effort first, but he encountered none. Everyone understood the Nazi top brass had assigned priority to eradicating the Jews.[6]

In 1947, a copy of the "Wannsee Protocol"—Eichmann's recorded minutes from the meeting—was found by an American prosecutor at the Nuremberg trials. There was no mention of killing, only that "different types of possible solutions were discussed." This wording was not fully understood until the trial of Eichmann in Israel in 1962. He admitted that as the Wannsee meeting was ending, cognac was served and the atmosphere became less formal. "The gentlemen were standing together, or sitting together, and were discussing the subject quite bluntly, quite differently from the language which I had to use later in the record," said Eichmann. "During the conversation they minced no words about it at all.... They spoke about methods of killing, about liquidation, about extermination."[7]

Here were fifteen grown men, most of them well-educated professionals, sipping brandy and casually plotting the death of an entire race. To be sure, many Nazi officials were school dropouts and street toughs. But at least eight of the fifteen senior bureaucrats at Wannsee held doctorates, six of them in law. Others were bankers or economists. One was the son of a minister. Most were from good Catholic or Protestant families.[8]

Germany as a whole was one of the most educated, advanced societies on earth at the time.[9] It boasted some of the world's leading universities and scientists, as well as a high rate of university graduates. This is why the Holocaust is such a chilling example of the great evil still lurking in our world today. How could a German populace so literate, educated, and advanced be seduced by such a diabolical figure as Hitler? He openly espoused radical racial theories that glorified one human race while vilifying another race as so inferior it deserved liquidation. Yet the people embraced him. Those gathered at Wannsee endorsed Hitler's vision so fully they had no moral qualms about butchering millions of Jews. Thus, Wannsee is a deeply disturbing indictment of modern humanity's enormous capacity for self-deception, no matter how smart or progressive we may think we are.

Where did the German people go wrong? How did they come to embrace the idea of Aryan superiority and unbridled anti-Semitism to the point of carrying out the industrial slaughter of over six million Jews? Many historians say the Nazis were driven by the mystical legend of an ancient superhuman race that could be revived by the modern triumph of the Aryan peoples. Most Germans were also steeped in classical Christian anti-Semitism, which was prevalent for centuries throughout Europe. This is all true! But the Nazis also justified their genocidal campaign against the Jews with scientific concepts developed only in modern times. Many Holocaust experts are cautious in assessing how direct an influence this had on the Nazis. But to their credit, the native German curators of the Wannsee Villa museum are honest in tracing the Nazis' scientific racism to the advent of Darwinian evolution.

The Nazis and Social Darwinism

On a wall in the Wannsee Villa museum hangs a plaque plainly stating that the Nazis' scientific racism was rooted in Darwinism. The museum's very informative catalogue, *The Wannsee Conference and the Genocide of the European Jews*,[10] reinforces this point:

> Racism and antisemitism had been central features of National Socialist ideology since…the 1920s, but stemmed from pre-existing prejudices and pseudo-scientific theories. In the 18th century, new scientific discoveries began to generate a modern, scientific world view which suppressed the monopoly of religion on explaining the world. Racism and modern antisemitism were negative consequences of this development. Those hostile toward Jews also modernized their arguments and asserted that their racist world view had a scientific basis.[11]

In 1859, naturalist Charles Darwin introduced his theory of evolution in *On the Origin of Species*. His landmark work sought to explain where the diversity of plants and animals came from, leaving his views on the origins of man for later. But his ideas quickly caught on among scientists, historians, and other "Social Darwinists," who used evolutionary concepts to bolster their own radical ideologies, including the notion of a hierarchy of races. Some even used biological arguments in support of government-run eugenics programs to "breed and weed" among the races.[12]

Though repugnant to us now, some of the scientific methods used to decide superior and inferior races were considered acceptable in those days. This included studying the shapes of human skulls in search of the ideal racial type. Besides phrenology, the new field of philology studied languages to determine which races were more advanced. The word *anti-Semitism* itself was a scientific term coined by the German publicist Wilhelm Marr in the 1870s in reference to research in the Indo-European languages. The German language was deemed to have a "superior" Aryan origin, while Hebrew was classified as a "lower" Semitic tribal language. The word soon became a catch-phrase for hatred toward Jews.

Classical anti-Semitism was largely a religious rejection of Jews as outsiders who had killed Christ. But from the late 1800s, new forms of racial anti-Semitism, based on Darwinian concepts, arose and targeted even assimilated Jewish communities. Many people sought to revoke Jewish emancipation and perhaps to expel Jews from Germany, while some even spoke of "eliminating" the Jews.[13]

This modern racial anti-Semitism had already infected German society before the "Great War." But when Germany lost World War I and then suffered a period of sharp inflation, it entered the political mainstream. Germans struggling under the Weimar Republic soon found a savior in Adolf Hitler and the Nazis, who fully embraced eugenics, Aryanism, and scientific anti-Semitism.[14]

As it gained power, the Nazi party went to great lengths to indoctrinate its members and the German public with their scientific racism. During the 1930s, every newlywed couple in Germany received a copy of Hitler's *Mein Kampf* as a wedding present. Respected universities were turned into key training centers for Nazi racist ideology. Some 80 percent of the commanders of the Waffen-SS and *Einsatzgruppen* roving death squads studied at the university level, and half completed their doctorates.

Thus, Reinhard Heydrich could easily discuss the mass slaughter of Jews with his colleagues at Wannsee using terms like *resistant strains* and *natural selection*. Today, scientists may cringe at the notion that the Nazi Holocaust was somehow linked to Darwinian evolution, and much revisionism has occurred to defend Darwin from this charge, since it could prove crippling to how evolution is perceived and taught. Yet even Darwin acknowledged that farmers breed horses and other animals to produce superior strains and keep weaker livestock from breeding.[15]

The "Silence" of Heaven

Sadly, the rancid fruit produced by Darwinism did not stop at the Holocaust. I am convinced the modern world's acceptance of Darwinian evolution—and particularly its refutation of the biblical high view of man as a special creation of God—has had many other dire consequences. By lowering our own self-image, considering ourselves descended from ape-like creatures and thus no different from the animals, we have devalued human life and made it expendable as never before. In the process, we also have cast God aside, seeing no need to answer to Him anymore.

These monumental changes have yielded an unending harvest of destructive fruit. It gave us the present-day scourges of abortion and euthanasia, as medical doctors have ditched their sworn oaths to preserve the most vulnerable human life. It has eroded our morals, as seen in the growing acceptance of homosexuality and other perversions. It fed the rise of atheistic Communism and is now fueling militant secularism. It is also driving the world to pursue biomedical advances that are tampering with our very nature as humans. Ultimately, it has triggered a growing rebellion against our Creator that will soon draw His wrath. We have breached the core command of the Noahide covenant, to treat all men as created in God's image, and thus divine judgment now awaits us.

Much of humanity today wants to be free of any godly standards and has turned to moral relativism. Most people believe there are no moral absolutes—and when we do make moral judgments, we invert right and wrong. Many have lost the fear of God and mock those who still believe in Him. Among those who do believe in a Creator, many see the world as so broken they feel they could have done a better job than God has. Yet when we lower our image of God, decide we no longer need Him, remove Him from our knowledge, and start leaving the natural order, it means we stand in peril of His wrath. According to the Bible, this happened in the pre-Flood world. And, as we have noted, Jesus Himself said our present age will end in a similar rebellion and divine judgment.

To be clear, I believe that, ever since the mainstream acceptance of Darwinian evolution, we have already entered that certain "waiting period" between God's decision to judge the world and the actual execution of that judgment—just as *"when once the Divine longsuffering waited in the days of Noah"* (1 Peter 3:20). In Noah's day, God waited a hundred and twenty years between His decision to judge humanity and the time of the actual Flood. As we have seen, He did this because His righteous character demands that He judge mankind in a certain way. He is always fair, He always gives warning, and He always gives time for repentance. And based on the Flood precedent, I believe He is doing the same today.

I am not setting dates here. I do not know exactly when God made this decision to judge us, nor do I know how long He will wait before releasing that judgment. But make no mistake—the growing moral rebellion against God is a clear sign He has already decided to let us go our own way, so that our sin might ripen to His just judgment! Meanwhile, He is storing up wrath for an unsuspecting world, and the "floodgates" of that wrath will soon open. Yet those who refuse to join this rebellion, but remain faithful to God and the redemption offered in Jesus, will be preserved as a righteous remnant in the earth, just as Noah and his family were.

I say this with much trepidation but also much certainty, since our modern moral slide so clearly fits the biblical pattern laid down by Paul and the Jewish sages—a pattern of idolatry leading to rampant violence and sexual immorality, and ultimately to divine wrath. We are arriving at the same place as the pre-Flood world, although by a slightly different path. The generations before the Flood left the worship of God and turned to idols. (See Genesis 4:26; Romans 1:20–23.) Today, we are too sophisticated for silly idol worship. Instead, we have jettisoned God by deciding our world came into existence by itself in the "Big Bang" some 13.8 billion years ago, and that humans later emerged as a random product of evolution. The worship owed to God is now directed at nature or at ourselves, and especially our human intellect. Because we have suppressed the truth (see Romans 1:18) and removed God from our knowledge (see Romans 1:28), He has given us over to our debased minds and wild imaginations, so that we come up with crazy theories about our world. We may profess to be wise, but we have become fools (see Romans 1:22), as some of our ideas on the origins of man and the universe are just as silly as idol worship. They also can be downright dangerous, as the Nazis so grimly demonstrated. God has also given us over to our *"uncleanness," "lusts"* (Romans 1:24), and *"vile passions"* (Romans 1:26), so that we are leaving the natural order and turning to homosexuality, transsexualism, and other perversions. Millions of women are going against nature by aborting their babies. All in all, God is giving us over to self-deception and moral decay because He fully intends to judge us. This process is far from over and will only get worse. But all in due time.

Meanwhile, God is storing up the wrath we deserve, and, as described earlier, one day it will burst forth in flames of fire, fire, and more fire. We only fool ourselves in thinking this is nonsense because nothing seems to happen from heaven in response to our rebellion. There is no lightning from heaven, no earth opening to swallow us up, so we continue our moral plunge. We are lulled into that false sense of optimism about the future that Jesus warned about from the days of Noah and Lot. And we fail to appreciate that God is holding back because of His longsuffering. (See Romans 2:4–5.) We misread our times, believing that only better days lie ahead, when we actually are headed for disaster.

All this started to become clear to me when I honestly questioned why Germany was never judged by God for the Holocaust. To be sure, man judged Germany. Man bombed its cities. Man divided the German nation for a generation. But Germany recovered and became an economic power within twenty years of its defeat. In contrast, when God truly judges, it is beyond repair. Remember that archeologists are still trying to find the remains of Sodom and Gomorrah. Thus, when Holocaust survivor and Nobel laureate Eli Wiesel anguishes over God's "silence" during the Shoah, I also wrestle with His silence afterward.

Seventy years after the Holocaust, Germany remains under a divine grace to allow its people time to show their nation has truly changed. Not to pick on this one people, but many Germans know the heavy responsibility they bear for what their forefathers did to the Jews. This is why German leaders often speak of their special duty to ensure Israel's existence.

Still, many Germans today resent having to continue to pay penance for the Holocaust. They no longer want to bear the guilt of past generations. Some even remain unrepentant for Hitler's atrocities, or project the evil of the Nazis onto Israel. This new brand of anti-Semitism obsessively vilifies the "collective Jew" represented by Israel. Whereas traditional anti-Semitism targeted the Jews as inherently evil, Israel is now perceived as the primary threat to world peace.

A series of recent studies has shown this new anti-Semitism is prevalent not only in Germany but throughout Europe. A survey by the University of Bielefeld in 2011 found that 48 percent of Germans believe Israel is conducting a "war of extermination" against the Palestinians similar to the Nazi genocide against the Jews.[16] An earlier study by the same university found that 51 percent of Germans agreed that "what the state of Israel does today to the Palestinians is in principle no different from what the Nazis did to the Jews in the Third Reich." The study concluded that such widespread criticism of Israel is to a certain extent a cover for anti-Semitic views.[17]

This certainly does not sound like a people who have genuinely repented. If God had truly judged Germany for the Holocaust, do you think so many Germans would be turning the tables so quickly on Israel today? Yet no one should think the German people are alone in their absurdly negative views of Israel. The 2011 poll by the University of Bielefeld asked citizens of six other European countries the same question regarding whether Israel is carrying out a "war of extermination" against the Palestinians, and the results showed a disturbingly high number agreed. For instance, Hungary (41 percent) and the United Kingdom (42 percent) came in just under the German figure (48 percent), while Portugal (49 percent) and Poland (63 percent) were higher.[18]

A 2003 Eurobarometer study also asked Europeans which countries they viewed as a threat to world peace, and Israel was cited the most, by 59 percent of respondents, above second place Iran and North Korea (both at 53 percent). Meantime, a BBC poll in 2013 found that 52 percent of Europeans viewed Israel as having a negative influence in the world, second only to Iran (59 percent).[19]

This makes one wonder if the world has truly learned anything from the Holocaust. We make sure to honor Jews who perished in that immense tragedy, yet many people turn around and denounce Jews alive today for trying to defend themselves in Israel. We declare that we will "never again" allow a people to be treated as subhuman and expendable, yet we excuse and ignore the genocidal incitement against the Jewish state spewing forth today from Iran and other quarters of the world. It is utter hypocrisy on a global scale!

So I ask: Have we truly learned the lessons of Nazi depravity? Do we really understand what they were all about? If so, how can so many today view Israel as being just as evil? Have we honestly turned the corner?

There is much moral confusion hanging over the modern world. Again, we have turned our backs on God, going on with our lives as if He never existed. As a result, God's Spirit is no longer dealing with us, but giving us over to our own delusions. The result is a world filled with moral compromise, lawless violence, and rampant sexual immorality, just as in the pre-Flood days. We think we are marching ever onward and upward, but on this, we are sorely mistaken. The proof is all around us, starting with the seething violence of our day.

9

THE BLIGHT OF VIOLENCE

"You can't say civilization don't advance...
in every war they kill you in a new way."
—Will Rogers[1]

"Deliver me, O LORD, from evil men; preserve me from violent men,
who plan evil things in their hearts;
they continually gather together for war."
—Psalm 140:1–2

If we take a wide-angle view of the past century, we first see humanity descending into an epic world war in which "civilized" European nations resorted to gassing enemy troops in a desperate bid to break the stalemate of trench warfare. The horrors of that conflagration led to international pacts banning chemical warfare. Nevertheless, a second global conflict erupted just two decades later, in which millions of innocent civilians were gassed for being "racially impure." Consequently, we enacted sacrosanct treaties banning genocide and ethnic cleansing. Yet that second war ended with the world crossing the nuclear threshold and destroying human life on an unimaginable scale. We also developed other means of cruelty and destruction, such as incendiary bombs and cluster munitions. And civilians became fair game in that resort to "total war."

Ever since, the world has witnessed an unbroken string of armed conflicts around the globe, crisscrossing every continent and impacting every nation on earth. Between the end of World War II in 1945 and the year 2007, there were 242 major wars fought with conventional forces involving at least one state actor, plus many other armed conflicts between non-state militias.[2] A number of these conflicts have been marked by ethnic cleansing and attempted genocide, such as in Cambodia, Bosnia, Rwanda, Sudan, and now Iraq and Syria. We have also seen the return of chemical weapons, most recently in the Syrian conflict. Many world leaders who vowed "never again" failed to take action, thereby inviting others to use nuclear, chemical, or biological weapons in the future.

It has not only been wars between nations that have claimed mass casualties. Professor Rudolph Rummel estimated that during the twentieth century, a total of 262 million people were murdered worldwide by governments in pursuit of secular humanist, colonialist, and Marxist aims. State-sponsored democide murdered six times more people than were killed in all the wars of the last century.[3]

Meanwhile, our best militaries are busy developing precision-guided munitions, laser weapons, and other advanced systems to more efficiently take out their foes. To offset that advantage, we are seeing asymmetrical warfare in which terror militias and even states fight in ways that neutralize the edge an opponent may have in conventional or high-tech weaponry. This type of warfare uses civilians as human shields while also deliberately targeting civilians, both of which methods are war crimes under the Geneva Conventions. One of the main engineers of this new asymmetrical warfare is Iran, the world's foremost sponsor of global terrorism and a looming nuclear threat.

The Real "Nazis" Today

I am careful about drawing analogies to the Holocaust, because it was such a uniquely horrendous event. But if anyone today deserves the Nazi label, it is the Islamic regime in Tehran. Iranian officials have repeatedly declared their intent to "wipe Israel off the map." Iran proudly displays this genocidal ambition on its missiles during military parades. Using inflammatory language similar to the vilest Nazi propaganda, they have labeled Israel and Jews as "the source of plague and typhus," "poisoners of wells," "parasites," "cancerous tumors that need to be removed," and "a germ of corruption," among other slanders.[4] They sponsor Holocaust denial contests while hosting conferences dedicated to a "World Without Zionism." Former Iranian president Hashemi Rafsanjani once referred to Israel as a "one bomb country."[5] While Western leaders bent over backwards in 2015 to reach a deal with Iran over its renegade nuclear program, Supreme Leader Ayatollah Ali Khamenei was leading chants of "Death to Israel."[6]

Given such vile anti-Semitic incitement, there can be little doubt that Iran's defiant nuclear program poses the gravest threat to the Jewish people since the rise of Nazism. Tehran may insist it is pursuing the "peaceful atom," but there is only one known use for uranium enriched to 90 percent purity—and that is for military purposes. And with half the world's Jews now regathered in their ancient homeland, Iran could potentially do in minutes what the Nazis took six years to accomplish. That is a chilling thought, but for the radical Shi'ite clerics in Tehran, it is actually a welcome idea, because they are driven by a *hadith* (Islamic tradition) that holds that Muslims must kill Jews *en masse* in order to hasten judgment day.[7]

The West's feckless response to Iran's genocidal plot against Israel again shows we have learned little from the Holocaust. The world is just as dangerous a place as when the Nazis were in power. No one thought Hitler would ever carry out his radical agenda, set out so clearly in *Mein Kampf*.[8] Yet he did, and because of that precedent, we have no excuse for ignoring the current Iranian threat to Israel. I actually believe there are powerful seducing spirits operating in the world today, just as when world leaders deceived themselves about Hitler's intentions. Indeed, the Bible warns of seducing spirits and powerful deceptions in the last days. (See Matthew 24:24; 2 Timothy 3:1, 13; 2 Thessalonians 2:9–12.) One such deception reasons that no nation has used atomic weapons for the last seventy years, enticing people to think it will never happen again. The experts also insist Iran launched its nuclear program merely as a guarantee against regime change, when its true purpose is as a frightening instrument of Islamic conquest. This brings us to the scourge of Islamic terrorism—and here again, the world seems strangely deluded.

The Sword of Islam

While it is true that fewer people are dying in armed conflicts today compared to past decades, no one feels safe anymore due to the pervasive threat of Islamic terrorism. It has become a chronic peril to all societies, and constant vigilance and innovation are required to stay ahead of the terrorists. Twenty years ago, if someone had suggested that people in airports must submit to security scanners that can see their entire naked bodies, we all would have objected. Yet after the September 11, 2001, terror attacks, almost everyone now does so willingly. This is because the sword of radical Islam now hangs over the entire globe. Still, many Western leaders are afraid to recognize this growing threat for what it is—an apocalyptic vision of world conquest. They repeatedly defend Islam as a "religion of peace," and insist jihadists like ISIS are not real Muslims.

Those who urge us to distinguish between moderate Muslims and the 10–20 percent who are radicals and jihadists have a fair point. Yet even most moderate Muslims believe in the Koranic vision and expectation that Islam will one day rule the world. Currently, there are three main radical Islamic movements competing over who will lead the Muslim masses into that promised "Golden Age," when the entire world will be placed under the dictates of *shari'a* law. Two are Sunni streams: the Salafists, represented by al-Qaida and ISIS, and the more mainstream Muslim Brotherhood. The third is the Shi'ite revolution led by Iran. Each group aspires to be the vanguard of that final jihadist surge that will lead all the Muslim faithful in a final world conquest. They each share a religious, ideological commitment to violence to achieve this end. And they also share the prophetic vision that this day of total Islamic hegemony will not come until the Jews are eradicated from the earth.

Thus, we see that many of the evils carried out by the Nazis, as well as facsimiles of their racist, genocidal ideology, are still present around the world today, especially in the Middle East, and the Jews remain the primary target of this monstrous spirit of violence. The world is still an extremely volatile place where there is rabid incitement, genocide, ethnic cleansing, the use of chemical weapons, an escalating nuclear arms race, and so much more.

It should trouble everyone that radical Muslims take pleasure in killing "infidels," and see it as pleasing to Allah. This means the divine imperative not to murder our fellow humans has been turned on its head, and the *everlasting covenant*" (Isaiah 24:5) God made with Noah to treat every person as made in the divine image has been seriously violated. When Islamists boast of their love of violence and death, when they view murder as morally right, when they shed so much innocent blood, and when so many others are still defending them and excusing their violence, then the world is moving beyond repentance, just as in the pre-Flood days. Can God's judgment be far behind?

Looking further afield, America is closely monitoring China as the next rival superpower, even while Russia has resurged militarily under the haughty and adventurous Vladimir Putin. I could go on and on cataloguing the violence and lawlessness plaguing our modern world, but I have focused on wars and threats that bear some link to the Nazi Holocaust, the worst atrocity in human history, just to give a sense of how much we are still spinning our wheels in the quagmire of anti-Semitism. Yet there also are drug wars, gang wars, conflicts over blood diamonds, race riots, and violent crimes happening all around the planet. There are growing concerns over food riots spawned by shortages and natural disasters. The international mechanisms to prevent nuclear and ballistic missile proliferation are breaking down. And many people fear that terror groups will use nonconventional weapons—including the release of viral agents—against urban centers. We may have seen only *the beginning of sorrows*" (Matthew 24:8).

This now brings us to another disturbing trend that the Bible says will happen if we rebel against God, and that is the rampant sexual immorality of our times. Much of what follows in the next chapter is unpleasant to read about, but it is necessary to do so if we are to take an honest look at our current irreversible moral slide.

10

THE SEXUAL REVOLUTION

"The fact that immorality is rampant throughout the nation
doesn't make it right!"
—Rev. Billy Graham[1]

*"The way of the wicked is like darkness; they do not know what
makes them stumble."*
—Proverbs 4:19

I believe that just as God has stored up the judgment due for the Holocaust, He is storing up His wrath over the world's unrestrained sexual immorality. Much like the rebellion in the pre-Flood world, signs now abound that God's Spirit is giving us over to our lusts and vile passions. As a result, we are leaving the natural order for twisted carnal pleasures, as seen in the growing acceptance of homosexuality, transsexualism, and other deviancies. Again, women are leaving the natural birthing function and aborting millions of babies. Meanwhile, Christians are frustrated that they keep losing key battles in the ongoing "culture wars." We wonder how evil can prosper like it does, as right becomes wrong, and wrong is turned into right. And we ask why God has not intervened. Well, it will happen one day! But first, God is allowing our sin to ripen to His just judgment. As we look at where all this is taking us, the conclusions are shocking.

The Sexual Revolution of the 1960s was a major turning point away from godly standards. In the Sixties, the pursuit of sexual pleasure was essentially divorced from the need to procreate, a pivotal social change that accelerated the moral decadence of recent generations. In America, this transformation hit a key moment in 1965 with the landmark US Supreme Court decision *Griswold v. Connecticut*, in which the justices suddenly discovered in the Constitution a penumbra of "privacy rights" the government cannot infringe upon. This ruling addressed only marital privacy rights, but it has since been extended to other relationships between consenting adults, including gay and lesbian couples. This loosening of morals in our laws and judicial decrees has meant that sexual practices once considered taboo are now being proudly paraded in public.

The biggest victim of this revolution has been the traditional family, and society at large is paying the price. Ever since no-fault divorce became readily available, divorce rates have soared to between 40 and 50 percent of all marriages in America.[2] This development has weakened the family unit, which was always the main source of stability in society, and the negative consequences are widespread.

A number of recent studies have shown that a healthy marriage is good for the couple's physical and mental health. Stable marriages are also good for children, protecting them from mental, physical, educational, and social problems.[3] Such benefits are now being eroded by high divorce rates. Fewer children have a model for what a healthy marriage looks like. Those from broken marriages tend to produce broken marriages themselves. Marital dysfunction leads to societal dysfunction, as children in such families quit school, wind up in drug or alcohol abuse, or turn to crime.

The Grim Reaper of Abortion

Another negative result of the Sexual Revolution is legalized abortion. Before the Flood, women left the natural order by mating with rebellious angels. Today, they are abandoning their natural ability to birth children in the name of liberating their bodies. Men share much of the blame for the scourge of abortion, as they have been irresponsible in their sexual practices and in their duties as husbands and fathers. Still, it is a sad reality that the price for women being "free" is the routine murder of millions of innocent lives.

In past generations, women considered it an honor to give birth. They sensed a special duty to do all they could to bring children into the world. These natural feelings arose from the strong maternal instinct engrained in all women. But that has now changed, and abortion is a clear example of modern humanity leaving the natural order set by God.

Abortions also began to increase when medical doctors wrested control over the child-birthing process from career midwives. From ancient times, birthing babies was almost exclusively the province of women, as they knew this delicate process first-hand. Indeed, midwives were common to nearly all cultures over all time periods.[4] Only in modern times have doctors assumed control of birthing procedures. This trend was motivated in part by the growing number of deaths among pregnant women turning to "backstreet" abortionists. But there also was a financial incentive, as prenatal care is a lucrative business.

There are now over forty million abortions per year worldwide, though many more go unreported. In a typical year, one of every five pregnancies is terminated by abortion. In developing countries, that figure often exceeds 25 percent.[5] Abortion is one of the most widely performed medical procedures in the world today. And if it were deemed the taking of a life, it would be the leading cause of death in America![6]

The total number of abortions in the US since *Roe v. Wade* legalized abortion in 1973 is over 56 million. That is roughly 1.3 million abortions per year in a nation where safe, effective methods to prevent pregnancies, such as pills and contraceptives, have been readily available and affordable for decades. Yet the mass disposal of precious young lives continues. This is the case even though most Americans still view abortion as morally wrong. According to Gallup, the percentage of those supporting abortion has never exceeded those morally opposed to it.[7]

Europe also has widely available and affordable means to prevent pregnancies, as well as aggressive sex education that starts as early as age five. Yet 30 percent of all pregnancies among European women still end in abortion, a shocking rate that runs even higher in Eastern Europe.[8]

More than half the world's annual abortions are performed in Asia, in part because the region contains roughly half the world's population. But one aspect of the abortion machinery in Asia is cause for added concern, and there is even a new term for this evil—"gendercide." Female fetuses are being aborted much more often than are male fetuses, leading to a huge deficit of girls in comparison to boys in many Asian nations, especially India and China. Baby girls have been aborted in the millions. In 1990, an Indian economist put the number at 100 million young women missing from the population, but that toll is even higher today.[9]

Acceptance of Homosexuality

Next we turn to the growing approval of homosexuality. In the West, sodomy was traditionally considered a transgression against divine law and a crime against nature, until social reformers like Havelock Ellis began challenging the notion that homosexuality is abnormal. Yet the gay rights movement as we know it today gained traction only during the Sexual Revolution of the 1960s, when the pursuit of sexual pleasure was detached from procreation. This new sexual freedom was largely forged in the context of heterosexual relations, but gays and lesbians jumped on the bandwagon to demand similar liberties. The Stonewall riots in Greenwich Village in 1969 are seen as the key moment when homosexuals first organized into a movement and started gaining public sympathy.

After decades of activism, in 1989, Denmark became the first country to allow same-sex couples to register as domestic partners. Then in 2000, Holland was first to recognize same-sex marriages. Since then, twenty-four additional nations have followed suit.[10] The US joined the list in June 2015 when the Supreme Court ruled in *Obergefell v. Hodge* that all state bans on same-sex marriage were unconstitutional. That same year, the Republic of Ireland became the first country to recognize same-sex marriages by public referendum.

The undeniable trend is toward ever wider acceptance of homosexuality and gay marriage. The annual Gallup values survey shows that approval of gay and lesbian relations rose from 38 percent in 2002 to 58 percent in 2015.[11] A Pew poll from 2015 found that millennials (born after 1980) accept same-sex marriage at an even higher rate of 70 percent.[12]

Thus, the mainstream acceptance of homosexuality is likely irreversible. That makes Paul's warning in Romans 1:32 quite serious, namely, that those who approve of such immoral practices are just as guilty as those who commit them. There can be no doubt that homosexuality is a willful departure from the natural order that will soon incur God's wrath. Just because it has not happened yet does not mean He is overlooking this great iniquity. And the fact that most people in Western countries now approve of homosexuality is a sign God has already decided to judge us and is merely giving us over to our vile passions and moral self-delusions, as He did with the pre-Flood world. This growing rebellion will only ripen until that day when *"the wrath of God is revealed from heaven against all ungodliness and unrighteousness of men…"* (Romans 1:18).

Child Sexual Abuse

A good measuring stick for the moral health of any people is how they treat women and children. By these standards, the world is in worse shape than many of us realize. The way our newfound sexual freedoms have impacted scores of vulnerable women and children is appalling! Today, tens of millions of women and children worldwide are victims of modern forms of slavery and sexual abuse. These twin evils often overlap; moreover, they rake in an estimated $200 billion per year.[13]

Child sexual abuse is more prevalent than many people know. One researcher estimates that as many as one in every five adult males in the United States has committed some type of child sexual abuse. Yet only about one-third of abuse cases are reported. Three-fourths of all child sexual abusers are relatives or acquaintances within the victim's "circle of trust."[14] Most abusers target girls, but offenders who molest boys usually seek out multiple targets over many years.[15] Sadly, sexual molestation of children is one of the most common crimes of our day, yet it is also the most underreported crime, since the victims are either too young, ashamed, or scared to tell others about what has happened to them.[16]

The problem of child sexual abuse, especially by trusted superiors, has garnered much attention lately due to such high-profile stories as the Catholic clergy child-abuse scandal and accusations against singer Michael Jackson and BBC presenter Jimmy Savile. Even the sports world has been rocked by this epidemic. In nearly all these instances, the crimes are invariably accompanied by cover-ups that only prolong the suffering of the victims. Yet despite all the public attention, child sexual abuse remains one of the greatest ills in our polite Western societies. It also has been recognized as deeply damaging to children due to its lifelong effects.

Because victims of childhood sexual abuse are so reluctant to come forward, one of the most accurate studies ever done on the problem was a survey conducted in the mid-1990s by the Kaiser HMO in San Diego. The health provider asked seventeen thousand members a series of confidential questions to determine how child sexual abuse was affecting their health as adults. In this anonymous setting, respondents were more candid, and the study found that approximately one in six boys and one in four girls were sexually abused before age sixteen.[17]

In Europe, a 2003 continent-wide study found that child sexual abuse is a significant public health problem requiring urgent attention. When broad definitions of sexual abuse were used, including exposure to pornography or unwanted touching of private parts, 50 percent of females and 25 percent of males reported instances of sexual abuse while minors.[18]

Other studies show this is a self-perpetuating malaise, as many of those abused as children end up abusing children themselves once grown. And the problem is only getting worse due to the easy accessibility of child pornography and other forms of "adult entertainment" on the Internet.

Meanwhile, child sex tourism is a booming, multibillion-dollar business, victimizing an estimated two million children per year. Pedophiles can easily seek out and trade information on-line about the best places to find child prostitutes. The majority of exploited children are under the age of twelve.[19]

Another growing problem is survival sex, in which poor and homeless women and children trade sex for food, a place to sleep, or drugs.[20] Researchers estimate that one in three homeless youth in North America have become enmeshed in some form of survival sex. This leads to greater odds they will engage in other criminal behavior, use illegal substances, attempt suicide, become pregnant, or contract a sexually transmitted disease.[21] Survival sex has also become quite common in refugee camps around the globe.[22]

The Push to Legalize Pedophilia

All this sexual abuse of children is happening even though most countries have strict criminal laws to protect minors from predatory adults. But these age of consent laws are under assault by an array of parties who want to decriminalize sexual activity with minors. This includes traditional Muslims who approve of child brides, as well as gay rights activists who unashamedly argue that children, too, have a "right to sex."

Now that the LGBT movement has won its battle to legalize same-sex marriages in many Western countries, the fear is they will now focus on making adult-child sexual relations lawful. Such efforts have been underway for decades in countries like Britain, Holland, and South Africa, often with support from prominent liberal politicians.[23] Some behavioral scientists have fueled this agenda by presenting pedophilia as "normal" if those involved can walk away unharmed.

This is fundamentally a battle over conscience. Gays and pedophiles want to be free from any sense of guilt for their actions. They especially do not want Christians reminding them that their actions are wrong. So they demand our tolerance or silence. But we must never surrender to their campaign to muzzle our moral voice and lower our standards.

Still, the slow erosion of our moral standards that led to the normalization of homosexuality is already occurring with transgenderism, and to some extent with pedophilia and polygamy. Some psychiatrists are already describing pedophilia as a "sexual orientation" that cannot be changed, the same argument that carried the day for homosexuality. The Boy Scouts, Girl Scouts, Big Brothers, YMCA, and others entrusted with our youth have been pressured to capitulate to the LGBT agenda. An organized assault on our age of consent laws, and our children, is already well underway.

Prostitution and Human Trafficking

This brings us to violence and sexual abuse against women. Many people want to turn a blind eye to prostitution and its attendant evils, glibly dismissing it as the "world's oldest profession." Western culture has tended to glamorize prostitution, as in the 1990 Hollywood film *Pretty Woman*. Yet the men who seek out prostitutes the most are not the rich, sensitive types like Richard Gere. Instead, they are usually the most violent toward women.

In her tell-all book, *Paid For: My Journey Through Prostitution*, Rachel Moran describes three types of men who patronize prostitutes: those who assume the women they buy have no human feelings, those who are conscious of a woman's humanity but choose to ignore it, and those who derive sexual pleasure from reducing the humanity of the women they buy.[24] Social researcher Melissa Farley says that very few women who become prostitutes (5 percent) make the choice freely. She notes that most female prostitutes, including those in escort services, were sexually abused as children. She also found the majority of prostitutes want to get out of the industry.[25]

Sadly, an increasing number of prostitutes today are lured into it by human traffickers. On a global scale, 77 percent of all trafficking victims today are females, many of them children. In 87 percent of all trafficking cases, the victims are forced into sexual exploitation.[26] According to the Global Slavery Index, there are currently 45.8 million men, women, and children trapped in modern slavery around the world. Human trafficking and slavery rake in around $150 billion in illegal profits per year.[27] The main goal of this forced slavery and trafficking is to feed the most depraved quarters of the sex industry.[28]

Slavery and sex trafficking are especially acute problems in the Middle East, largely due to raging conflicts, political upheavals, and the Islamic culture's traditional approval of slavery and the suppression of women. The region has the world's highest levels of abuse against women, as exemplified in the widespread practices of forced marriages and child brides.[29]

This brief look at the sexual exploitation of women and children has not even touched on gang rapes in Asia, child soldiers in Africa, or child drug couriers in Latin America. Nor has it addressed such sordid trends in Western cultures as date rape and domestic violence. So, are we really morally superior to the Romans, or to those who perished in the Flood?

Much of the material in this chapter is not suited for polite conversation. But I trust it has confronted the reader with the reality of our present moral slide. We may think mankind has progressed with our modern sexual liberation. Yet the Jewish sages viewed sexual immorality as the most crippling sin of the Flood generation, largely because the people came to believe what they were doing was right. When those in rebellion reach this point, they are beyond recovery.

All the elements of corruption present in the Flood story can be found in our modern world. In the days of Noah, people went from idolatry to lawless violence and rampant sexual perversity. Today, we are turning away from God, suppressing truth, leaving the natural order, inverting right and wrong—and ending up in moral confusion and compromise. Yet despite this grave moral collapse, we remain optimistic about the future, totally unaware that the roof is about to cave in on us. God has yet to judge us for the death factory of abortion or the sins of homosexuality and child abuse. He has yet to punish us for the Holocaust or the endless violence and mayhem still plaguing the world. But judgment is coming! The "floodgates" will open once more, and God's wrath will be revealed from heaven on an unsuspecting world.

How did we get into this predicament? Where exactly did we go wrong? We will explore these questions in the next chapter.

11

WHERE WE WENT WRONG

"Could it be possible!
This old saint has not heard in his forest that God is dead!"
—Friedrich Nietzsche, *Thus Spoke Zarathustra*[1]

"We should not trust in ourselves but in God who raises the dead...."
—The apostle Paul (2 Corinthians 1:9)

Many people promote the fallacy that science and religion are fundamentally incompatible. The truth is that modern science was birthed by Christians during the Reformation. Researcher Rodney Stark analyzed the fifty-two leading figures behind the scientific revolution and found that fifty were Christians.[2] In *The Book That Made Your World*, philosopher Vishal Mangalwadi explains that these pioneers of science studied the universe because they believed God had created it, gave it order, set the laws of nature in motion, and made man to have dominion over creation.[3]

Many of these early scientists—Copernicus, Kepler, Galileo, and Newton—were astronomers who believed the greatest mysteries of creation were to be found in the heavens. Their inspiration came from the psalmist: *"The heavens declare the glory of God; and the firmament shows His handiwork. Day unto day utters speech, and night unto night reveals knowledge"* (Psalm 19:1–2). So they focused on the stellar bodies and unlocked the laws governing their motion.

After solving many of the celestial mysteries, the focus of science turned to the earth itself. The new field of geology, however, came across signs the earth was older than once thought. So scientists began to challenge not just the Creation account in Genesis but the entire Bible, while looking for other explanations about the origins of life on earth.

This was also an era when many people began to question the divine right of rule by the church and crown. This initially started with courageous reformers like Martin Luther and John Calvin, who challenged the monarchs and papacies for being corrupt and oppressive. They asserted that there were scriptural laws and truths that were above men, including kings and popes, a principle that led to our constitutional limits on government. Later, secularists and atheists sought to undermine kings and clergy by undermining the authority of Scripture.

It was during this Enlightenment period, when human reason was exalted over divine revelation, that a new middle view became popular—Deism. This belief system still made room for a Supreme Being, but held that He had created the universe, set it in motion, and then stepped back like a grand watchmaker and let it run its course, content to observe from afar. Thus, it rejected traditional claims that certain royal or clerical figures were divinely appointed to rule the world.

Finally, this was an era of great exploration around the world, which gave rise to yet a third factor for many people to begin questioning the Bible. European travelers, in particular, discovered starkly different races as they ventured around the globe, and wondered how they all could have come from one couple—Adam and Eve. In time, these "civilized" Europeans developed condescending views of other races, especially black Africans, whom they came to view as having inferior, though still unexplained, origins. This all set the stage for Darwinian evolution.

The Dawn of Darwinism

Charles Robert Darwin (1809–1882) was born into a wealthy English family; he was the son of a physician and the grandson of noted poet and abolitionist Erasmus Darwin. Charles studied medicine at the University of Edinburgh and theology at Cambridge, but was drawn to the natural sciences, like his grandfather Erasmus, who made one of the first attempts to explain how the world evolved.

While in Edinburgh, Darwin became acquainted with geologist James Hutton, originator of the concept of "geological time." Fellow Scotsman Charles Lyell built on Hutton's work in *Principles of Geology*, where he sought to explain changes in the earth's surface over great lapses of time due to forces still in operation today. His book, read closely by Darwin, was among the first to use the term *evolution* in the context of biological speciation.[4]

A second influence on Darwin was Sir John Herschel, a Cambridge professor who advocated a scientific approach based on careful observation and theory-building, to identify the single unifying explanation for a phenomenon. Herschel was a major inspiration to Darwin, which he duly noted in the opening lines of *On the Origin of Species*.[5]

The third major influence on young Darwin was Alexander von Humboldt, the greatest scientific traveler of his day. Humboldt journeyed throughout the world, later describing its diverse landscapes, plants, and animals from a scientific viewpoint in an enormous, multivolume travel journal written over twenty-one years. His flowery prose and keen insights into nature inspired not only scientists like Darwin, but also novelists and poets like Wordsworth and Thoreau. He has gone down as one of the most feted figures in history, and some even credit him with predicting man-made climate change.[6] Darwin would later admit that, if not for Humboldt, he probably would never have taken up an invitation in 1831 to board the HMS *Beagle*, a sailing ship bound for South America on an official charting expedition.

This five-year voyage would end up changing the world. The route took Darwin around South America and across the South Pacific, with stops on the Galapagos and other South Sea Islands, as well as New Zealand and

Australia, finally docking back in Cornwall. Darwin kept a detailed diary of his journey, which served as a major source for his later publications.

Continuing to study plants and animals back in England, Darwin's imagination was stoked when reading an essay by the Reverend Thomas Robert Malthus, warning that human population growth was multiplying so fast that, unless somehow checked, it would soon outstrip food production. From this, Darwin later surmised that the reason why some species survive while others do not is due to environmental forces that serve as agents of "natural selection." This selection process was the primary mechanism, along with inheritance of traits, for explaining the slow altering of species from one original form of organic life to its many varieties today—the idea of macroevolution. These principles of heredity and adaptation, also termed "descent with modification," would become the twin pillars of Darwin's theory of evolution.[7]

However, Darwin was reluctant to publish his ideas, not only because he was cautious by nature, but also due to the public outrages stirred by two earlier works on the subject. In 1809, French naturalist Jean-Baptiste Lamarck published *Philosophie Zoologique*, an early attempt at a cohesive theory of evolution based on natural laws, primarily the inheritance of acquired traits. But his ideas were widely rejected, as even scientists were skeptical of his belief that evolution was inherently progressive. After Lamarck, biologists and naturalists pondered three main questions: (1) Was evolution innately progressive or random, or perhaps even regressive? (2) Could the evolutionary process be impacted during the lifetime of an organism or was heredity set in concrete? (3) Was God involved by direct intervention or by merely setting the laws of nature in motion, or did He even exist at all? In due time, Darwin would contend that the evolutionary process was slow, random, and brutal, with no God to miraculously intervene and only the most fit and adaptable life forms managing to survive, thus begrudgingly giving way to a "vague yet ill-defined sentiment" that progress is possible over vast amounts of time.[8]

The second major work on evolution to get skewered pre-Darwin was *Vestiges of the Natural History of Creation*, published anonymously in 1844 by Robert Chambers.[9] *Vestiges* was the first scientific work to combine the astronomical discoveries of Newton and Galileo with the more recent findings of geologists and biologists to arrive at one broad theory of how the world came into being. Chambers proposed that God had set the natural laws in motion for the mutation of species and then let it run its course, so that man would eventually develop. His theory of "Designed Transmutation" meshed well with Deism but broke from the traditional view that God created man as a separate and crowning act of Creation. Thus *Vestiges* was widely criticized by clergymen and conservatives. Still, it was a huge best seller, creating a sensation in the royal courts of Europe, with Prince Albert reading the entire work aloud to Queen Victoria.[10]

Vestiges remains noteworthy because Chambers first proposed an order for the appearance of life on earth that evolutionists accept to this day. He saw the universe as a chaotic mass that came into order by the laws of nature; as the earth cooled, plant life appeared; then came animal life, starting out in the water; aquatic life forms then mutated into birds, and later moved onto dry ground to become land animals; and finally man appeared. Still a believer in a biblical Deity, Chambers undoubtedly took this progression from the Creation account in Genesis, since he followed its sequence exactly. Thus, one of the great ironies of the debate over evolution today is that its advocates insist the world evolved in the same stages as are given in the Bible. So the question is this: how could the author of Genesis have known the order of evolution thousands of years before science unraveled it?

Wary of the heated controversies surrounding these earlier works, Darwin hesitated to publish his own theory of evolution until he could answer all possible objections. But he was forced to go public in 1858 when a colleague in the field, Alfred Russel Wallace, arrived at the same conclusions concerning natural selection. To avoid any dispute, the two agreed to submit papers to the Linnean Society in London announcing their co-discovery of the principle.[11]

The following year, Darwin published *On the Origin of Species*, outlining his theory in detail.[12] The theory was still controversial, even among scientists, who questioned whether natural selection was sufficient enough to result in speciation, and if evolution was as unguided as Darwin maintained. But *Origin of Species* quickly found an audience. Part of what gave Darwin credibility was his many long years spent painstakingly observing plants and animals, both at home and abroad. Yet Darwin never addressed man's ancestry in *Origin*, merely suggesting that with his new theory, "light will be shed on the origin of man...."[13]

More than twelve years would pass before Darwin openly connected his theory to humans, in his 1871 book *The Descent of Man and Selection in Relation to Sex*.[14] Yet in those intervening years, at least six other scientists and theorists published their own books applying Darwin's theory to the human race.[15] One was Thomas Henry Huxley, who wrote the first book devoted exclusively to human evolution. But a second figure to quickly embrace Darwin's theory and apply it to mankind proved to have a much greater impact. This was the flamboyant German biologist Ernst Haeckel, the first scientist of note to unequivocally claim that Darwin's evolutionary process also explained the origins of man.

Crossing the Line

Tall, blond, and blue-eyed, Ernst Heinrich Philipp August Haeckel (1834–1919) served as professor of zoology at Jena University for forty-seven years, attaining fame in Germany and throughout Europe. When Haeckel read *Origin of Species* in 1860, he found the answer to all his questions in "one magic word—evolution." He visited Darwin in London and began lecturing to overflow audiences on natural selection. An avid artist, Haeckel supplemented his lectures with drawings that brought to life the bland field of biology. His illustrated textbooks sold hundreds of thousands of copies, far more than Darwin's books did. In fact, it was common at the time to refer to Darwin's theory as "Haeckelism."

Haeckel's first major work was published in German in 1868; it was published in English in 1876 under the title *The History of Creation*. The book became the chief source for promoting Darwinism in Germany for the next fifty years.[16] At the outset, Haeckel lauded Darwin's theory as applied to plants and animals, but insisted that its value was almost eclipsed by a single deduction to be drawn from it—"the *animal descent of the human race*" [italics in original].[17] He added, "We are now in a position to establish scientifically the groundwork of a *non-miraculous history of the development of the human race*...traced to ape-like mammals..." [italics in original].[18]

Haeckel also maintained that racial inequalities were biologically determined, and thus it was futile to try to educate and improve primitive races. Rather, he predicted that all lower races "will sooner or later completely succumb in the struggle for existence to the superiority of the Mediterranean [European] races...."[19] He also said, "Even if these races were to propagate more abundantly than the white Europeans, they would inevitably be eradicated."[20]

Haeckel—unlike Darwin—had no reservations about taking on the religious establishment, and, in fact, openly mocked them. In his second major work, Haeckel focused squarely on man's evolutionary origins and took direct aim at the "arrogant" belief in a biblical Creation. In *The Evolution of Man* (1874), Haeckel scoffed at the "utterly baseless" notion that man is "the real main-purpose and end of all earthly life."[21]

Haeckel identified twenty-two separate stages of mankind's slow development from a spontaneously generated single-cell amoeba to its present human form. The twenty-first stage is now referred to as the "missing link"—what Haeckel identified as an "ape man without speech."[22]

Haeckel then bared his racial prejudice, describing black Africans as among the "lower races of men" because they still climbed trees with both hands and feet gripping the trunk, much like apes. His illustration of this point was even less subtle—a drawing of a small "negro" man squatting in a tree alongside a gorilla, an orangutan, and a chimpanzee, all four in similar crouches.[23] [Please go to the web address in endnote 23 to see Haeckel's illustration of the evolution of man.] Haeckel added that what set humans apart from apes was a larynx for speaking and a larger brain for greater language skills. However, some races had evolved faster than others, and the more complex languages belonged to the higher races (meaning Aryans).[24]

Others before him had already noted the similar anatomies of apes and humans and inferred their common ancestry. But Haeckel stands out as the first notable figure with scientific credentials to publicly declare it as proven fact, and to directly challenge the prevailing view of man as made in God's image. Where Darwin was timid to go, Haeckel went brashly!

If I had to put my finger on exactly where humanity went wrong in modern times and started getting in trouble with its Maker, this would be it! Ernst Haeckel, a popular university professor, using Darwinian arguments soaked in racism, crossed a line with God—and mankind has been following this rebellion ever since.

It seems odd that so few people know this important fact of scientific history. Most people just assume Charles Darwin was the first to link apes with humans. He is revered as one of the great luminaries of modern science. Yet if Darwin were somehow connected to this racist German scientist, then it could taint him and his theory of evolution. I believe so few people know about Haeckel's central role in developing and promoting Darwinian evolution because the scientific community has tried to bury it. But Haeckel's input gets even worse, as we will see later when we saddle him with inspiring the racist ideology of Adolf Hitler.[25]

A Family Affair

Darwin's ties to Haeckel and others who started steering evolutionary thought toward such malignant ends are actually extensive. In *The Descent of Man*, Darwin made eleven references to Haeckel and praised his views on human evolution to the point he almost felt his own book was superfluous. Darwin was especially grateful to the German celebrity scientist for propelling his ideas into the public consciousness. After all, it was Haeckel who brought Darwinism to the masses and forced its teaching in German public schools.[26]

Another link between Darwin and the dark side of evolutionary thought lies within his own family, by way of his cousin Sir Francis Galton (1822–1911). Galton was a remarkably talented man who was proficient in anthropology, geography, psychology, sociology, and other disciplines of science. He also helped to pioneer criminology, meteorology, and statistics—coming up with such concepts as standard deviation, the correlation coefficient, and regression toward the means. Last, but not least, Galton was the father of eugenics.[27]

When he read *Origin of Species*, Galton was gripped by the ideas of his "Uncle Charles" and began studying evolution in earnest, especially heredity. He was the first to study twins as a means to determine the impact of heredity versus environment, concluding that nature is more important than nurture in determining one's characteristics. By extension, he argued that "if talented men were mated with talented women...generation after generation, we might produce a highly-bred human race." Conversely, if alcoholics, paupers, and criminals were prevented from mating, their unfortunate traits could be bred out of the race.[28]

In 1883, Galton coined the term *eugenics* to describe his program for improving the human race through controlled breeding. He envisioned a two-pronged strategy: "positive eugenics" would encourage the fittest members of society to have more children, while "negative eugenics" would discourage reproduction among the unfit. Later eugenicists would casually refer to this agenda as "breed and weed." Galton even suggested that the state employ the ancient Spartan practice of disposing of inferior infants— an idea already proposed by Haeckel.[29] For all his distasteful and racist views, Galton remained a Victorian-era icon. He was elected a fellow of the Royal Geographical Society at age thirty-one, and was later knighted by the king.

Many of Galton's ideas were fully sanctioned by his cousin Charles, and the two regularly exchanged views on eugenics, including whether white Europeans should actively strengthen their race. In *Descent of Man*, Darwin extolled the "ingenious" work of Galton, and affirmed central tenets of eugenics.[30] He also agreed that "the reckless, degraded, and often vicious members of society, tend to increase at a quicker rate than the provident and generally virtuous members." Darwin worried that this could lead to racial degeneration, and he came dangerously close to endorsing negative eugenics. In *Descent*, he wrote:

> We civilised men...build asylums for the imbecile, the maimed, and the sick; we institute poor-laws; and our medical men exert their utmost skill to save the life of every one to the last moment.... Thus the weak members of civilised societies propagate their kind. No one who has attended to the breeding of domestic animals will doubt that this must be highly injurious to the race of man.[31]

The Rise of Social Darwinism

So we see Darwin himself flirting with radical proposals to intervene in the natural course of human evolution to steer it in favor of the more "noble," white European races. Today, Darwinian evolution has been thoroughly sanitized by historic revisionism and is presented solely as pure science. But Darwin was well aware that his theory was more than just a biological concept, and in the ensuing decades, many of its early proponents sought to extend its application to all spheres of life. Within a quarter century of the publication of *Origin of Species*, there was an eruption of writings by scientists, historians, and political theorists, applying his ideas to all aspects of society. This expanding circle of "Social Darwinists" insisted mankind was subject to the same laws that govern nature, including natural selection and the struggle for survival. The great seduction of Social Darwinism was that it gave a scientific way to explain away old institutions and social orders—including the aristocracy and the church.[32]

Darwin knew that others were using his biological concepts to promote some truly radical ideas, such as the superiority of the Aryan race or the notion that warfare is a beneficial motor of progress. Other recurring themes among Social Darwinists included: disparaging the intelligence of nonwhites; calls to isolate, sterilize, or eliminate the sick, insane, infirm, and criminals; and the theory that human history is the history of racial struggle. Many Social Darwinists eventually gave up on programs for educating and caring for the lower classes and foreign races, which were largely seen as misguided Christian charity. Better to let these inferior peoples fade into extinction—or even to help the process along by state-enforced negative eugenics, if not by outright warfare.[33]

Darwin himself did not articulate any racial theories, as such, but like most Europeans of that day, he did distinguish between the superior "civilized" races and the lagging "savage" races. Nevertheless, he also opposed African slavery and hoped his research would eventually prove that the lower races were just as capable of learning and improvement as white Europeans.[34] Yet the great irony is that Darwin's apparent efforts on behalf of one race ended up laying the groundwork for the near annihilation of another race—the Jews.

12

THE TIPPING POINT

"Darwin did not know what a bitter satire he wrote on mankind."
—Frederich Engels[1]

*"For thus says the LORD of hosts: 'He sent Me after glory,
to the nations which plunder you;
for he who touches you touches the apple of His eye.'"*
—Zechariah 2:8

The turn of the twentieth century was a heady time for the world. At the World's Fair in Paris in 1900, the French hosts proudly marked *la fin de siècle* by trumpeting *art nouveau*, while a number of new inventions were showcased, including talking film, the telegraphone, and the diesel engine. At the French government's eco-sensitive request, the diesel prototype ran on peanut oil.[2] Thanks to all the new styles and fancy gadgets, life was beautiful and the future wide open.

But the "millennial fever" also had a dark undercurrent. In 1899, no less than six major books were published, each with ominous tones for civilization, and especially for Jews. Their concurrent release amounted to a very bizarre moment of convergence. The advances of science during the 1800s held great promise. These included Darwin's theory of evolution, which was unlocking many mysteries in the natural sciences. But it was also being used to justify racial bigotries and radical ideologies. This troubling trend reached a tipping point in 1899, as the series of new books released that year would not only shape public opinion going forward, but already reflected the spirit of the times. Darwin's concepts were now stoking eugenics and scientific racism. This was also an age of nationalism, and the mixing of science with racial biases would soon prove to be a dangerous concoction.

Germany, in particular, was being swept along by a nationalistic longing for its mythical past. At the same time, the nascent Zionist movement, led by Theodor Herzl, was desperately seeking a national homeland for Europe's unwanted Jews. Herzl was motivated by the twin perils of anti-Semitism and assimilation. Religious-driven pogroms in Russia were an ever-present hazard. But after covering the Dreyfus trial in Paris in 1894, Herzl realized even emancipated Jews in Western Europe were not truly welcome. Many were blaming their social and economic problems on the mixing of native Europeans with lower races, especially Jews. There were growing calls for racial purity and for purging the weak from society. The most extreme brand of this racial elitism was Aryanism. Surely, Herzl rued the sight of books promoting Aryan supremacy and Jew-hatred on scientific grounds, selling like hotcakes at the turn of the century.

The Rise of Aryanism

Aryanism viewed the white Aryan race as superior to all other races, the creator of all progress, and the possessor of the natural right to dominate the world. In Germany, it was more common for people to refer to their ancestors as the legendary Teutons, while in America, the preferred term was Nordics. But they all pointed to the stereotypical tall, blond-haired, blue-eyed, northern European. The man the Nazis credited with originating their Aryan racial theory was the French diplomat Joseph Arthur, Comte de Gobineau (1816–1882). Born into an aristocratic family, Count Gobineau blamed democracy for his nation's decline after the

French Revolution. In response, he turned to his Germanic roots for so-lace. In the mid-1850s, he published the influential, yet bitterly pessimistic, four-volume set *Essay on the Inequality of Human Races*, the first attempt to explain human history primarily in terms of racial struggle.[3]

Gobineau divided humanity into three unequal races: white, black, and yellow. White Europeans were by far the superior race, noted for their "monopoly of beauty, intelligence, and strength." Yet racial mixing was di-luting their stock, with the Aryans still the purest race.[4] He believed that when a superior race mixes with an inferior one, it experiences decline, as ancient Rome did. Gobineau felt a duty to warn his Aryan brethren of this danger. But, for him, the inferior "savages" were not just black Africans, but also the peasant Gauls of southern France who had deposed the noble Aryans, or northern Franks, in the French Revolution. The Aryan race now risked extinction, which would repel the world back to its primitive state.[5] Having sullied most of his countrymen, he found few readers for his *Essay* in France. But he did find fans in Germany, including Friedrich Nietzsche and Richard Wagner. Another receptive reader was Adolf Hitler, whose debt to Gobineau is evident in *Mein Kampf*:

> History...shows, with a startling clarity, that whenever Aryans have mingled their blood with that of an inferior race the result has been the downfall of the people who were the standard-bearers of a higher culture.... All the great civilizations of the past became decadent because the originally creative race died out, as a result of contamination of the blood.... Every manifestation of human cul-ture, every product of art, science and technical skill, which we see before our eyes today, is almost exclusively the product of the Ary-an creative power.... Should he be forced to disappear, a profound darkness will descend on the earth; within a few thousand years human culture will vanish and the world will become a desert.[6]

Lapouge and the Aryan Duty

Gobineau won over many more enthusiasts, and in the pivotal year of 1899, a fellow French nobleman penned a ringing endorsement of his Aryan creed, entitled *L'Aryen: Son Rôle Social* [The Aryan: His Social

Role]. Basing his racial hierarchy on skull shapes, Count Georges Vacher de Lapouge (1854–1936) also placed the Nordics at the top, followed by the shorter, darker, flat-faced Alpine and Mediterranean peoples of southern Europe, who were accustomed to using their brawn in instinctive servitude to the Aryan brain.[7]

Like Gobineau, Lapouge resented how the upper-class Franks were deposed in the French Revolution, and he, also, retreated into his Germanic roots. Yet he was more optimistic, citing the eugenic policies of Haeckel and Galton as the means to restore the Aryan nobility to power. These were needed because the Alpines were reproducing faster. Yet Lapouge also faulted the Aryans themselves for refusing their duty to breed, and even warned of "race suicide."[8] The answer was state-enforced eugenic programs to breed pure Aryans and limit the growth of other races.[9]

As for Jews, Lapouge viewed them not as a distinct race but as an ethno-religious group known for being ruthless, greedy, crafty, and arrogant. Even worse, the parasitic Jews were in league with the lower European races to keep the Aryans down—via democracy, fraud, and other means.[10]

A respected anthropologist, Lapouge became one of the foremost champions of Aryanism. Among his biggest admirers was Kaiser Wilhelm II, who hailed him as "the only great Frenchman."[11] Lapouge's 1899 treatise *L'Aryen* was also treasured by the Nazis, who kept issuing reprints of it into the 1940s.[12] Lapouge also stands out for being eerily prescient about where he saw the racial struggle in Europe heading: "The conflict of races is now about to start," he ominously forecast in 1887. "I am convinced that in the next century people will slaughter each other by the million because of a difference of a degree or two in the cephalic index."[13]

Haeckel and the Aryan Faith

The second book of note published in 1899 was *The Riddle of the Universe at the Close of the Nineteenth Century*, by our old friend Ernst Haeckel.[14] The celebrated German biologist had already declared that man came from apes, with black Africans still resembling simians. Now it was time to put down other races—especially Jews. First released in German as *Die Welträtsel* and offered the next year in English, *Riddle of the Universe* was a runaway best seller, ringing up more sales than the Bible over the next three decades.[15]

In a nutshell, *Riddle* profoundly reshaped the mind-set of the modern world with its rigid Social Darwinist message. Haeckel asserted that politics is "applied biology," Jews were inherently inferior to Aryans, Christianity promoted weakness, and eugenic action was needed to protect white society. Yet the book offered a highly positive outlook, as Haeckel claimed that science had solved or would soon solve all the riddles of the cosmos. Nothing lay beyond the ability of science to comprehend, meaning it could be trusted like a religion.[16]

Haeckel arrived at his Aryanism via polygenism. Darwin had viewed all races as originating in one common source. In contrast, Haeckel relied on language studies to contend that different races had evolved independently from different simian ancestors over separate time periods. Haeckel identified at least ten distinct races, with Aryans the most advanced, and the more primitive races lagging behind and headed for extinction.[17]

Haeckel especially feared the dilution of Aryan blood through mating with inferior types. He insisted the state must step in to enforce the laws of evolution and preserve the biological purity of the German people. The first step was halting the mass influx of "filthy" eastern Jews, whom he viewed as the most immediate threat with regard to intermixing. He added that since the inferior races are "nearer to the mammals (apes and dogs) than to civilized Europeans, we must, therefore, assign a totally different value to their lives."[18]

When some noted the Jewish contributions to Western civilization, Haeckel countered that "recent historical investigation" had proven Jesus was not Jewish, but Aryan.[19] At the same time, Haeckel fumed against Christianity, chiefly for viewing all men as created equal by God. He also feared that Judeo-Christian principles, especially caring for the weak, coupled with medical advances, would reverse the evolutionary process.[20]

Always anticlerical, Haeckel posited that the "supreme question" was not whether Germany should be a monarchy or a democracy, but "shall the modern civilized state be spiritual or secular?"[21] He even proposed a new secularist religion to replace Christianity, called Monism. This worldview held that any spiritual energy in the universe had been absorbed long ago into the material world. Worship of God was replaced by a mystical worship of nature.[22] He even elevated the sun to a cult object, to be revered as the source of all life.[23]

A frontal assault on Christianity in the name of science and progress, *Riddle* became the leading anti-Christian manifesto of the early twentieth century.[24] German romanticism in the late 1800s longed for the pre-Christian paganism of their ancient folklore. Haeckel managed to link the conservatives behind this movement with progressives who valued science and modernity. This would eventually give the National Socialists a much broader foundation to build upon, especially in militarizing German society.

Flush with *Riddle's* success, Haeckel became a hero of German national and racial regeneration. The Kaiser awarded him the title of Excellency in 1907, while the Linnean Society of London gave him its prestigious Darwin-Wallace Medal in 1908.[25] But his most significant endorsement came a few decades later from Adolf Hitler, guardian of the Master Race. Indeed, it is fair to categorize Haeckel as a main progenitor of Nazi ideology.

Chamberlain and the Aryan Hero

Another popular book published in 1899 was authored by Houston Stewart Chamberlain (1855–1927), entitled *The Foundations of the Nineteenth Century*. Chamberlain had a unique story as a Brit who moved to Germany and became enraptured by its Teutonic lore. He was especially captivated by the music and philosophy of Richard Wagner, and became the chief popularizer of the Bayreuth cult—a major fount of German anti-Semitism. Chamberlain got so close to Wagner, he eventually married his daughter Eva.

While living in Vienna, Chamberlain encountered waves of Russian Jews escaping czarist pogroms, and his anti-Semitism only deepened. With their strange dress and customs, he saw them as dirty human vermin who were threatening the superior native Aryans by racial mixture. So Chamberlain warned in *Foundations* that this Jewish "pest" must be cut off, lest they "spread like a poison over the whole earth."[26] They were a "mongrel" people, and universal corruptors.[27] He added that Jews were a threat not just to the body politic, but to the actual human body. Obsessed with cleanliness, Chamberlain seemed to project all his fear of contamination onto the squalid Jews. So he urged his fellow Teutons to purge themselves of any Jewish strain, lest they become "a herd of pseudo-Hebraic mestizos."[28]

Yet Chamberlain held out hope for the Aryan race due to his intense studies of the works of Charles Darwin. He reasoned that the same practices employed in animal husbandry to produce thoroughbred race horses and champion hunting dogs could be used in the propagation of human beings. Hence, he sunnily points out in *Foundations* that by wisely planning their mating habits and outlawing interracial couples, the Teutons could stem their degeneration.[29]

Chamberlain also turned on the God of the Jews, as well as Christianity. He compared the harsh God of the Bible with the heroic *Übermensch* of German paganism. He even dedicated a whole chapter to proving the case for an Aryan Jesus.

A patchwork of rambling ideas, *Foundations* reduced the history of Western civilization to a prolonged conflict between the progressive, moral Aryans and the mercenary, materialistic Jews.[30] The Germanic people were in decline due to mixing with inferior races, but they could be salvaged by decisive state intervention, and he eventually found the man who could save Germany.[31]

Chamberlain's book was a huge success, both in Germany and abroad. In America, it was highly regarded by Teddy Roosevelt and other prominent figures. In his adopted homeland, Chamberlain's acclaim skyrocketed. Kaiser Wilhelm II lauded *Foundations* as a marvelous "Hymn to Germanism."[32] He ordered that it be read aloud at court, and distributed free copies to army officers, as well as to schools and libraries across the land.[33]

When World War I broke out, Chamberlain renounced his British citizenship and spent the war years blasting the Semitic-loving Allies. He was deeply depressed by Germany's defeat in 1918, and his health deteriorated rapidly. For the last ten years of his life, he was bedridden. But his spirits were lifted in 1923 by a visit from a young rabble-rouser named Adolf Hitler. Afterward, Chamberlain wrote this to him:

> My faith in Germandom has not wavered for a moment, though my hopes were—I confess—at a low ebb. With one stroke you have transformed the state of my soul. That Germany, in the hour of her greatest need, brings forth a Hitler—that is proof of her vitality.... I can now go untroubled to sleep.... May God protect you![34]

Though Chamberlain never explicitly advocated violence against Jews, he did much to fuel German hostility toward them. He magnified the Aryan myth and gave it an intellectual and pseudo-scientific facade. Chamberlain also was the first prominent figure to endorse the Nazi movement, and the Führer never forgot it. When he died in 1927 at Bayreuth, a mournful Hitler was among the many notables who attended his funeral.

Ripley and the Aryan Migration

A fourth title published in 1899 showed that America was not immune to the toxins being spread by Social Darwinists. William Zebina Ripley (1867–1941) was a respected economist and the foremost authority on America's mighty rail industry. He also ventured into anthropology and the science of racial differences, and set forth his views in *The Races of Europe*.[35]

The book opens with the now-familiar ordering of the European races, with the northern Teutons atop the pyramid, followed by the southern Alpines and Mediterraneans. Ripley next warned that the masses of southern and eastern Europeans then streaming into America were endangering the nation's Anglo-Saxon majority. Around this time, nearly one million new immigrants per year were pouring into the country from Europe, and Ripley saw this tide of foreigners as a source for disease, overcrowding, moral corruption, and Aryan degeneration.

Ripley cautioned against one particular group arriving in massive numbers—Jews. He noted their peculiar physical features, beginning with their large, hooked noses. Their "rather full" eyebrows revealed their "suppressed cunning." Finally, Jews were "prone to nervous and mental disorders; insanity is fearfully prevalent among them."[36] With millions more still in Eastern Europe waiting to join the great migration to New York,

Ripley feared allowing the "great Polish swamp of miserable [Jews], terrific in its proportions...to drain itself off into our country."[37]

Ripley's book put him on the map as an authority on racial problems in America just at the time the nation was absorbing these waves of destitute immigrants. While welcoming these newcomers in her famous poem *The New Colossus*, Emma Lazarus still referred to them as "your tired, your poor, your huddled masses..., the wretched refuse of your teeming shores." Meanwhile, a new play by Israel Zangwill celebrated America as "the great melting pot" of the European races. But Ripley's book struck a different chord with many Anglo-Saxon natives, feeding their fears that their days as rulers of North America were numbered.

Among those awakened by Ripley's alarmism was Madison Grant, father of the conservation movement. Grant launched the first campaigns to save California redwoods, American bison, bald eagles, and whales. Yet thanks to Ripley, his greatest cause became saving the white Nordic race, which he championed in the most influential book ever published in America on Aryan superiority, *The Passing of the Great Race*. A glowing tribute to the "Master Race," the book soon caught the eye of Adolf Hitler. The two became close friends, and Hitler drew inspiration from Grant as he began to plot the conquest of Europe and the solution to its Jewish problem.[38]

The Russian Contribution

The year 1899 also saw the appearance of a notoriously anti-Semitic pamphlet purporting to be the inside account of a Jewish conspiracy for world control. While it lacked any legitimate scientific angle, *The Protocols of the Learned Elders of Zion* was an extremely potent ingredient to add to the noxious mix of publications then taking direct aim at the Jewish people at the turn of the twentieth century. Forged by the Russian secret police, *The Protocols* pretends to be the minutes of a secret meeting of Jewish leaders, held at the 1897 First Zionist Congress, in which they plotted to use Communism, materialism, world wars, economic depressions, pornography, and other means to achieve global control. The tract was later spread abroad by Russian expatriates who blamed Jews for the fall of the Romanov dynasty in 1917. This charge resonated with anti-Marxist elements in Europe and America. *The Protocols* had a huge influence on such key figures as American auto baron Henry Ford and, of course, Adolf Hitler, who relied on it heavily in writing *Mein Kampf* and developing Nazi ideology.[39]

Rohling and the Spreading Net

That same year, a sixth book appeared, portraying Jews as an evil and disruptive force in world history. *The Talmud Jew*, by August Rohling, was actually a three-decades-old treatise that gave existing anti-Semitic prejudices a spurious intellectual and scientific legitimacy. But its translation into Arabic and release in Cairo in 1899 was yet another timely dagger aimed at the heart of European Jewry. In *The Talmud Jew*, Rohling falsely charged that Jews were permitted by their religious writings to practice all manner of sins and vices, including falsehood and chicanery, usury and theft, murder and adultery. Besides its classic Christian anti-Semitism, Rohling also threw in a dose of modern conspiratorial anti-Semitism, warning of Jewish plots to control the world.[40] Long discredited for its phony scholarship, the book still became a primary source for spreading traditional European anti-Semitism among the Arab and Muslim people.[41] According to historian Martin Gilbert, the appearance of *The Talmud Jew* in Arabic in 1899 was an added worry for Theodor Herzl, as it threatened to arouse anti-Semitism in a region he needed to welcome Jews fleeing pogroms and prejudices in Europe. If the door to Palestine were to close, that would spell disaster for his Zionist movement.[42]

Ultimately, the cavalcade of these six different publications in one year—all disparaging and dehumanizing the Jews on scientific, racial, religious, and conspiratorial grounds—reflected the spirit of the times. Jews were under universal derision and increasing threat, and yet even their efforts at self-preservation were being twisted into evidence of their evil nature. What is truly remarkable is how so many similar yet bizarre ideas were being arrived at by one author after another, all at the same time: the dangers of racial mixture that had doomed Rome, the Aryan mastery as seen in the Aryan Jesus, the biological defects of the Jews, the weakness of Christianity. These ideas carried a common thread, as each was drawn from the lessons taught by nature's cruel, unyielding struggle for existence as revealed by Darwinian evolution. That is where things stood at the dawn of the twentieth century, just before these unsavory ideas leapt beyond the lab in ways few people at the time could imagine.

13

FRUIT OF THE POISON TREE

"Be brave!... God has never deserted our people. Through the
ages Jews have had to suffer.... The weak shall fall and the strong
shall survive and not be defeated!"
—Anne Frank, *The Diary of a Young Girl*[1]

"A good tree cannot bear bad fruit, nor can a bad tree bear good fruit."
—Jesus of Nazareth (Matthew 7:18)

Again, it is a sensitive subject to connect Darwinism to the Nazi Holocaust. Not only scientists, but even some Jews are offended by this
charge. The Anti-Defamation League has described such claims as outra-
geous and trivializing of the many complex factors behind the Shoah.[2] Yet as
the series of books released in 1899 reveal, there is a direct link between Social Darwinism and the Nazi genocide against the Jews. True, other factors
were involved, most notably German mysticism, Christian anti-Semitism,
and modern conspiratorial anti-Semitism. Religious anti-Semitism certainly helps explain why Hitler had so many willing Christian accomplices, as

for centuries Europe's established churches had taught that the Jews were cursed for killing Christ. Yet Christianity still viewed Jews as humans, since the Bible teaches that all men were created in God's image. They were even redeemable, if they would only convert.

In contrast, the Nazis used Darwinian concepts to degrade Jews to a subhuman level, as being closer to rats than to the higher human races. This went beyond traditional Christian anti-Semitism, twisting biological concepts to justify exterminating a "genetically defective" race. No doubt, Christian anti-Semites had committed many atrocities against the Jews— inquisitions, pogroms, expulsions, forced conversions—but nothing on the scale of the Holocaust.

Moreover, the Nazi core rejected Christianity as weak and passé. This was a general trend in Germany at the time, and some theologians tried to remold Christianity to fit the new Aryan ideology. But the Nazi inner circle was not impressed. In fact, Hitler's *Mein Kampf* is bereft of any New Testament quotes and thin on any traditional appeals to Christian bias against Jews.

The Nazis also shared a mystical belief in Aryan superiority, rooted in the German Romanticism of Goethe, Bismarck and Wagner. Yet they also went to extraordinary lengths to build a scientific foundation for their racial views. This was not just an intellectual veneer, but a purposeful use of science to achieve diabolical ends—taking evolution to what they thought were logical conclusions. Thus, many scholars now concur that the Nazis used Social Darwinist ideas to underpin their policies on war, eugenics, and race.[3]

Still, many recoil at the notion that Darwinian evolution was somehow behind the Holocaust, and revisionists have tried to shield Darwin from this weighty charge. Surely, they argue, he never anticipated state-sponsored mass genocide. Yet, in *Descent of Man*, Darwin himself fretted over biological decline were society to cushion the unfit from the beneficial weeding process of natural selection, warning that "excepting in the case of man himself, hardly any one is so ignorant as to allow his worst animals to breed."[4] From this thought flowed the idea of artificially impacting the natural evolutionary process to solve social ills via state-run programs. Such efforts were launched decades before the Nazis, including in England and the United States. Haeckel described it as "applied biology" by active and passive means. Others knew it by the catchphrase "breed and weed." Alas, the science of eugenics had arrived!

The Eugenics Explosion

Eugenics had been a scientific pursuit ever since Galton coined the term in 1883. Its early focus was on protecting and improving individual bloodlines, but around 1900 eugenics shifted its emphasis to group preservation, due to several coalescing factors. First, statistics indicated a sharp decline in birthrates among northern Europeans. Second, there was a general sense of moral degeneracy in Western society, which many blamed on racial mixing. A third factor was an advance in science known as the Mendel-Weismann synthesis, which seemed to confirm that our physical and mental traits are fixed by heredity. Thus, programs to assist the weaker members of society or lesser races in hopes they would produce better offspring were suddenly deemed futile. Instead, everything now had to be done to keep their tainted seed from mixing with the stronger individuals and races. Almost overnight, eugenics became the means to ensure human progress and safeguard the higher European races.[5]

In the first decade of the twentieth century, groups promoting eugenics sprang up in over thirty countries worldwide, but America was where the movement made its greatest strides in the pre-Nazi era. By the time Hitler took power in Germany in 1933, thirty US states had adopted laws to involuntarily sterilize the "feebleminded," petty criminals, vagrants, paupers and other "undesirables." US Supreme Court decisions defended these laws; in its infamous ruling in *Buck v. Bell*, the Court sanctioned a compulsory state program to cut the Fallopian tubes of mentally disabled women, with Justice Oliver Wendell Holmes declaring, "Three generations of imbeciles is enough."[6] Such forced sterilization programs continued in America even into the 1970s.[6] Eugenics became so trendy in the US that it was common to see "fittest family" contests at county fairs.[7] Prestigious universities, such as Harvard, Yale, Stanford and Princeton, all hosted eugenic research departments. Corporate titans like Carnegie and Rockefeller provided funds for these eugenic programs, as well as for pioneering German research on twins by Josef Mengele and others.[8]

Meanwhile, Madison Grant was instrumental in shifting eugenics from a struggle against individual contaminants to a war against unfit races. His book *The Passing of the Great Race*, published in 1916, alerted America's Anglo-Saxon elite that, unless they embraced eugenics, the great Nordic race would soon vanish due to mixture with inferior immigrants. For Grant, admired for saving the redwoods and buffalo, this was no different than a wildlife manager thinning out a herd of overpopulating deer.[9] After reading his manifesto on scientific racism, one would have felt that the biological threat posed by inferior races was no longer a speculative theory, but a palpable danger. And the greatest threat was from the Jews. The patriotic Nordic race was being "elbowed out of his own home...by the swarms of Polish Jews," who take his language, steal his clothes, and now "are beginning to take his women."[10]

In stark language soon echoed by the Nazis, Grant made this decree:

> The laws of nature require the obliteration of the unfit.... This is a practical, merciful, and inevitable solution of the whole problem, and can be applied to an ever widening circle of social discards, beginning always with the criminal, the diseased, and the insane, and extending gradually to types which may be called weaklings rather than defectives, and perhaps ultimately to worthless race types.[11]

His book had a huge impact on political leaders in Washington, including on presidents Calvin Coolidge and Warren G. Harding. Congress began enacting ever stricter immigration laws, cutting the flow of new immigrants from almost one million per year to barely twenty thousand by the mid-1920s. This critical escape outlet for European Jews would be kept shut even amid the Holocaust.[12]

By keeping imperiled Jews out of America, Madison Grant effectively dumped them back into the lap of his great admirer, Adolf Hitler. The two corresponded regularly, and Hitler glowingly referred to *Passing of the Great Race* as his "Bible." Hitler studied other American eugenic literature and laws, and praised them in *Mein Kampf*. For many Germans, the Nazis' ruthless racial policies were more palatable once they were shown to have American precedents. Yet under Hitler, Germany took the lessons of Darwinism to an unconscionable extreme.[13]

The Science of Nazism

A defeated Germany struggled after the First World War, and many people blamed the Jews for the defeat and the stagnant economy. One of the most radical anti-Semitic elements was the National Socialist German Worker's Party (NSDAP), now known as the Nazis. Its brash young leader, Adolf Hitler, championed a fight against the Jews as the cure for all of Germany's problems. Jailed in 1923 for an attempted *putsch*, he used the time to perfect his oratory skills and write *Mein Kampf*, a dark treatise setting out his aims of ensuring a "pure race" and the "elimination" of Jews from German society. Finding sympathy among the Weimar elite, Hitler was released early, and his party quickly gained a national following. Despite limited electoral success, Hitler managed in early 1933 to manipulate an ailing President Hindenburg, exploit the Reichstag fire, purge his Communist rivals, and have himself declared—in essence—dictator for life.[14]

Once in power, the Nazis immediately began enacting laws to isolate Jews from the nation's political, economic and social life. Any explanations for these anti-Semitic policies apart from the influence of Social Darwinism always tend to break down. Indeed, ongoing research has increasingly confirmed the connection between Nazi ideology and scientific racism. In particular, historian Daniel Gasman has established a direct link through the person of Ernst Haeckel.[15] Similarly, Harvard paleontologist Stephen Jay Gould insists that Haeckel's "evolutionary racism… contributed to the rise of Nazism."[16] Others note that Haeckel's appeals to "applied biology" appear often in Nazi propaganda.[17]

Thus, it was Ernst Haeckel—the venerated German biologist who preempted Darwin in declaring man's descent from apes, who insisted that the different races evolved separately at different paces, and who believed blacks and Jews were still closer to their original simian ancestors than to the glorious Aryan race—it was this man, more than anyone else, who provided the scientific justification for the Nazis to view Jews as subhuman and in need of extermination.

Most people see Alfred Rosenberg's book *The Myth of the Twentieth Century* as the primary exposition of Nazi ideology. Yet it was never endorsed by Hitler and his inner circle as official party doctrine. Instead, it was Hitler himself who articulated the core party philosophy, and his writings and rhetoric were filled with Darwinian biological concepts taken to lethal excesses.

In Hitler's Own Words

Throughout Hitler's writings and speeches, there are repeated references to the phrase "struggle for existence," by which he invariably meant the biological fight a person or race wages to survive when pitted against the unkind forces of nature. In fact, his most well-known work, *Mein Kampf*, means "My Struggle." This did not refer to political contests but to Darwinian principles. The phrase "struggle for existence" also appears in a little-known book he wrote in 1928 that was published only after the war as *Hitler's Secret Book*.[18] Here, he insisted that nations and races face the same "struggle for existence" as the lowest organisms.[19] A third surviving direct literary source of his views, entitled *Hitler's Table Talk, 1941–1944*, records his statements as Reich Chancellor made to core Nazi officials during the war years. Among them, Hitler asserted that "it is the struggle for existence that produces the selection of the fittest."[20]

In *Mein Kampf*, Hitler explained that race meant more than culture—it meant bloodline, which must be collectively preserved. Thus, it was heroic for individuals to sacrifice themselves for the survival of the whole race. Since nature did not assign land to any particular nation or race, it was up to the race to acquire the land and resources needed to survive by engaging other nations in conflict. So Hitler called for Germany to acquire *Lebensraum* ("living space") to the East, a Darwinian-based concept he adopted from geologist Friedrich Rolle.[21] War was necessary to acquire this land, and was beneficial in toughening and purifying the German race. "For the good of the German people, we must wish for a war every fifteen or twenty years," he once said.[22]

By the "brutal" and recurring "process of thorough-going selection," nature eliminated the weak and improved the strong.[23] This struggle was the highest driving force for progress.[24] It also had forged a hierarchy of superior and inferior races, and Hitler's task was to ensure German society understood and mirrored this iron principle of nature. Thus, he wrote in

Mein Kampf, his ideology "by no means believes in the equality of races, but...demand[s] the subordination of the inferior or weaker in accordance with the eternal will that dominates this universe."[25]

One hardened rule of nature was the negative impact of racial mixture, which had to be avoided at all costs. "The stronger must dominate and not blend with the weak."[26] Of course, the strongest, most progressive race was the Aryan, or Germanic, race, while the greatest threat of racial mixing came from the Jews. This Jewish threat was presented in biological terms—as a parasite, a bacillus, and a "world plague" threatening to poison the pure Aryan bloodline. Thus, Jews had to be purged from the German homeland.[27]

In a speech at a Nuremberg party rally, Hitler also decried the "sentimental humanitarianism" which was breeding the weak and killing off the strong.[28] Elsewhere, he denied the ability of education and other efforts to improve the weaker individuals and lesser races.[29] Accordingly, he launched merciless eugenic programs to protect and purify the Aryan race. The Nazis made sterilization mandatory for certain criminals, those with mental and physical defects, hereditary alcoholics, homosexuals, unwed mothers, and others with "moral weaknesses." By 1945, an estimated three hundred and sixty thousand Germans had been involuntarily sterilized, many by castration. Even more brutal was the euthanasia program against the mentally disabled, with thousands of retarded children slowly starved to death and tens of thousands of adults gassed.[30] Scores of elderly Germans were taken from old-age homes and asphyxiated with chemical agents.[31]

But the most extensive state-sponsored campaign for purging German society of any undesirable elements was the mass extermination of over six million Jews between 1938 and 1945. A half million gypsies and millions of Slavic Poles and Russians were also targeted. Hitler had stated in *Mein Kampf,* "All who are not of good race in this world are chaff."[32] The Nazis made sure much of that chaff went up in flames.

Connecting the dots from Darwin to Hitler, it appears the Führer adopted Haeckel's polygenism. This meant the various races had different origins and evolved at different paces, and thus superior races must never mix with inferior bloodlines, even if it meant resorting to mass executions. He even questioned whether Aryans were descended from apes, and looked for some as yet unexplained higher origin.[33] Heather Pringle's recent book, *The Master Plan*, follows the bizarre expeditions of Nazi archeologists to find proofs of this mystical Aryan ancestry.[34]

Even so, Hitler still kept to a rigid reading of Darwinian evolution, which ironically may have contributed to Germany's defeat. Some scholars assess that Nazi leaders persistently undervalued Russian abilities in battle, based on their view of the Slavic peoples as genetically inferior to Aryans. Even at the end, Hitler was still presenting the war as a Darwinian struggle, telling his people that if they lost, it would be because they had proven themselves weaker and unworthy of victory.[35]

After Hitler took his own life in April 1945, many of his chief lieutenants were tried by the Allies for war crimes at Nuremberg. There, the Nazi defendants cited an array of sources in their defense, including Madison Grant's book *The Passing of the Great Race*. They also cited US sterilization laws and eugenic programs. Ultimately, as the unearthed minutes of the Wannsee Conference reveal, the Nazis committed mass genocide against the Jews to prevent racial mixture, based on their understanding of such Darwinian concepts as natural selection and resistant strains. So the Nazi Holocaust is unavoidably a part of the legacy of Darwinism.

Darwinism as Idolatry

Once the Nazi atrocities against the Jews were uncovered, the actual science of biology retreated sheepishly back into the lab room and refocused on what we now call genetics. Yet Darwinian evolution fundamentally changed how we view the world, ourselves as humans, and our Creator. Darwinian thinking has so permeated the modern mind-set that we reflexively use its terminology in everyday life. (How ironic to find Anne Frank writing in her diary about the weak perishing and the strong surviving.) Even the business world today is seen as an animalistic "jungle" where only the fittest rule. Yet many proponents of evolution are not content with this cultural saturation and are pushing the envelope further. They have removed the acknowledgment of God from our classrooms, and now seek to eradicate Him from all public life. So the poisonous tree of Darwinism is still bearing destructive fruit to this day, with serious implications for our world.

I sense that something even larger has happened since the advent of Darwinian evolution. As this falsehood has gained wider acceptance over the past hundred and fifty years, I believe that somewhere along the way we have entered the "days of Noah" again. We have breached the prime condition of the Noahide covenant, to treat every human with dignity as created in God's image. As a result, God has passed judgment over us but is storing up the punishment for a final day of reckoning with mankind. He is still making sure His purposes are accomplished in the affairs of men. But again, something has changed since we entered the "days of Darwin." Consider how the First World War became locked in the stagnant slugfests of trench warfare, leaving both sides to resort to gas warfare. Apparently, human life had become so cheap that soldiers could be poisoned and choked to death by the thousands. This devaluation of human life had a source—the lowering of our image of mankind from a special creation of God to an animal like any other.

In the Second World War, human life became even cheaper, as this time innocent civilians were the ones gassed—by the millions—all justified by Darwinian principles. Thankfully, the right side won that war, too. But Germany has yet to be truly judged by God for perpetrating the Holocaust. And by war's end, mankind had entered the nuclear age. Thus, so far in the age of Darwin, we have gassed, nuked, rocketed, napalmed, carpet-bombed, cluster-bombed, and stealth-bombed each other. And soon we may be radiating, lasering, microwaving, or spraying viral agents at each other. But what does it matter if we are no different than the animals?

It is true that Darwin never used evolution to advocate such violence, nor to promote atheism. But he was well aware that his theory meant the degrading of mankind's value and the discarding of belief in God. After all, he was swamped by letters and visitors urging him to recant his heretical theory. Yet Darwin was proud of the way he had identified natural selection as a transcendent force—often referring to it as his dear "child." The concept of natural selection had a profound impact on the world, as it challenged traditional beliefs in nature's order and goodness, in man's elevated place and purpose in creation, and in a benevolent Creator.[36] Even liberal philosophers like Nietzsche and Hegel were troubled by the negative effects of "killing off" God. Nietzsche realized it meant losing any sense of the cosmic order or any basis for moral absolutes, leading to nihilism.[37]

Many Darwinists did realize Darwin's ideas had truly revolutionary potential, and even relished the fight against established church dogmas. Some went so far as to propose new religions to replace Christianity, such as the Monism of Ernst Haeckel. Today, this immanence approach—the ancient Greek idea that God was absorbed into nature—is readily seen in Gaia worship and other eco-cults. Still, it is not necessary to flesh out an entirely new religion from Darwinism, as by default it transfers the worship due the creator God to some other object. Whether it is nature, man's intellect, or another false god, the end result is idolatry.

Dr. Randy Guliuzza makes the case that Darwinists have indeed fallen into the trap of idolatry. He notes that the cardinal axiom of evolution is that "nature selects." However, this requires a conscious agent with a mind and will to choose among options. Thus, Darwinists ascribe to nature mysterious powers to "select for," "operate on," "punish," or "favor." This is humans projecting mankind's own mental and volitional abilities onto the inanimate world, and crediting it for what only God can do.[38]

Further, when we declare God "dead," then there is no need to fear Him or answer to Him, and moral absolutes are also dead. Once freed of these restraints, will a liberated humanity ever come back under His moral authority?

It is my contention that the mainstream acceptance of Darwinian evolution in modern Western societies is fueling a rebellion against God that is every bit as idolatrous as the pre-Flood rebellion. In the antediluvian world, the abandonment of God led to lawless violence and rampant sexual immorality, and then divine judgment, and the same process of corruption and degeneracy is already well underway in our day. As the Christian West has slowly lost its biblical compass of truth and morality, the malevolent fruit of the Darwinian rebellion has stretched from the Nazi gas chambers of the 1940s to the unrelenting abortion mills of our day.

Mankind crossed a line with God when we lowered our self-image and said we were descended from apes, rather than being the crown of

His creation. We violated the lone command of the Noahide covenant. Therefore, God has been giving us over to our own self-deceptions and vile passions ever since in order to judge us. The sexual revolution today is constantly in search of new ways to break all boundaries of decency. We are leaving the natural order and turning to homosexuality, transsexualism, and other deviancies. Anyone who challenges this immoral behavior is denounced as phobic and intolerant. The rebellious feel that what they are doing is not sinful but morally right, placing them beyond repentance.

Christians who still uphold biblical values need not be frustrated with how we seem to be losing the current culture wars. Evil might be prospering, and we might wonder why God has not intervened yet. But it will happen one day soon. Still, I believe there is one more line for mankind to cross before its rebellion has fully ripened to God's just judgment. And that has to do with the ways we are tampering with our very nature as humans, all as a result of Darwinian evolution.

14

THE NEXT REVOLUTION

"If I had known they were going to do this,
I would have become a shoemaker."
—Albert Einstein, after Hiroshima[1]

"I will praise You, for I am fearfully and wonderfully made."
—Psalm 139:14

The first modern work of science fiction was the 1818 novel *Franken-stein*, by Mary Shelley. It came out when electricity was still a new breakthrough, and many people were captivated by its mysterious properties. Likened to a second discovery of fire, science was rushing to unlock its secrets and harness its power, believing it would dramatically change the world. An Italian biologist named Luigi Galvani noticed odd muscle contractions in animals when electrical currents were passed through their bodies. His nephew held a macabre public demonstration featuring a stone-dead corpse that twitched when placed under its strange spell. Thus was born the tale of eccentric scientist Victor Frankenstein, who "galvanized" to life a hideous creature sown together from assorted cadavers.

Today, the "fiction" is being removed from science fiction. Our world is driven by a confidence in the steady and inevitable progress of humanity, because of a belief that science can and will solve everything. German biologist Ernst Haeckel had already voiced this optimism in his runaway best seller *Riddle of the Universe* in 1899.[2] A century later, Princeton philosopher Francis Fukuyama declared that "there could be no end to history unless there was an end to science."[3]

This buoyant faith in science and progress is fueled more than ever today by the ideas of Darwinian evolution. Many people are seized by the notion that evolution has brought mankind to a point where we are now able to grasp its secrets, empowering us to control and even hasten the evolutionary process going forward. Our human nature is no longer subject to random forces or "chance," as Darwin maintained.[4] Rather, our own intellect and resolve will now guide our future.

The US intelligence community publishes a periodic assessment of global trends to inform government decision-makers about what to expect in coming decades. The National Intelligence Council's latest "Global Trends" estimate from 2012 claims that advances in information and biomedical technologies are rapidly moving the needle on human potential.[5] Enhanced computer power and massive data storage are now affordable and available in ever smaller platforms. The possibility of a technological/biological merger could trigger a quantum leap in human intelligence and physical abilities. For instance, new types of "human augmentation," such as bionic arms or brain chip implants, could become optional—like plastic surgery.[6]

In the Digital Age, the ability of computers to collect and analyze data has compressed the time needed for science to overcome obstacles once deemed insurmountable. In 1965, Intel cofounder Gordon Moore assessed that computing power was doubling every eighteen months. Moore's Law, as it became known, meant that we could acquire more knowledge and achieve greater technological advances in shorter time frames. We see this today in the way many mobile devices hitting the market are virtually obsolete within two years, due to the rapid pace of technology.

Meanwhile, new biomedical advances, made possible by the cracking of our genetic code, will soon lead to smarter, stronger, healthier humans. By mapping the human genome, we can now develop cures for diseases faster than before. Some people even foresee a time of expanded longevity, if not immortality, for our species. This could even be accomplished by merging man and machine into an indestructible union. Thus, futurists seductively speak of reaching the point of "singularity," achieving "convergence," and approaching our "transhumanist" destiny—when we finally transcend the limits of our finite bodies to create the superhuman.

Yet this allure of curing diseases and making humans better and brighter has to be approached with great caution. For in the process, we are tampering with our nature as human beings made to be like Adam— our prototype. This is crossing a line with God, just as those in the ancient world crossed a line by mating with rebellious angels, thinking they would give birth to immortals, and ended up producing mutated bullies known as the *Nephilim*. God decided that was enough, and He sent the Flood. I fear we now stand in peril of divine judgment by seeking to alter our human nature through scientific means. We do not really need the fallen angels this time to create hybrid humans. It is within our own hands, yet it is a grave offense against our Maker. And it is now happening in a myriad of ways, as medical and technological advances propel science forward.

Genetic Mapping and Crossbreeding

Since its discovery in 1953, we have known that all living organisms have a double helix of genetic information encoded in their DNA, which serves as an in-built instruction manual for life.[7] Launched in 1990, the Human Genome Project sought to map out the complete human genome, a massive project completed in 2003. But scientists soon realized there is another whole complex layer to the human genome called RNA, which we are just beginning to understand.

A recent breakthrough computer program known as CRISPR/Cas9 has enabled researchers to map out gene sequences faster and more cheaply, not only of humans but animals as well. Animals have often been used in labs to study diseases and test new drugs for later use in humans. But researchers are now using new gene-editing tools to compare and rewrite the genetic codes of both humans and animals in hopes of finding cures for human ailments faster. This is leading to new experiments that are blurring the lines between humans and animals as never before.

For instance, due to the chronic shortage of organ donors worldwide, medical researchers are now trying to grow human organs inside pigs, to be later transplanted back into humans in need of organ transplants. A patient could even donate his own DNA to produce an organ in a pig that would more likely be accepted once back in the patient's body. This might sound eerily reminiscent of *The Island of Dr. Moreau*, but big pharmaceutical companies have begun to invest heavily in this field.[8]

Such "chimera" research has actually been around for a while. For decades, young mice have been "humanized" by the insertion of human cells to render them more biologically like us for drug testing.[9] In 2007, a university professor created a sheep with 15 percent human cells.[10] Scientists recently used human stem cells to grow an adult-size human ear on the back of a rat. This so-called tissue engineering is being used to grow other body parts, like noses and windpipes.[11]

Conversely, scientists are implanting animal tissue into humans for medical purposes. For example, the procedure of using pig tissue for skin grafts on humans has been around for decades, even though the FDA has warned that most major epidemics start with an animal pathogen that jumps to humans.[12] Yet, armed with the newest gene-editing tools, scientists are mixing and crossbreeding human and animal cells as never before. Researchers have now sequenced the genomes of over two hundred and fifty animals, and are squabbling over which ones are most like humans and thus more suitable for research on human diseases. Some say pigs, others say chimpanzees, sheep, cows, mice or frogs.[13] The genetic similarities between humans and animals is thus enticing scientists to increasingly cross human and animal tissue. This practice might seem commendable to some people as a way to end suffering and disease. But I fear it is a "corruption" of human flesh like that which occurred in the pre-Flood world.

Human Stem Cells and "Designer Babies"

For decades, we have known that our bodies contain generic "stem cells" which can turn into specific cell types—bone cells, brain cells, skin cells, and so forth. These "adult" stem cells reside in many organs and tissues of a grown person and are a major component of our body's self-healing capabilities—proof that we are *"fearfully and wonderfully made."* When a bone breaks, for instance, neural messages wake up these dormant, multipurpose stem cells and direct them to the break. Once there, they read the type of cells around them and turn into those cells, filling in the fracture. Thus, adult stem cells have been used successfully in transplants and to treat a variety of diseases, such as cancer, multiple sclerosis, arthritis, stroke, spinal cord injury, Parkinson's disease, and heart disease.[14] But they are difficult to locate, as they are often hidden in "niches" throughout the body, and once found they must be artificially awakened, moved, and activated to treat injury or disease.[15]

In 1998, scientists discovered a rich, easy-to-find source of these generic stem cells inside human embryos. Ever since, there has been a drive to tap embryonic stem cells for medical purposes, although it means the embryos will never develop into a human life. So scientists have been harvesting stem cells from cloned embryos in test tubes. Advocates of this research believe it will lead to cures for some of humanity's worst diseases. But opponents insist this medical research should not be pursued when it destroys a potential life, especially with other alternatives available.[16] Opponents also charge that scientists pushing embryonic stem cell research are doing it largely for pecuniary gain, as there are huge profits at stake if they can patent and sell these stem cell lines, whereas adult stem cell lines cannot be patented.[17]

Yet now, the incredible new CRISPR gene-editing program is enabling more precise modifications of DNA in human embryos, a move that has eager scientists launching a whole new wave of experiments. A recent *Time* cover feature highlighted the explosion of new research in human genetic modification.[18] In response, some scientists are demanding an urgent public debate about the ethics and pitfalls of "designer babies" and related issues.[19] But a stem cell researcher at King's College in London predicted the experiments in editing human genomes will continue unabated. "You cannot stop science," he insisted.[20]

This may prove true. Potentially, the new technology could produce designer babies with greater intelligence, enhanced physical abilities, or even less need for sleep. But critics say the process is still unproven and unsafe, and would only be available to the rich at first, with some parents mortgaging their homes to make sure their child was not at a competitive disadvantage. One critic even labeled it "consumer eugenics."[21] So, despite the potential benefits, the dangers and ethical concerns of this tampering with our human nature are enormous and will not go unnoticed by heaven.

The Quest for Longevity

Another new field of research is "life extension" science, also known as anti-aging medicine, which aims to slow down or reverse the aging process and thereby extend human life spans. Some now see this quest for longevity and even immortality as the new holy grail of science. They believe breakthroughs in tissue rejuvenation, stem cells, regenerative medicine, molecular repair, gene therapy, cloning, drugs, and organ replacement will eventually enable humans to have indefinite life spans in a healthy, youthful condition.

Much of the current research in this area is simply trying to understand the aging process. One cause of aging has to do with the Hayflick limit, a built-in quota for cell division in the somatic cells which make up the vast majority of our bodies. The average somatic cell divides around sixty times before it dies. Yet this innate limit on cell division also appears to prevent genomic instability, as there is slight damage or distortion in the copying of our DNA information each time a cell divides. These errors accumulate over our lifetime, and thus our skin turns rough, our immune system collapses, our organs fail, and we eventually die a natural death.

If our cells were allowed to divide forever, we would shrivel into twisted shapes due to the accrued corruption of our DNA. But some scientists hope to override the built-in quota on cell division so that our bodies could replenish their cells indefinitely. Yet this requires regenerative methods to reverse or repair all the DNA damage that builds up over time. Some experts say this will prove impossible.[22] But that is not stopping some very determined people from trying. They have even formed political parties to promote their drive for immortality.[23] In 2013, Google joined the quest for longevity by launching the new company Calico to study the biology of aging.[24] The next year, wealthy biologist Craig Venter jumped in the race by founding Human Longevity, Inc.[25] Fellow researcher Aubrey de Grey provocatively claims the first humans who will live to be a thousand years old have already been born.

The areas of life-extension research with perhaps the greatest potential at present are cloning and body-part replacement, though these also remain controversial. Over recent decades, scientists have conducted cloning experiments on a variety of animals. In 1996, after 276 attempts, Scottish researchers finally produced Dolly, a lamb made from the udder cell of a six-year-old sheep. Ever since, researchers have cloned cats, cows, deer, dogs, horses, monkeys, rabbits and rats. The idea now among some researchers is to insert adult human cells or DNA coding into the cells of a human embryo to try to clone a person.[26] Others, including those in the US Department of Defense, are just trying to clone replacement body parts.[27]

There is nothing wrong with wanting to live a longer, healthier life. One of the greatest achievements of modern medicine is the raising of life expectancies.[28] But many of these new life extension strategies are deeply troubling. Some fear the world would become overpopulated or that an eternally young population would pose its own set of problems. My concern, however, is with how we are tampering with our human makeup in a bid to cheat death, which is a defiant act against God. The apostle Paul proclaims that God *"alone has immortality"* (1 Timothy 6:16). Thus, to seek eternal life outside of God is both futile and rebellious. He will never allow it! But science is pursuing it, just the same, and this quest for immortality is largely a product of Darwinian evolution, making it yet another bad fruit of that poisonous tree. I believe we are crossing a final line with God that will demand divine intervention. Even as God judged mankind for "corrupting" its flesh and altering its Adamic nature in Noah's time, so God will not tolerate our genetic mutations and scientific bid for immortality today.

The Hubris of Transhumanism

In 1970, Alvin Toffler predicted in *Future Shock* that the speed and scope of scientific advances would soon bring about such profound changes that many people would become overwhelmed by them. Today, transhumanism is a movement that not only welcomes technological changes, but it even wants to accelerate the pace in order to birth a superhuman race. Futurists like Max More have explained that transhumanists seek to control and quicken human evolution to produce a radically new, higher species.[29] With obvious Darwinian inspiration, adherents hope to use technology to extend human life spans, augment our senses, boost our memory capacity, and eventually ascend to a post-human state. It may sound like sci-fi nonsense, but there are techno-wizards at Google and professors at Yale, MIT and Oxford buying into this vision. The technologies under-girding transhumanism are all currently part of the biotech explosion and include genetics, neuropharmacology, robotics, cybernetics, artificial intelligence, and nanotechnology.

The real guru of the movement is Ray Kurzweil, a computer scientist at MIT and the director of engineering at Google. He predicts we are approaching the moment of "singularity," when artificial intelligence surpasses human abilities and begins to design new technology on its own. Within a very brief period, perhaps even days, the world might be transformed almost beyond recognition, due to a theoretical positive feedback loop caused by smarter systems designing ever smarter systems.[30] Kurzweil also sees machines gaining a human-like consciousness by 2029.

He and others insist the next step in human evolution is the union of man and machine. Thus, brain-machine interfaces are popular with trans-humanists. Already, tiny brain implants are allowing paraplegics to control artificial limbs with their own minds in order to walk again. Instead of using such technologies just to help the wounded or handicapped, however, some people want to use them to enhance the mental and physical abilities of healthy humans. Kurzweil and others also are fixated on "uploading"—transferring a human's intellect from their brain to a computer, perhaps by an ultra-precise scanning of brain wave patterns onto software that is then uploaded onto a hard drive, in order to achieve virtual immortality.[31]

Yet transhumanists admit that biotechnology, nanotechnology, and artificial intelligence pose serious risks of accidents and abuse.[32] Perhaps that is why the US military recently jumped on the bandwagon. DARPA, the Pentagon's research arm that brought us the World Wide Web, is now funding an array of projects aimed at merging humans and computers. The transhumanists could not be happier![33] Thus, instead of a nuclear arms race, the US now seems locked in a biotech race with Russia and China to be the first to reach the "convergence" of man and machine. Yet transhumanists contend even more is at stake.

Kurzweil claims that once the Singularity arrives, computer intelligence will be infinitely more powerful than all human intelligence combined and will radiate outward from the planet until it saturates the universe, creating in essence an omnipotent god where none existed before. In *The Singularity Is Near*,[34] Kurzweil predicted that once the universe is saturated with knowledge, it will "wake up" and become sublimely intelligent. "That's about as close to God as I can imagine."[35] So transhumanists are pursuing self-transcendence to a higher life form as a logical extension of Darwinian evolution, with science giving us eternal life and even creating an all-seeing, all-knowing deity.[36]

Frankly, transhumanism is hubris—a haughty exaltation of man and his genius over our Creator. In *Mere Christianity*, C. S. Lewis describes hubris as a blinding arrogance pitting the self directly against God.[37] It is committed when humans attempt to rise above their natural limitations to attain a godlike status. This was the temptation offered by the serpent to Eve in the garden of Eden, with the false claim that if she ate of the forbidden fruit, she would *"be like God"* (Genesis 3:5). The same temptation was faced—and also succumbed to—by those before the Flood who mated with rebellious angels, thinking their offspring would be gods. Transhumanism is the same old seductive promise of self-deification. It offers immortality outside of Jesus. Anyone buying it?

Actually, I believe that many people today have such confidence in science that they will indeed put their trust in this futuristic dream. Hollywood and pop culture are already selling it wholeheartedly. The transhumanist agenda has been woven into so many movies in recent years, it is hard to keep track of them all, including the portrayal of Kurzweil's core ideas in the recent hit film *Lucy*. Thus, the masses are being programmed to both expect and accept these bio-tech innovations as they come. Yet transhumanism will never be able to deliver on its utopian promise of eternal life, as it is a counterfeit to faith in Jesus. And those who are casting God aside and seeking immortality through scientific means are automatically shutting the door on themselves to that glorious future in a new immortal, incorruptible body that is available only in Christ. Those who will receive these incredible new bodies in the age to come are the next topic of discussion.

15

THE RIGHTEOUS REMNANT

"There are many wells today, but they are dry. There are many
hungry souls today that are empty. But let us come to Jesus and
take Him at His Word and we will find wells of salvation...."
—William J. Seymour, father of modern Pentecostalism[1]

"When the whirlwind passes by, the wicked is no more,
but the righteous has an everlasting foundation."
—Proverbs 10:25

For the days of Noah to be a complete analogy for the end of days,
there must be a righteous remnant whom God preserves through the
dark times ahead and uses to start over, just as He preserved Noah and
his family so that they survived the Flood and repopulated the earth. This
concept of a "righteous remnant" actually appears throughout Scripture
and is a core doctrine of the Christian faith. In every generation, God has
always kept for Himself a faithful remnant, in numbers great and small.
The fullest teaching on this principle is in the ninth to eleventh chapters of

Romans, where Paul explains how God always preserved a believing remnant within Israel. He points to Elijah, who fled to the desert after challenging the prophets of Baal, fearing he was the last servant of the Lord left. But God responded, *"I have reserved seven thousand in Israel, all whose knees have not bowed to Baal..."* (1 Kings 19:18; see also Romans 11:2–4). He also quotes Isaiah 10:22: *"Though the number of the children of Israel be as the sand of the sea, the remnant will be saved"* (Romans 9:27).

So, in every generation, God has preserved a believing remnant. Not everyone who claims to belong to the family of God actually does, but only those who remain faithful to Him. (See Romans 9:6–8, 30–32.) Paul also told Timothy, *"Nevertheless the solid foundation of God stands, having this seal: 'The Lord knows those who are His'..."* (2 Timothy 2:19). Additionally, the apostle Peter said, *"The Lord knows how to deliver the godly out of temptations and to reserve the unjust under punishment for the day of judgment"* (2 Peter 2:9). God is well able to distinguish between the upright and the wicked, between light and darkness, wheat and tares; and He is perfectly capable of preserving the just and punishing the unjust. But before we identify the righteous remnant today, it will be helpful to look at how God separated them out in Israel's past. It was by a continual sifting process, just as wheat is sifted so that the grain is separated from the chaff.

The Sifting Process

After the northern kingdom of Israel had broken away from the southern kingdom of Judah, Hebrew prophets were sent by God to warn the people that their sinful ways would soon lead to exile. But they did not leave the land of Israel without also being given hope. Isaiah repeatedly promised that a remnant would return from exile one day to resettle the land. (See Isaiah 10:20–21; 11:11–16; 37:31–32.) Jeremiah concurred: *"I will gather the remnant of My flock out of all countries where I have driven them, and bring them back to their folds"* (Jeremiah 23:3). Amos described what lay ahead as a sifting process: *"'I will not utterly destroy the house of Jacob,' says the LORD. 'For surely I will command, and will sift the house of Israel among all nations, as grain is sifted in a sieve; yet not the smallest grain shall fall to the ground'"* (Amos 9:8–9).

This sifting process started well before Israel's exile to Assyria. The northern Israelites were in greater rebellion, as they had set up their own royal line outside the House of David, built a temple on Mount Gerizim to rival the one in Jerusalem, and fallen into Baal worship. So the Hebrew prophets warned they would be the first ones exiled. Yet many in the northern tribes still feared God and heeded the prophets by fleeing south into Judah. They also remained loyal to Jerusalem as the proper place of worship, and still believed the true successor to King David was in Judah. All this is confirmed throughout the books of Kings and Chronicles, which speak repeatedly of many from the northern tribes fleeing south even before the Assyrian assault in 722 BC. (See, for example, 2 Chronicles 11:16–17 and 2 Chronicles 15:9.)

Many more fled southward once Assyria laid siege to the northern tribes. Archeologists have verified that the population of Jerusalem grew ten times in size in this brief period due to the mass influx of northern refugees.[2] Even in the period between the Assyrian invasion of the north and the Babylonian siege of Jerusalem in 586 BC, the Bible confirms that many northern Israelites were left in the land and continued to join Judah. In 2 Chronicles 30, for example, King Hezekiah invites them to keep Passover in Jerusalem. Yet Judah was eventually exiled as well because they, too, lapsed into idolatry.

The books of Ezra and Nehemiah then attest that small bands from both Israel and Judah began returning to resettle the land and rebuild Jerusalem. Thus, we see Ezra thanking God for bringing back a humble *"remnant"* (Ezra 9:8, 15). Yet when some of the returning Israelites again began taking Canaanite wives and worshipping their idols, Ezra stopped the practice immediately, knowing it was a core reason why they had been exiled in the first place. (See Ezra 9–10.) We find that from about the end of the Babylonian exile, the Jewish people finally left idol worship and be-came strictly monotheistic. This can be attributed to the sifting process that God was putting them through among the nations, just as foretold in Amos 9:8–9. It was a steady refinement, whereby God constantly sorted out those faithful to Him from those who were not, and it has continued ever since. He accomplishes this by always giving people clear moral choic-es to reveal just how closely they are willing to follow Him.

We again see this in how the Israelites in exile had a clear choice regarding whether to go back to the land or not. The most faithful returned to Zion, while many who chose to stay in exile were lost to history. Even today, Jews now have a choice regarding whether to return to the land of Israel. I believe those making *aliyah* have come home to be part of incredible changes and miracles in this reborn nation. There are more amazing prophetic promises for Israel still to be fulfilled, and those who stay in the Diaspora may miss out. They also risk getting caught up one day in God's judgment of the Gentile nations for always being arrogant and unmerciful toward the Jewish people. (See, for example, Jeremiah 51:6; Zephaniah 3:8–13.) In this way, the land of Israel actually serves as a modern-day ark of protection for the Jewish people. Ultimately, I believe a regathered Israel is destined to be part of that righteous remnant that God preserves in the day of wrath.

The Remnant Today

Meanwhile, even amid the grave moral slide all around us today, we still should be able to identify a righteous remnant among the nations. And in fact, since about the year 1900—right when Darwinian evolution was going mainstream—there has been an explosive growth in the evangelical Christian movement worldwide. I believe this is the righteous remnant that God is now preparing for the dark times ahead, so that we might shine as the stars in the heavens. (See Daniel 12:3; Philippians 2:15 NIV.) Jesus Himself said, "*You must be born again*" (John 3:7); otherwise, you "*cannot see the kingdom of God*" (verse 3). So that is the number one prerequisite to being a part of the righteous remnant. This knowing of God through the forgiveness of sin is the essence of the "*new covenant*" promised in Jeremiah 31:31–34. The same passage also identifies the second requirement—to have His law written on our hearts. That is, we need to remain faithful to God and His standards. No moral compromise and no falling away.

Many of the growing numbers of Evangelicals today are from peoples and lands that never really had a chance to hear the gospel before. In parts of Africa, Asia and Latin America, there are more people being saved in this generation than in all the previous generations combined. Paul foresaw such a "*fullness of the Gentiles*" (Romans 11:25) in the last days—meaning a great end-time harvest out among the nations. On the other hand, in many traditionally Christian nations, there is a great falling away from the faith, and some have even entered a post-Christian era. Many people still identify culturally as Christians, but they no longer truly believe in the power of the cross. As the divine sifting process confronts them with moral choices meant to keep us on the straight and narrow, they prefer to fall by the wayside. In so doing, they are fulfilling a separate prophetic warning of a great apostasy among those in the body of Christ in the last days. (See 2 Thessalonians 2:3; 2 Timothy 3:13–14.) Thus, we see this prophetic paradox in Scripture playing out in modern times: the *"fullness of the Gentiles"* is being harvested in the developing world, even while a great *"falling away"* (2 Thessalonians 2:3) engulfs the Christian West.

There are an estimated 2.2 billion Christians in the world today, about one-third of the global population.[3] Roughly one billion identify as Catholics, while the Eastern Orthodox and mainline Protestant traditions number around two hundred million each. But the fastest-growing stream of Christianity is the Evangelical movement, which now includes some seven hundred million people. An outgrowth of the Protestant Reformation five centuries ago, the Evangelical movement has seen phenomenal expansion over the past hundred years. If current trends continue, within twenty years, there will be more Evangelicals than Catholics worldwide. This dramatic growth is being fueled mainly by the Pentecostal/charismatic revivals in Latin America, Africa and Asia.

The definition of what constitutes an evangelical Christian varies widely, but a simple formula would be someone who (1) claims a genuine "born-again" experience with God through Jesus, and (2) respects the Bible as the true Word of God. This very inclusive definition would also extend "Evangelical" credentials to many Catholic, Orthodox and mainline Protestant believers.

As a sustained global movement, Evangelicalism can actually be traced back to the Hussites in Bohemia in the fifteenth century, who presaged the Reformation by birthing some of the first "free churches" of Europe.[4] Yet it has been the Pentecostal/charismatic movement that has drawn unprecedented numbers into the Evangelical fold over the past century. Pentecostalism alone now accounts for over six hundred million adherents worldwide, including denominational and independent Pentecostals and Charismatics.[5] If current growth rates continue, the Evangelical stream will surpass one billion within two decades.[6]

With the dramatic Evangelical growth in Latin America, Africa and Asia, the center of Christianity is shifting away from Europe and North America toward the South and East. Those driving this expansion are no longer Western missionaries but indigenous ministries. Africa alone has seen an astonishing increase in Christian identification from 10 million in 1900 to 493 million in 2010. One source projects that the growth in Africa will exceed one billion by 2050.[7] Again, similar Evangelical growth can be seen in Latin America and Asia. According to the World Christian Database, Latin America had 62 million Christians in 1900, but that number will reach 655 million by 2050. In Asia, there were an estimated 22 million Christians in 1900, with a projection of 601 million by 2050. Even in Arab and Muslim countries, unprecedented growth is being reported in Evangelical churches.[8] The overall global figures project an estimated 3.19 billion Christians by 2050.[9]

The Sifting of the Western Church

Meanwhile, there is an opposite trend in Europe and North America—the traditional bastions of Christianity. In America, the number of Christians is expected to keep growing, but it will become a lower percentage of the overall population. The Pew Research Center found that between 2007 and 2014, those identifying as Christians dropped from 78 percent to just under 71 percent, and they will continue declining to 66 percent by 2050. While Evangelical churches are still growing, mainline Protestant and Catholic churches are steadily losing parishioners. Nearly a quarter of those raised as Christians no longer identify with the faith. Meantime, the ratio of the unaffiliated (atheists, agnostics, and other non-religious) is expected to rise to 26 percent by 2050. Millennials (18–33) are even more atheist/agnostic, at 35 percent unaffiliated.[10]

The Barna Research Group also has tracked Christianity's waning influence in America. Rising numbers of the religiously unaffiliated, a steady drop in church attendance, and tensions over religious liberty all point to a secular trend sweeping the nation. Barna gauged that the number of

Americans who qualify as "post-Christian" rose by 7 percent in just two years, from 37 to 44 percent between 2013 and 2015. Although 78 percent of Americans still identify as "Christian," many are wavering in their faith. Barna found they either no longer believe in God, do not consider faith important in their lives, have stopped praying and attending church, have no commitment to Jesus, no longer read or trust in the Bible, or have become outright atheists or agnostics. Those most faithful to God in all these areas tended to be Evangelicals.[11]

In Europe, not only is the percentage of Christians dropping, but the actual number is falling, as well. Europe had 588 million Christians in 2010, but that figure will decline to 530 million by 2050. By then, nearly a quarter of Europeans (23 percent) will have no religious affiliation. Yet much of Europe is already staunchly secular, refusing to let religion have any role in public life.

Part of the impetus for this parting from Christianity is that many people no longer want to adhere to biblical morality lest they be seen as intolerant. So there is much moral compromise on key social issues of our day, whether abortion, homosexuality, evolution, school prayer, or support for Israel. Science also is eroding their faith. But all this is little more than the age-old sifting process that God continually uses to filter out the faithful from the fickle, the righteous remnant from those whose faith becomes shipwrecked. (See 1 Timothy 1:19.)

It is easy to discern this sifting process even among many church leaders today, as they wrestle with the latest moral questions, such as gay ordination and transgenderism. The faithful remnant stick with the proven godly standard, while those weak in faith compromise with the world. Other issues are arising to test our faithfulness, such as whether Islam also offers a valid pathway to heaven, or if the Allah of the Koran is the same as the God of the Bible. No true Evangelical can ever compromise on Jesus being the only way of salvation. (See Acts 4:12.) Yet we could face persecution and even jail time for staying true to our beliefs.

Polling data consistently shows Evangelicals are much more likely to uphold biblical standards regarding today's most divisive moral issues. For instance, a 2015 Pew poll found that while an overall majority of Americans

(55 percent) now support gay unions, 76 percent of Evangelicals still oppose it.[12] On abortion, a 2013 Pew survey found that most Evangelicals (75 percent) still view abortion as morally wrong, while mainline Protestants actually favor it more than the general public.[13] In other nations around the world, Evangelicals tend to be even more conservative than their American counterparts on abortion, gay marriage, and divorce.[14]

All this shows that a genuine born-again experience makes a huge difference in the life of a believer. That personal encounter helps cement one's faith in God and trust in His Word. Once you are aware of His gracious and holy character, it is easier to agree with His standards, no matter what the world says. The righteous remnant in our day must remain true to Him and not join the growing rebellion around us, just as Noah was faithful and obedient to God in the midst of an evil and perverse generation. (See Hebrews 11:7.) And the moral questions arising out of this rebellion against God will not get any easier.

Amid all this sifting, I encourage every true Christian to stick to your convictions. There is a glorious future awaiting those who stay faithful to God. The Bible promises us an immortal, incorruptible body. (See, for example, 1 Corinthians 15:53–54; Romans 2:7.) And in the age to come, the whole earth will be renewed and at peace, as never known before. The nations will "*beat their swords into plowshares*" and "[will not] *learn war anymore*" (Isaiah 2:4; Micah 4:3). "*The earth shall be full of the knowledge of the* LORD *as the waters cover the sea*" (Isaiah 11:9). Even the animal kingdom will be transformed, as "*the wolf also shall dwell with the lamb,…the lion shall eat straw like the ox.*" (See Isaiah 11:6–8.) So, just as God preserved a righteous remnant in the days of Noah to make a new start, He will do the same with us today to prepare us for eternity. But we must remain faithful!

In the story of the Flood, righteous Noah and his family were preserved inside the ark because God instructed Noah to seal the vessel inside and out with pitch. The Hebrew word for "*pitch,*" or seal, in Genesis 6:14 is *kaphar,* which has the same Hebrew root as *kippur,* or atonement. Thus, the pitch represented a covering for sin, like that provided by Jesus on the cross. The righteous remnant had this covering and were spared, but the unrighteous perished in the Deluge. In the same manner, those Israelites who placed blood as a seal on their doorposts on the first Passover were spared from the Death Angel. (See Exodus 12:1–28.) Likewise, the New Testament tells us the judgment at the end of days will distinguish between the righteous and unrighteous. The righteous are *"sealed for the day of redemption"* by the Holy Spirit. (See Ephesians 4:30.) God also has a *"seal"* by which He *"knows those who are His"* (2 Timothy 2:19). This *"seal of the living God"* will be placed on all the righteous saints still present on the earth before the wrath of God is ultimately poured out on the unrighteous. (See Revelation 7:2–3.) In fact, this fiery judgment cannot take place until the righteous remnant is first "sealed" for divine protection. Thus, if we are still here to see that day, we can trust God to preserve us, no matter what happens to our mortal bodies.

In contrast to these great promises to the righteous remnant, there is only woe for the unrighteous. Yet there is an especially grave warning to those who once knew Christ but have turned their backs on Him. They have no hope or future! In fact, the New Testament warns that if someone has been *"enlightened"* to the grace available in Christ and has *"tasted the heavenly gift,"* but then turns their back on the cross, it is *"impossible"* to restore them. Rather, their *"end is to be burned."* (See Hebrews 6:4–8.) Additionally, Peter cautions it would have been better if they had never known Jesus in the first place. (See 2 Peter 2:20–21.) So, I especially fear for those who think they can just walk away from the Christian faith as if it bears no consequences. They will face the worst fate of all—even worse than those who perished in the Flood, or in Sodom and Gomorrah.

16

THE BUILDING UP OF ZION

"In Israel, in order to be a realist you must believe in miracles."
—David Ben-Gurion[1]

"For the LORD *shall build up Zion; He shall appear in His glory."*
—Psalm 102:16

There is still one more element for the Flood paradigm to be complete, and that is the ark of Noah. God is always just and fair, and thus He gave the ancient world a clear warning sign that they needed to repent or perish in the Flood. From Hebrews 11:7, we know that Noah's upright life and faithful building of the ark was the means by which God *"condemned the world"* to its watery fate. The apostle Peter also presents Noah's construction of the ark as an act of divine patience and fair warning. (See 1 Peter 3:20.) Ultimately, the ark was visible to all and removed any excuse the people of the ancient world might have offered that they had not been warned. So, where in the earth today can we find such an unmistakable warning sign visible to all that judgment is soon coming? The answer is the point where the Flood analogy comes full circle.

I am convinced that the building up of Zion—the modern-day restoration of Israel—is the clearest sign to all the world that we are about to be judged. This promised restoration of Israel, and its connection with God's last-days judgment of the nations, is foretold throughout Scripture—from the books of Moses through the Psalms and Prophets, and over into the New Testament. And I believe Jesus likened His return to the days of Noah due to certain Old Testament passages concerning Israel's end-time restoration.

Jesus knew the Hebrew Scriptures well, and nearly everything He said came directly from them. So where did He get the idea that there would be a repeat of the "days of Noah" in the last days? This is a highly relevant question, given God's solemn promise never to flood the earth again. In chapter six of this book, we noted that the only place in the Old Testament where the phrase *"days of Noah"* appears in a prophetic, futuristic sense is in Isaiah 54. Here, God likens His covenant promise to restore the nation of Israel in the last days to His covenant with Noah, saying:

> *"For a brief moment I forsook you, but with great compassion I will gather you. In an outburst of anger I hid My face from you for a moment, but with everlasting lovingkindness I will have compassion on you," says the* LORD *your Redeemer. "For this is like the days of Noah to Me, when I swore that the waters of Noah would not flood the earth again; so I have sworn that I will not be angry with you nor will I rebuke you."* (Isaiah 54:7–9 NASB)

Putting this passage in context, God promised Noah even before the Flood that He would make a covenant with him after it was all over. (See Genesis 6:17–18.) So Noah entered the ark with the assurance he would survive the Deluge and become part of the new beginning God planned for the earth. In a similar manner, Isaiah informs Israel even before their exile that they will survive the ordeal and be regathered to the land one day to become part of the glorious new age to come. And since it is impossible for God to lie (see, for example, Numbers 23:19; Hebrews 6:18), Israel's restoration in the last days is as sure as anything in Scripture.

The prophet Jeremiah gives this same assurance that Israel's restoration in the last days is as sure as the *"fixed order"* of the sun and moon giving light by day and night. (See Jeremiah 31:35–36 NASB.) This present order was set by God in His covenant with Noah, in which He said, "*While the earth remains, seedtime and harvest, cold and heat, winter and summer, and day and night shall not cease*" (Genesis 8:22). It appears again in Jeremiah 33:23–26 as standing proof of God's unbreakable promise to preserve Israel and fully restore her in the last days.

So the Hebrew prophets are clear that Israel has a uniquely central role in the end of days, just like the ark in the Flood story, and this role will be fully visible to all mankind. In addition, the psalmist had an incredible vision about the building up of Zion in the last days.

> *You will arise and have mercy on Zion; for the time to favor her, yes, the set time, has come.... So the nations shall fear the name of the* LORD, *and all the kings of the earth Your glory. For the* LORD *shall build up Zion; He shall appear in His glory.... This will be written for the generation to come, that a people yet to be created may praise the* LORD. (Psalm 102:13, 15–16, 18)

Here, the psalmist foresees a predetermined season of favor and restoration for Israel that is uniquely connected to the Lord's appearing. All nations and rulers will see and know about it, and they will finally come to serve the Lord. This was written for a "*generation to come*," which in the original Hebrew reads *dor acharon*—meaning "last generation."[2]

The Bible is totally transparent that the restoration of Israel taking place in our day was foreordained and specifically timed for the end of the age, as it is intended to help usher the world into the age to come. This means those of us watching it happen must take it seriously as an inescapable sign that the end is near, for it also means God is about to show up to judge humanity. It's no wonder, then, that the Hebrew root of *tzion* means "a conspicuous mark or sign."[3]

Thus, the building up of Zion serves a similar purpose to the building of the ark in the days of Noah, as a sign of God's looming judgment. In addition, Israel is an ark of refuge for the Jewish people from what is about to take place out among the nations. (See Zechariah 12:8; Joel 3:16.) Yet the ark was something that actually had to be built; it required the grit and labors of those acting in obedience and reverence before God. In the same way, the building up of Zion is an ongoing process that has required the courage and actions of men and women humbly aligned with God's purposes today. The psalmist said, *"The LORD shall build up Zion"* (Psalm 102:16), but we are invited to be partners with Him in this great prophetic venture.

What is most remarkable is that the practical movement to restore the Jewish people to their land was launched around 1900. This happens to be the same time period when Darwinian evolution went mainstream, as well as the time when the outbreak of the Pentecostal revival spurred the rapid growth of the Evangelical movement. So all three developments have progressed parallel to each other over the past century or so. This is no coincidence, but the perfect timing of God!

The Zionist movement was birthed by Theodor Herzl in 1895, when he published a tract entitled *Der Judenstaat* [The Jewish State], calling for a renewed Jewish national homeland. Herzl was not a particularly religious Jew, but he soon realized the Hebrew Scriptures had already planted deep within the Jewish people a great longing to return to their own land one day. This prophetic hope became the engine driving the Zionist movement to its eventual success, despite the many obstacles arrayed against it.

The Promise of Israel's Restoration

There is so much more that could be said about the prophetic rebirth of Israel in modern times, but first consider some simple, yet extremely profound, historic facts. The Jews are remarkable in that they are the only people to be violently uprooted from their homeland not once but twice, only to return each time to reestablish their national sovereignty. It is hard to find another people who have achieved this even once, and yet the Jews have done it twice! And what makes this even more remarkable is that they gave us a Book that said all this would happen before it ever took place. The Bible declared beforehand that there would be two Jewish scatterings—first to Babylon and then to all nations—and two returns. And indeed, this has been the testimony of history. The first return came after the Babylonian exile. Then, over the past one hundred and twenty years or so, more than 3.5 million Jews have returned to the land of Israel from all

over the world—from the north, south, east, and west—in literal fulfillment of God's promises. (See Isaiah 43:5–6.)

So the Bible is a truly amazing book that tells the story of a truly remarkable people. It is not a collection of fables, but the proven Word of
God! And Israel's restoration is indisputable proof of its reliability, as well
as of God's rule over the affairs of men. As we have seen, it also serves
as the most unmistakable sign that the judgment at the end of the age is
near. Many of the biblical passages that foretell of Israel's last days' return
also speak of the judgment of the nations at that time for their rebellion
against God and resistance to His purposes for Zion (Jerusalem). The two
are inseparably linked. To ignore these truths is to seal our own fate, just
as happened with those who paid no heed and even mocked Noah as he
faithfully built the ark.

Frankly, this promised restoration of Israel in the last days happens
to be one of the most widely addressed themes in the entire Bible. Most of
these prophetic passages involve the timing and fulfillment of divine promises made in the Davidic covenant. Beginning with 1 Chronicles 17, we find
God promising King David that He would establish his throne forever.
Later passages assure that one day the people and land of Israel will be
reunited and restored beyond that which David had built, and that Israel
will finally enter their rest in the land from all their enemies. In fact, this
will be an everlasting kingdom presided over by a promised Messiah, the
Son of David, who will rule from Jerusalem over all the earth in righteousness and peace.

Plainly stated, the Jewish people are being restored to their land in our
day in order to fulfill a prophetic role exclusively reserved for them, which
is to help birth the world into the messianic age in fulfillment of the promises of the Davidic covenant. As with any birthing process, it will involve
suffering, which the Bible warns will impact all nations. Yet the dawning
of that blessed messianic age will be glorious, and it remains the world's
greatest hope for peace.

The Partners of Israel's Restoration

Another feature of the promised last-days' restoration of Israel is that
it would be marked by Gentile assistance. The same Hebrew prophets

who foretold of the final Jewish ingathering also saw Gentiles positively involved in their return. This theme was especially emphasized by Isaiah, who foretold that *"the sons of foreigners shall build up your walls, and their kings shall minister to you"* (Isaiah 60:10). He added that *"the sons of those who afflicted you shall come bowing to you, and all those who despised you shall fall prostrate at the soles of your feet"* (verse 14). It is hard to find a more apt description of the modern-day phenomenon of Christians coming in humility to assist a people whom our forbearers in the faith once severely oppressed. Isaiah also said:

> *Behold, I will lift My hand in an oath to the nations, and set up My standard for the peoples; they shall bring your sons in their arms, and your daughters shall be carried on their shoulders; kings shall be your foster fathers, and their queens your nursing mothers.*
>
> (Isaiah 49:22–23)

This literally means God is shouting and waving at the Gentiles to get involved in the restoration of Israel. Thus, Christians have little excuse when we fail to answer that call.

History shows that Gentile kings and queens indeed made key contributions to the Zionist cause. In 1865, for example, the Palestine Exploration Fund was founded, with Britain's Queen Victoria as its royal patron, to study the feasibility of settling Jews back in their homeland.[4] The British government later endorsed Jewish national aspirations in the Balfour Declaration of 1917. Meanwhile, American presidents, such as John Adams, Woodrow Wilson, and Harry Truman, openly supported Israel's restoration. Herzl owed much of his success to a Christian clergyman named Rev. William Hechler. Christians also helped to train Jews in how to farm and to defend themselves again. Both skills are critical to nation-building, as a people must be able to feed and protect themselves. The Jews had lost the ability to do either over the centuries of the Dispersion, but thanks to Christian supporters, the Jews of Palestine learned these skills once more.[5]

Since Israel's rebirth, the Christian Zionist movement has swelled into the tens of millions worldwide. Most Evangelicals hold a favorable view of Israel today, as we simply believe it is the same nation as the Israel of the

Bible. By standing with the Jewish state, we are privileged to be active partners with God in building up Zion. Israel's ingathering is not just a private
matter between God and the Jewish people. Gentiles also are invited to
help build the ark of our day.

In the end, the modern ingathering of the Jewish people holds great
promise for both Israel and the world, as it heralds the soon coming of the
messianic kingdom—that promised new beginning for the world, similar
to what Noah once helped to birth. Israel's return is also irrefutable proof
of the reliability of God's Word. It shows His faithfulness to His promises, which are being fulfilled with great accuracy and precision. Finally,
this great ingathering demonstrates that God remains sovereign over the
affairs of men. Even when much of the world has resisted the return of the
Jews to their homeland, it is still coming to pass, just as He said it would:
"*Hear the word of the* LORD, *O nations, and declare it in the isles afar off, and
say, 'He who scattered Israel will gather him, and keep him as a shepherd does
his flock'*" (Jeremiah 31:10).

17

REASON AND REVELATION

"If false, [Darwinian evolution] has been the most insidious and
destructive thought system ever devised by man. Yet, if true, it is
at best meaningless, like everything else."
—Cornell geneticist John C. Sanford[1]

*"Why do the wicked renounce God? He has said in his heart,
'You will not require an account.'"*
—Psalm 10:13

Before wrapping up, some serious questions have been raised in this
book that still need to be addressed. For instance, has Darwin's theory of evolution held up in the light of the latest discoveries in science?
Can we reconcile the apparent advanced age of the earth with the biblical
account of Creation? And how can we be sure there is a loving God who
created us?

From the moment Darwin published his theory in 1859, a clash erupted between the mavericks of science and the guardians of religion. Within

months, Darwinian defender Thomas H. Huxley and Anglican bishop Samuel Wilberforce engaged in a high-profile debate in England. The most dramatic showdown in America occurred in the 1925 "Scopes Monkey Trial." Despite the eventual triumph of evolutionists in our educational systems, the row between science and faith continues to this day. Yet it is wrong to think scientists uniformly reject belief in God.

For instance, Francis S. Collins, the respected geneticist who chaired the Human Genome Project, is a professing Christian who advocates "theistic evolution."[2] A survey of his scientific colleagues found some forty percent believe in a creator God.[3] More than eight hundred prominent scientists also signed a statement questioning the creative power of Darwin's selection/mutation mechanism to explain life and the universe.

Among the wider public, a Zogby poll from 2009 found 52 percent of Americans agree that "the development of life was guided by intelligent design."[4] A Gallup poll from 2014 also found a strong majority of Americans still believe God was involved in creating man, though some allow for a lengthy process of evolution, while only 19 percent deny any role for God.[5]

This indicates there is still a lot of confusion and hedging when it comes to Darwinism. His theory is now part of a wider scientific view that holds the universe came into being on its own in the "Big Bang" around 13.8 billion years ago. This is seemingly supported by the apparent old age of the earth and its fossil record, which still present a challenge to anyone holding a biblical view. On the other hand, Darwinian evolution has come under closer scrutiny due to new findings in genetic research, as the complexity of the human genome points increasingly to both an intelligent Designer and to a human race much younger than anyone expected. So which one is correct? First, we will peer inside the human genetic code and see what it is revealing to us.

Darwinism and Human Genetics

It seems nothing has evolved more than the theory of evolution itself. In recent decades, new discoveries in genetics keep forcing the scientific community to adjust the Darwinian consensus. Darwin first identified mutation and natural selection as the primary factors driving evolution. After crossbreeding pea plants, Gregor Mendel placed more weight on heredity due to what we now know as genes. Eventually, scientists were forced to regroup around the modern evolutionary synthesis, combining Darwin's natural selection and Mendelian genetics to offer a refined theory of slow, gradual, undirected human evolution.[6] More recently, the Human Genome Project, completed in 2003, mapped out the sequencing of our DNA code. The new ENCODE project is now looking deeper into the mysterious RNA messengers. Based on their findings to date, it turns out the human genome is far more complex and multilayered than ever imagined, throwing a major wrench into Darwin's theory.

One major problem has to do with "junk DNA," a term biologists started using to describe large segments of the human genome with no apparent function. For decades, atheist Richard Dawkins and other neo-Darwinists raised the junk DNA argument to deny the existence of God, since why would He design useless segments into our genes?[7] But the ENCODE team has now discovered these supposedly inactive regions of our DNA are actually packed with over four million "switches" that turn genes on and off, and control how cells, organs, and other tissues behave. Researchers now estimate at least 80 percent of the human genome has a "biochemical function," and, in time, uses will likely be found for the remaining 20 percent.[8] These complex layers of the human genome also contain volumes of information. Made of chemicals designated by the letters A, T, C, and G, the genetic code in a single human cell, if printed in standard type, would cover 75,490 pages of the *New York Times*.[9] Yet these vast DNA codes are just the surface layer beneath which messenger RNA and other biochemical agents do the real work of sustaining life in ever more complex, integrated arrangements.

Meanwhile, scientists who promote Intelligent Design have put atheistic evolutionists on the defensive. For instance, Stephen C. Meyer, in his book *Signature in the Cell*, makes the case for Intelligent Design based on emerging evidence that shows not only man's biological complexity but also that the entire universe is fundamentally operating on encoded information.[10]

Cornell geneticist John C. Sanford, in his book *Genetic Entropy*, establishes that Darwinian evolution is unable to explain how so much genetic information got into our cells in the first place, nor how it can be retained there over such vast amounts of time given the proven rate of degeneration within the genome.[11] Sanford describes the human genome as having multiple loops and overlapping branches, and even genes that can rewrite our genetic code. There is no humanly conceived information system that can even come close to it. And according to Carl Sagan, each human cell contains more information than the Library of Congress. So where did all this vast information come from, how did it get in our cells, and how has it stayed there?

Yet Sanford also explains that as our cells divide and copy the DNA code for use in new cells millions of times over, there are always mutations in the A-T-C-G sequence due to "misspellings," deletions, duplications, insertions, and other copying errors. These errors accumulate over our lifetimes, which means the human genome is deteriorating and has been from the start. Thus, humans could not have evolved from lower life forms; we actually came from a higher life form, resulting in "backwards evolution." Sanford insists there is no selection scheme that can reverse this damage, as any "beneficial" mutations in nature are so extremely rare as to defy measurement and so small as to be un-selectable. That means, without divine intervention, the human race is doomed to extinction within three hundred generations. As a result, Sanford labels Darwinian evolution the most "sacred cow" within academia, which they refuse to abandon even though it has become indefensible.[12]

Similarly, biochemist Michael J. Behe has proven that the maximum positive mutation rate any biological life form can achieve in earth-like conditions is two random mutations, thus seriously undermining the notion of macroevolution.[13] His book *Darwin's Black Box* also identifies the problematic hurdle of "irreducible complexity," the point beyond which complex life forms cannot be reduced or they will cease to exist. Irreducible systems have to come together at once, and not one piece at a time, and life itself is the very essence of irreducible complexity. Thus, both abiogenesis (life springing from nonliving material) and "spontaneous generation" (life springing out of nothing) are impossible feats for nature. Darwin himself warned of the challenge that irreducible complexity posed to his theory of natural selection. In chapter six of *Origin of Species*, he wrote, "If it could be demonstrated that any complex organ existed, which could not possibly have been formed by numerous, successive, slight modifications, my theory would absolutely break down."[14] The empirical evidence now shows this to be the case, and the prime assumptions underlying Darwinian evolution are crumbling in the hands of science itself.

The Bigger Picture

Research into the human genome also has revealed some startling new facts about the age of the human race. Recent DNA analysis indicates our race is extremely young, rather than the product of millions of years of evolutionary change. As a result, the hypothesis that our species originated in East Africa around two hundred thousand years ago is now untenable. This important finding was made possible by the study of a special gene called "Mitochondrial DNA," which is inherited solely from the mother and mutates more slowly compared to other genetic markers. Yet recent research has shown it mutates much faster than previously thought, forcing scientists to recalibrate the evolutionary clock and conclude that all humans came from one woman, dubbed "Mitochondrial Eve," a mere six thousand years ago, just as the Bible says.[15]

Further, two separate studies of the male Y chromosomes show there was a second bottleneck within the genetic history of the human race soon after this Mitochondrial Eve lived. Both studies found that all humans can trace their ancestry back to at least one of three males who lived about five thousand years ago.[16] Some scholars call this the "Noah's Ark Theory," in reference to his three sons.[17]

Thus, both the male and female chromosomes tend to corroborate the biblical accounts of man's origins and the Flood. The genetic evidence also points to the prototype man and woman (Adam and Eve) as having a more perfect genetic makeup than we do today, due to the accumulated damage to our DNA code built up over succeeding generations. This can be attributed to Adam's sin and the moment when death *"entered the world,... and thus death spread to all men..."* (Romans 5:12; see also Genesis 2:17). This death or aging process has been degenerating our human genome ever since.

This also means all those depraved theories about superior and inferior races, and different origins for different races, are totally dispelled.

Every person on earth can trace their ancestry back to the eight people on Noah's ark. And as Paul proclaimed, "[God] *has made from one blood every nation of men to dwell on all the face of the earth*" (Acts 17:26).

We also can put to rest the theory that mankind is descended from apelike creatures. In the 1970s, DNA studies led some to claim that the genomes of humans and chimpanzees are 98 percent the same. But recent data indicates there are major, even unbridgeable, genetic differences between chimps and people that defy evolutionary time-scales.[18]

This leaves us with the apparent old age of the earth and its fossil record, including all those hominin skeletons supposedly linked to human evolution that have been found all over the world, such as Peking Man, Java Man, Neanderthal Man, and Cro-Magnon Man. So far, all these fossil remains represent hominid lines that went extinct, and they bear no markers indicating they are our direct human ancestors.[19] Still, if that is the case, then what were they? And what about the evidence that our planet is many millions of years old?

Some Christians argue that God made the world "mature" from the start, just as Adam was an adult from the moment he was made. True or not, the fossil record testifies to what is known as the "Cambrian explosion," a moment about five hundred and forty million years ago when all kinds of complex plant and animal life suddenly appeared out of nowhere. From that point forward, evolutionists have established an order for the appearance of life forms on earth that fits the Genesis account of Creation exactly. Yet such a sudden explosion of higher life forms runs counter to the evolutionary theory, which sees only an extremely slow process of gradual change. Thus, I do not get too worked up about these things. For me, the Genesis account is absolutely correct; it is just a question of how we interpret its wording. Some people can be very dogmatic in sticking to a strict, literal interpretation of six twenty-four-hour days of Creation about six thousand years ago. Other Bible scholars have identified a number of "gaps" in chapters 1 and 2 of Genesis that could possibly account for a much longer passage of time. This debate between Young Earth versus Old Earth creationists has even set Christians at loggerheads with each other.

I tend to agree with those creationists who identify several "gaps" in the Creation story that help explain some of the expansive time periods.

For instance, in Genesis 1:1–3, we do not know how long the heavens and the earth were here before God said, *"Let there be light."* In addition, there was no sun or moon until the fourth day of Creation week (see Genesis 1:14–19), so how could one mark the passing of a twenty-four-hour day until then? A third substantial gap occurs in the second chapter of Genesis, between verses 3 and 4. Before this, there were two primary actions taking place in the six days of Creation—God spoke things into existence out of nothing (described by the Hebrew verb *bara'*) and also gave them order. Then He rested on the seventh day. But starting with Genesis 2:4, something new is happening. In chapter 1, man was spoken into being three days after plants had appeared on the earth, but in chapter 2 he is *"formed"* out of the ground before there were any plants. (See Genesis 2:5–7.) The Hebrew word used here is *yatsar*, which means to fashion something out of that which already exists.[20]

I cannot answer all the questions about how old the earth is and whether there were ages past that were perhaps destroyed by global catastrophes like the Flood. But I also do not think we should be expected to. I go back to the words of Moses, who was given special revelation about the Creation and the Flood, and still said, *"The secret things belong to the LORD our God, but those things which are revealed belong to us..."* (Deuteronomy 29:29). That is, God has given us all that we need to know for now to live upright lives before Him. Let us appreciate the revelation we do have, and trust it! After all, the Bible keeps proving to be true time after time.

In the end, we know this: We all came from Adam and Eve. Anything that might have come before them is dead and gone. We are only responsible for what happens in this age. And even if we are not given the whole picture, the Bible still gives us answers to life and the universe that Darwinian evolution will never provide. Evolution only strips life of any purpose and meaning. And it can never truly tell us how the universe got here.

In a recent *Wall Street Journal* column, Christian author Eric Metaxas laid out the amazing facts now accepted by astrophysicists concerning the miraculous origins of the universe and the rarity of our planet Earth.[21] Today, scientists have identified over two hundred necessary requirements for a planet to be able to produce and sustain life, and the fact that our Earth has them all is beyond explanation. Yet the fine-tuning necessary for life to exist on a planet like ours is nothing compared to the fine-tuning required for the universe to exist at all. For example, we now know that the values of the four fundamental forces—gravity, the electromagnetic force, and the "strong" and "weak" nuclear forces—were determined less than one millionth of a second after the "Big Bang." Alter any one value, and the universe could not exist. This reality led theoretical physicist Paul Davies to conclude that "the appearance of design is overwhelming," while Oxford professor Dr. John Lennox said, "The more we get to know about our universe, the more the hypothesis that there is a Creator...gains in credibility...." Even astronomer Fred Hoyle, who coined the term "Big Bang," has admitted that crediting life on earth to natural, random causes is like believing that a tornado sweeping through a junkyard could assemble a Boeing 747.[22]

The God Question

This brings us to the ultimate question: How can we truly know there is a God? Some of the world's most brilliant scientists, such as Albert Einstein, unlocked some of the greatest wonders of the universe and still retained their belief in a Supreme Being. Others have made it their life mission to prove God does not exist. Those efforts spring from an overinflated trust in human intellect and our sensory perceptions, which are both flawed and finite.

Besides this misguided pride in science, many are drawn to Darwinism simply by a desire to break free from God. They refuse to be answerable to Him, a rebellion that is as old as mankind itself, but in modern times is cloaked in a scientific veneer. And even though Darwinian assumptions are being shattered, these individuals will never admit it because it would mean having to come back under God's moral authority. This they will never do. Yet make no mistake, *"God requires an account of what is past"* (Ecclesiastes 3:15). Surely, we will all have to give account for our lives one day. (See Matthew 12:36; Romans 14:12; Hebrews 4:13.)

This may be blunt, but the Bible defines an atheist as a *"fool."* The psalmist wrote, *"The fool has said in his heart, 'There is no God'"* (Psalm 14:1). This means that to deny God's existence, you have to actually talk your own heart into it. Atheism does not come naturally, as everyone has been given a measure of faith in God. (See Romans 12:3.) The evidence of His existence is all around us in the handiwork of nature. (See Psalm 19:1–2; Romans 1:20.) I offer a simple proof. The sun is massive at 109 times the diameter of the earth and sits some 93 million miles away, while the moon is one-quarter the diameter of the earth and is roughly 239,000 miles away. And yet to the naked eye of a human standing on the surface of our planet, the sun and moon look exactly the same size. This is demonstrated every time there is an eclipse, as their circumferences match up perfectly. Now, the odds that this just happened by chance are "astronomical." Only an incredibly intelligent Designer could have worked out the geometry to ensure such a result, much less make it happen. It also shows the centrality of man in Creation—God perfectly placed these signs in the sky for us to appreciate. He loves us and is not far from any of us, if even by chance we should seek after Him. (See Acts 17:27.) And have no doubt, God wants to be found.

The Bible actually contains a great paradox concerning belief in God. There is nothing more certain in its pages than the existence of God. Yet the Bible also readily admits that He is "in hiding" from mankind. (See Job 34:29; Exodus 33:20; 1 Timothy 6:16; Hebrews 12:14.) But why is God hiding from us? The answer begins in the garden of Eden. Because of man's disobedience, the Creator removed Himself from everyday contact with human beings. This was actually an act of mercy on His part, since were He to stay around us, His holy character would constantly be tested by our sinfulness. It is still possible to know Him by faith, and He has since made many appearances and visitations—most notably in an approachable human form in Jesus. But the Bible readily acknowledges that God took a step back from humanity for our sake, lest we perish.

The Bible also promises that He is going to come out of hiding one day. The world has witnessed this already in Jesus, who is described as "the brightness of His glory and the express image of His person" (Hebrews 1:3). And there is an even fuller revelation to come. The prophet Isaiah foresees a time when God "will destroy…the surface of the covering cast over all people, and the veil that is spread over all nations" (Isaiah 25:7). The result will be that "the earth shall be full of the knowledge of the LORD as the waters cover the sea" (Isaiah 11:9). Indeed, the Bible promises a day is coming when "the mystery of God would be finished" (Revelation 10:7).

When God finally does reveal Himself, it will be a glorious day for the redeemed. *"The pure in heart...shall see God"* (Matthew 5:8). The righteous *"shall see Him as He is"* (1 John 3:2)! But for the unrepentant, this will be an awesome and terrible day.

CONCLUSION

"Science reckons many prophets,
but there is not even a promise of a Messiah."
—Thomas H. Huxley[1]

*"The Lord knows how to deliver the godly out of temptations and to
reserve the unjust under punishment for the day of judgment."*
—The apostle Peter (2 Peter 2:9)

Many people have pointed to the Flood of Noah as an apt analogy for our day, and rightfully so. It is a prevalent theme in Scripture, and no less an authority than Jesus affirmed it as a template for the end of the age. I have attempted to lay out in a thorough and systematic way just how accurate a model it is for our modern era. It turns out that the "days of Noah" are a full and complete paradigm for the contemporary world, with serious consequences for us all. So what are the main takeaways from this book?

First, there is ample evidence that the Flood of Noah was a real, global event. There have been too many sightings of an ancient wooden ship frozen in a glacier high atop Mount Ararat to ignore. Stories of a catastrophic flood can be found in hundreds of cultures worldwide, with Genesis providing the most detailed and accurate record of this major calamity in human history. The geological record also indicates a massive deluge once engulfed the entire planet. Finally, recent studies of human languages and genetic patterns reinforce the biblical account of the Flood.

Second, the Bible describes the Flood in paradoxical terms, as an act of both severe correction and abundant mercy. It was a necessary divine intervention to arrest mankind's moral slide and rebellion against our Maker, which was fueled by idolatry, rampant violence, and sexual depravity, thereby opening the door for an intrusion by disobedient angels. Those who perished in the Flood were blinded to their corrupt ways, looking ahead with optimism and totally unaware of what was about to befall them, despite clear warnings of impending judgment. Yet the Deluge also provided the opportunity for a fresh start for humanity and all life on earth. Thus, the New Testament consistently presents the period before the Flood as a time of divine patience and longsuffering, of fair warning and hope for the future.

Third, the same Bible that faithfully recounts the Flood of Noah also gives clear warning of a similar divine judgment of humanity at the end of this age, though this time it will be by fire rather than by water. The Hebrew prophets repeatedly use Flood allusions when speaking of this perilous time to come. Their prevalent use of Flood typology, along with the intertestamental book of Enoch, greatly influenced Jesus and the apostles Peter, John, Paul and Jude to also warn of a cataclysmic judgment in the last days, just "as in the days of Noah." The New Testament's repeated use of the phrase *"days of Noah"* invariably refers to the divine waiting period between God's decree to judge the world and His actual execution of that judgment.

Fourth, there are worrisome signs that we have already entered that divine "waiting period," as evidenced by humanity's growing rejection of God. The primary impetus for this modern-day rebellion was the mainstream acceptance of Darwinian evolution, which denies the divine origins of the universe and of mankind. In so doing, we have breached the core condition of the Noahide covenant to respect every human as created in God's image. Our surrender to Darwinism has produced much malevolent fruit, including the Nazi Holocaust, the Sexual Revolution, and so much more. We see it in how abortion has become one of the most widely performed medical procedures in the world today, while sexual molestation of children is one of the most common crimes being committed worldwide. The growing acceptance of homosexuality is yet another sign that God is giving mankind over to our own vile passions. These ruinous consequences stem from the fact that much of humanity has used evolution as an excuse to walk away from God. Many people no longer sense any accountability to our Maker. Instead, they substitute their own morality, such that right is now seen as wrong, and wrong is deemed right and even celebrated. When one feels such moral superiority to God, that is a dangerous place in which to be. And although Darwinian evolution has been discredited as a scientific theory, a "liberated" humanity will never come back under God's moral authority. Thus, this is an irreversible slide, meaning much of humanity is moving beyond repentance.

Fifth, this sad state of affairs has left God with little alternative but to resort to a predetermined response rooted in His righteous character, as evidenced in the Flood story. Whenever mankind has moved beyond repentance, the righteousness of God demands that He hold us accountable in a certain way—by allowing our sin to ripen to His just judgment. If we persist in our sins, view them as morally right, and even take pleasure in them, His Spirit stops striving with our conscience, and He allows the rebellion bound in our hearts to run its course. He turns us over to our lusts and desires, all the while storing up His wrath against us. And by the time He does show up to deal with us, we are without excuse and always get what we deserve. Yet the Flood story reminds us that even in these times when God withdraws before bringing corrective judgment, He is always longsuffering and waits for those who would turn back to Him. Likewise, He always gives fair warning, He always preserves a righteous remnant, and He always remembers His mercy and brings about a fresh start. This is the enduring lesson of Noah and the Flood, and how we need to heed it today!

Sixth, there is an extraordinary congruence between the moral slide triggered by the acceptance of Darwinian evolution and two parallel historic developments, which date to around the start of the twentieth century. One such phenomenon is the separating out of a righteous remnant in the earth, as seen in the explosive growth of the Evangelical movement worldwide, especially since the Pentecostal revival was ignited in 1906. The other parallel development is the modern-day restoration of Israel, which dates to the rise of the Zionist movement in 1897 and serves as the most unmistakable sign that the age is closing and judgment is looming, much as the building of the ark by Noah was a sign that the days of the antediluvian world were numbered. Taken together, these three trends provide the central elements for the Flood analogy to be rightly applied to our day.

Seventh, there is little doubt we are at a crossroads in human history. Medical and technological advances hold incredible promise for improving and enhancing our race, but also could bring great peril. Some even insist that we can gain control of the evolutionary process and transform the human race into a vastly superior and even immortal species. Yet there are equally valid concerns these revolutionary innovations could lead to our own extinction. This paradox was captured concisely on a plaque that I encountered at the end of a special exhibition, "A Brief History of Humankind," on display at the Israel Museum in Jerusalem in May 2013. Entitled "The Future," the plaque read:

> At this very moment, innovators from various disciplines—scientists, programmers, entrepreneurs—are busy engineering our future, using cutting-edge tools such as nano- and bio-technology, cloning, synthetic biology, artificial intelligence, and virtual reality…. Genetic engineering and technology are progressing at breakneck speed—but are they a double-edged sword? Will the yearning for eternal life and an enhanced memory affect the evolution of the human species? Can the ability to clone animals and plants, make physiological changes in our bodies, and revive extinct species usher in a better world? When we become able to recreate a more intelligent species, society will have to set the limits. Will our own creative power, like the legendary golem, spell doom or redemption for humankind?

Sadly, I believe the future spells doom for those who have rejected the redemption offered in Jesus Christ. Any human efforts to achieve immortality or self-deification will surely fail. This brings us back to the introduction to *Floodgates*, in which I described this book as a "tale of two ships," and challenged everyone to decide which boat they were on. Would it be the ark of Noah or the HMS *Beagle*? So, which ship are you now on?

Those traveling with Charles Darwin on the HMS *Beagle* have basically accepted his theory of evolution and no longer believe in a God who created and cares about this world. Instead, you believe in science and its ability to solve all human problems. You also probably have great concerns about the way we are treating the environment. I care about nature, too. I have always been especially attached to the ocean, as I grew up along the seashore and love to fish and surf. I also believe we need to take better care of our world. But when we worship creation more than the Creator, we have lapsed into idolatry. The irony of this truth is that to cherish nature more than God is to consign our planet to judgment and destruction. And make no mistake, science and human intellect will not be able to save you from what is coming on the earth!

The Bible is clear that nature and mankind are inexorably linked, and that nature suffers because of man's sins. (See Romans 5:12, 8:18–22.) Therefore, I do believe there is something to the threat of global warming. But the real dangers from climate change and its underlying causes are different from how many understand them. Environmental pollution is a serious concern, but the greater problem is mankind's moral pollution. That is what should worry us! And the consequences of our rebellion will be much worse than rising sea levels and holes in the ozone layer. As Paul explained long ago, this present age will end with creation groaning and travailing for the consummation of the age and the revealing of the righteous children of God. I believe nature can already sense the increase in sin around it, and is going a little haywire. At some point, these birth pangs will lead to catastrophic events, with the earth trembling and staggering and even splitting. The fountains of the deep will break open once more, as will the "floodgates" in the heavens above, to release their fiery judgment upon mankind. Revelation warns that all plant life and all the fish in the sea will die. Multitudes of humans will also perish. And all this will occur because mankind turned from God and sought its own way. That is the tragic destiny of those who choose to stay aboard the HMS *Beagle*.

On the other hand, there is great promise ahead for those who seek shelter on the ark with Noah. For these travails of nature are just the birth pangs of the messianic age, when all things will be made new under the glorious reign of the Messiah. Those who have placed their faith in Jesus will have new bodies that are incorruptible and eternal. There will be no more wars. Even nature will be renewed, as it is freed from the sin and death that entered the world through Adam's fall. The animals will once again dwell in harmony with each other. That amazing new world is the destiny for those who find refuge on the ark of Noah.

Some may still not be sure which boat they are on. But the sifting process will eventually force everyone to decide on one ship or the other. We live in a day when God is making sure there is no gray area. He is again dividing light from darkness, the just from the unjust, which makes it easier for Him to judge humanity. For *"the Lord knows how to deliver the godly out of temptations and to reserve the unjust under punishment for the day of judgment"* (2 Peter 2:9).

Right now, the dividing line is between remaining faithful to God or accepting any number of moral compromises, such as abortion and gay marriage. We are mocked as religious extremists if we believe Jesus is still the only path to God. Soon it could be a choice between Jesus and enhanced human capabilities. Ultimately, we will be compelled to choose between Jesus and taking the mark of a false messiah just in order to buy and sell. (See Revelation 13:16–17.) So if you are weak in faith when it comes to today's moral choices, you will never be able to stand when the options are between Jesus and your belly.

We need to understand just how stark this coming choice will be. In the Flood story, mankind's lapse into idolatry allowed the entry of a band of disobedient angels into the world who only accelerated humanity's rebellion, most notably by mating with women and producing the *Nephilim*, or giants of old. But this time, the Bible warns the door will be opened for Satan himself and certain other demonic forces to enter the world and deceive humanity. Revelation says Satan will one day be cast down from heaven to the earth, and that he will arrive *"having great wrath, because he knows that he has a short time"* (Revelation 12:12). His immediate purpose will be to destroy the people who gave birth to the Messiah (Israel), and having failed in this, to make war on those who have the testimony of Jesus. Meanwhile, Revelation 11:7 warns of a great *"beast"* who *"ascends out of the bottomless pit,"* also known as the Abyss. Two "beasts" also are mentioned in Revelation 13—one is seen *"rising up out of the sea"* (verse 1), while a second beast is seen *"coming up out of the earth"* (verse 11). The first beast will demand that all humanity worship him. Paul warns of this same day of grave deception in 2 Thessalonians 2:3–4, in which a false messiah will set himself up in the temple and demand to be worshipped as God. Yet Paul also warns that it will be God Himself who allows this *"strong delusion"* to test humanity, in order to differentiate more easily between those who love the truth and those who take pleasure in unrighteousness. (See 2 Thessalonians 2:9–12.)

What is most interesting to note is this demonic intrusion that is meant to test mankind will come through the same gateways that once allowed in the waters of judgment during the Flood. Satan falls from the heavens above, while demonic beasts arise from the Abyss deep within the earth. This lowest part of *Sheol*, or Hades, is where the rebellious angels from the Flood story were once chained in darkness until the day of judgment. Nonetheless, the ultimate fate of Satan and his evil cohorts is to be chained up as well in the bottomless pit, until the day they are cast into the lake of fire. (See Revelation 20:1–10.)

A short word on this lake of fire: some say it does not exist, or they wonder how a God of love could create such a place. Well, every single day we look up in the sky at a lake of fire called the sun. Additionally, the earth's crust is floating on a sea of molten lava. It takes no stretch of the imagination to believe there is such a place of eternal punishment. Jesus says it was prepared for the devil and his angels, but He warns humans can wind up there, too, if we also rebel against our Creator. (See Matthew 25:41; also, Matthew 5:22, 7:19, 13:40–43, 47–50, 18:8–9; Mark 9:43–48; John 15:6.)

That is why you need to make doubly sure you are on the ark with Noah. To be a passenger on this vessel, the first step is to accept Jesus and

His atoning sacrifice on the cross—which assures that your redemption is "sealed," just as the ark was sealed inside and out with pitch. Being part of the righteous remnant of our day also means we should examine Noah's life and character before the Flood and mirror his message and actions. This necessitates that we do the following:

1. We should be humble and obedient before the Lord. In Genesis, Noah is called *"a just man"* (Genesis 6:9). He also is praised twice for his obedience, first in building the ark and then in caring for all the animals. Moreover, Noah was grateful to God, giving thanks by way of sacrifice after he left the ark. In the New Testament, Noah again is lauded for his faith, obedience, and fear of the Lord. May we follow his example in our own lives as the day of reckoning draws near.

2. We must search our hearts and root out any rebellion against God, lest we get swept up in the moral downfall of humanity. Before the Flood, the Spirit of God stopped striving with men, even while Noah found "favor" in God's sight. In the original Hebrew, this word *chen* means the Lord granted Noah the ability to see right from wrong, and the power to choose what was upright and pleasing to God. Thus, he did not become part of the wickedness and corruption around him, and in particular his bloodline was not tainted by mating with fallen angels. In this way, he qualified to be the progenitor of future generations in the new beginning that followed the Flood. Today, we need to keep ourselves clean from the world and not cave in to the spirit of revelry and lawlessness around us. We also need to be grateful that the Holy Spirit is still dealing with our conscience about sin, since it means God has not given up on us. And if we remain faithful to God in these ways, we will surely be part of the new world to come.

3. We should be actively involved in the building up of Zion. Noah was tasked with building an ark, which served not only as the vessel that rescued him from the coming Deluge but also as the most unmistakable warning sign to his generation that judgment was coming. Thank heaven for his obedience in carrying out this command. Today, the faithful remnant is tasked with the building up of Zion, meaning the restoration of Israel. This restoration process has two phases, involving the physical return of Jews to their land and then their spiritual return to God. The restored nation of Israel is destined to be a safe haven for the Jewish people,

as well as the greatest sign to our generation that the end of the age is upon us. So we need to not just profess a love for Israel, but do something to make a difference in securing her future and destiny in God.

4. Finally, we should be faithful in telling others about God's goodness and love, but also about His holy and just character. The apostle Peter called Noah *"a preacher of righteousness"* (2 Peter 2:5). This meant Noah had a balanced message concerning both the mercy and wrath of God, which meet together in His righteous character. The apostle Paul had a similar message when he declared in Romans 11:22, *"Therefore consider the goodness and severity of God."* Given the day in which we live, it is imperative that we offer a message of hope and love, while also warning of the serious consequences ahead due to humanity's rebellion against our Maker.

This last point is critical! Today, there are many ways of preaching the gospel, and yet so few Christians are truly "preachers of righteousness." Some Christians preach a God who is so loving and gracious that He comes over as a complete pushover who no longer cares about sin. Yet even after the cross, the New Testament writers repeatedly warn of "the wrath to come." Revelation even foresees a time when many people will cry out to be spared from *"the wrath of the Lamb."* (See Revelation 6:15–17.) So much for those who can only envision a meek Jesus.

On the other hand, many Christians today go to the other extreme by preaching only a God of wrath. They are so heavily into divine judgment that they detect the Lord doling out His wrath in nearly every natural disaster, a little here and a little there, because of our growing immorality. Yet the Flood paradigm cautions us to view these natural catastrophes in a different light—that God is actually storing up His wrath, even while nature senses the increase in sin around it and is travailing for the end of the age. Under such circumstances, we need to have a compassionate message that there is, indeed, mercy and forgiveness with God, and He has provided a way to escape the coming judgment.

Meanwhile, we also have those believers who promote a "prosperity gospel," or a "social gospel," or the hyper-faith message of "kingdom now." Sadly, none of these movements are truly preparing the followers of Jesus for what lies ahead.

It is time for Christians to realize we are already living in the "days of Noah"—the divine waiting period between God's decision to judge the world and His actual carrying out of that judgment. This interim period is marked by God setting human beings free to fully pursue the rebellion bound in their hearts, even while He looks for a righteous remnant to repent and remain faithful to Him. I cannot say exactly how far along we are in this period of divine longsuffering, and I am certainly not setting any dates for the Lord's return. But I do believe we have been living in a different world since around 1900. Again, that is when Darwinian evolution first found mainstream acceptance, even as the restoration of Israel gained steam and the Evangelical revival caught fire. I believe God has been storing up His wrath ever since, and that man is now crossing one final line with our Maker in the way we are tampering with our nature as humans.

If we truly understand the Flood paradigm, it means God's decision to judge the world is final. It is *res judicata*—a matter decided with no more avenue of appeal. We might temporarily delay His wrath through prayer and repentance, but we can never cancel it. That means judgment is nearing, but so is deliverance for those who fear God and love His appearing. (See 2 Timothy 4:8.)

Some Christians may still question whether this is an irreversible process. They point to such verses as 2 Chronicles 7:14 as an ever-present invitation for the people of God to intercede for their nations and deliver them from divine correction. They should be commended for their faith and stand for righteousness. But when one has entered a time like the "days of Noah," things have changed. When God finally decided to judge the northern kingdom of Israel for their idolatry, which He described as *"persistent unfaithfulness,"* He declared through the prophet Ezekiel that even if Noah, Job, and Daniel—three of the most righteous characters in Scripture—were there interceding for the nation, they would only spare themselves. (See Ezekiel 14:12–14.)

Then came the turn of the southern kingdom of Judah. Although they had the fresh example of their brethren to the north, Judah also lapsed into idolatry to the point that God decreed judgment on them as well. As their rebellion grew worse, the day of reckoning drew ever closer. Then we see in Hezekiah a king who repented and was given another fifteen years to live and reign. (See 2 Kings 20:1–6; 2 Chronicles 32:24–26.) Next we have King Josiah, who also repented and followed the Lord so faithfully that God promised he would not see in his lifetime the calamity determined for Jerusalem. Yet at the same time, God also decreed that His wrath against Judah would not be "*quenched,*" and was just a matter of time. (See 2 Kings 22:16–20; 2 Chronicles 34:23–28.) This whole episode is described succinctly in 2 Chronicles 36:15–16:

> *And the* LORD *God of their fathers sent warnings to them by His messengers, rising up early and sending them, because He had compassion on His people and on His dwelling place. But they mocked the messengers of God, despised His words, and scoffed at His prophets, until the wrath of the* LORD *arose against His people, till there was no remedy.*

So the biblical principle is clear: there are times when God decrees divine judgment on a people or generation, and from that moment on, the righteous might be able to temporarily postpone the inevitable judgment by repentance, but they cannot cancel it. I believe we are living in such a time already. Yet this does not mean we should become fatalistic and abandon our place and godly role in the world. We need to continue to be salt and light, and speak truth to power. We need to continue to believe our own countries will be sheep nations and not goat nations. (See Matthew 25:32–33.) But we should no longer become frustrated when the majority of people around us are lapsing irreversibly into sin and immorality. Rather, we need to realize that God may be in it, because He actually is determined to bring an end to the rebellion through divine correction. Thus, my final plea and prayer is that we would all heed the sure warning of Scripture that the floodgates of God's wrath are soon to open!

ACKNOWLEDGMENTS

The content of this book has accrued over the past twenty years while I have been living and working in Jerusalem. Many of the biblical insights came by revelation, so I can only credit heaven for that which I have freely received. (See 1 Corinthians 4:7.) I have always been a student of history, but I had a lot to learn when it came to the history behind modern science. As for the material on current affairs, I gleaned much of it from my stints as a news editor and radio show producer/host. It all slowly began to crystallize into a comprehensive thesis about our prophetic times, and a final year of intense research filled in the details.

I do owe a debt of gratitude to two individuals who made key contributions to this book. First, my friend and colleague Rev. Malcolm Hedding deepened my appreciation for the inexhaustible riches of God's Word, and also further opened my understanding about mankind's moral decline before God's calling of Abraham. Also, some twelve years ago, I had an encounter with a kind Dutch doctor named Wim Croughs, which turned out to be crucial to this book, as he urged me to study further the links between Darwinian evolution and the Nazi Holocaust through the persons of Ernst Haeckel and Houston Stewart Chamberlain. Once I had time to fully research Darwin's impact on the modern world, as well as the many biblical references to another Flood-like event at the end of the age, everything else seemed to fall into place.

I am also indebted to my colleagues at the International Christian Embassy Jerusalem, particularly to our president, Dr. Jürgen Bühler, for allowing me the time I needed to finish researching and writing this book. A special note of thanks also goes to Hans Jongsma, who translated portions of Dr. Croughs's book for me, as well as to Isabella Henkenjohann, a student intern at the Hebrew University of Jerusalem who assisted with some of the research.

Additionally, I need to credit Jerusalem itself for being such a place of inspiration and enrichment, as I could not have written this book anywhere else. I have benefitted immensely from engaging with many scholars and authors linked to the city's great institutions, such as the Hebrew University of Jerusalem, Yad Vashem, the Shalem Center, and the Jerusalem Center for Public Affairs. I also appreciate the professional relationships established with David Horovitz, Steve Linde, and many others during my time coediting a magazine at the *Jerusalem Post*.

In addition, I owe much to my family back home in North Carolina, who have always been so supportive and sacrificial in sending me forth to pursue my calling, wherever it has taken me.

Finally, my deepest gratitude is reserved for my wife, Josepha, and my son, Yonathan Amos, for all their boundless love, patience, encouragement, and practical assistance in seeing this book through to completion. Only they know how massive an undertaking it has been for me, and only I know how indispensable they have been to the final product.

NOTES

N.B.: All URL links cited in these notes were verified as still active and valid as of August 10, 2016.

Introduction

1. Charles Dickens, *A Tale of Two Cities* (London: Chapman and Hall, 1859), chapter one, http://etc.usf.edu/lit2go/22/a-tale-of-two-cities/108/book-the-first-recalled-to-lifechapter-1-the-period/.

2. Francis Fukuyama, "The End of History?" *National Interest*, Summer 1989, 2–3, https://www.embl.de/aboutus/science_society/discussion/discussion_2006/ref1-22june06.pdf.

3. Ibid., 23.

4. Francis Fukuyama, "Second Thoughts: The Last Man in a Bottle," *National Interest* 56 (Summer 1999), 16–33, https://www.embl.de/aboutus/science_society/discussion/discussion_2006/ref2-22june06.pdf.

5. Francis Fukuyama, *Our Posthuman Future: Consequences of the Biotechnology Revolution* (London: Profile Books, 2002).

6. John F. Kennedy, Inaugural Address (Washington, D.C., January 20, 1961), http://www.presidency.ucsb.edu/ws/index.php?pid=8032&.

Part One: The Flood of Noah

Chapter 1: The Divine Nature

1. C. S. Lewis, *Mere Christianity* (Quebec, Canada: Samizdat, 2014), 21–22, http://samizdat.qc.ca/vc/pdfs/MereChristianity_CSL.pdf.

2. Christian Zionism is a contemporary global movement of Christians who support the modern-day restoration of the nation of Israel in their ancient homeland based on biblical principles and promises.

3. For all of these Gallup findings, see Jeff Jones and Lydia Saad, "Gallup Poll Social Series: Values and Beliefs: Final Topline," Gallup News Service (May 8–11, 2014), http://www.gallup.com/file/poll/170798/Moral_Acceptability_140530.pdf, and Rebecca Riffkin, "New Record Highs in Moral Acceptability," Gallup News (May 30, 2014), http://www.gallup.com/poll/170789/new-record-highs-moral-acceptability.aspx.

Chapter 2: Proof of the Flood

1. Bob Cornuke, foreword to *The Unsolved Mystery of Noah's Ark*, by Mary Irwin (Bloomington, IN: WestBow Press, 2012), xi–xii.

2. Biographical entry for James Irwin on the website of Arlington National Cemetery, http://www.arlingtoncemetery.net/jbirwin.htm.

3. Henri Nissen, *Noah's Ark: Ancient Accounts and New Discoveries*, trans. (from Danish) Tracy Jay Skondin, et al. (Copenhagen: Scandinavia Publishing House, 2012), referenced in chapter 10, https://books.google.co.il/books?id=ygFrBgAAQBAJ&printsec=frontcover&source.

4. Steve Boggess, *The Search for Noah's Ark* (Mustang, OK: Tate Publishing and Enterprises, 2009), Introduction, https://books.google.co.il/books?id=KTTPtlWrSdsC&printsec=frontcover&source; "Ed Davis, "Ararat Adventure and Ark Sighting," as told to Robin Simmons, noahsarksearch.com, n.d., http://noahsarksearch.com/ed-davis.htm.

5. See "Mount Ararat Photo Album," noahsarksearch.com, http://www.noahsarksearch.com/LeeElfred/LeeElfred.htm.

6. See YouTube videos posted at https://www.youtube.com/user/NoahsArkSearch; Alan Boyle, "Noah's Ark Found? Not so Fast," NBC News, April 27, 2010, http://www.nbcnews.com/science/noahs-ark-found-not-so-fast-6C10404024; Chanan Tigay "Ex-Colleague: Expedition Faked Noah's Ark Find," AOL News, April 29, 2010; Stefan Lovgren, "Noah's Ark Quest Dead in Water—Was It a Stunt?" *National Geographic News*, September 20, 2004, http://news.nationalgeographic.com/news/2004/09/0920_040920_noahs_ark.html.

7. Andre Mitchell, "Experts to Present New evidence on Noah's Ark on Oct. 15 in Special Christian eEvent," *Christianity Today*, October 11, 2015, http://www.christiantoday.com/article/experts.to.present.new.evidence.on.noahs.ark.on.oct.15.in.special.christian.event/67195.htm.

8. "Does New Evidence Point to Noah's Ark?" Fox News report, October 16, 2015, http://video.foxnews.com/v/4561729115001/does-new-evidence-point-to-noahs-ark/?#sp=show-clips.

9. For example, see the list of sightings posted at http://www.home.earthlink.net/~arktracker/ark/Quotes.html#Dr.%20FriedrichParrot.

10. Edwin B. Greenwald, "Turk Reports 'Ship' Atop Mt. Ararat," Associated Press, November 13, 1948, http://www.noahsarksearch.com/reshit.htm.

11. Hillary Mayell, "Noah's Ark Found? Turkey Expedition Planned for Summer," *National Geographic News*, April 27, 2004, http://news.nationalgeographic.com/news/2004/04/0427_040427_noahsark.html.

12. Stefan Lovgren, "Noah's Ark Quest Dead in Water—Was It a Stunt?" *National Geographic News*, September 20, 2004, http://news.nationalgeographic.com/news/2004/09/0920_040920_noahs_ark.html.

13. For those seeking more background material on the search for Noah's ark, visit: http://www.noahsarksearch.com.

14. Irving Finkel, "Noah's Ark: The Facts Behind the Flood," *Telegraph* (London), January 19, 2014, http://www.telegraph.co.uk/culture/books/10574119/Noahs-Ark-the-facts-behind-the-flood.html.

15. Ibid.

16. "Flood Legends from Around the World," Northwest Creation Network, http://nwcreation.net/noahlegends.html.

17. Ibid.

18. Maria Trimarchi, "Was There Really a Great Flood?" *How Stuff Works*, n.d., http://science.howstuffworks.com/nature/climate-weather/storms/great-flood.htm.

19. "Flood Legends from Around the World."

20. Ibid.

21. C. H. Kang and Ethel R. Nelson, *The Discovery of Genesis* (St. Louis: Concordia Publishing House, 1979).

22. David Pawson, *Unlocking the Bible* (London: HarperCollins Publishing, 2007), 75.

23. "Flood Legends from Around the World."

24. Brian Godawa, *When Giants Were upon the Earth: The Watchers, the Nephilim, and the Biblical Cosmic War of the Seed* (Embedded Pictures Publishing, 2014); Kindle e-book, 97–113.

25. Peter Enns, *The Evolution of Adam: What the Bible Does and Doesn't Say About Human Origins* (Grand Rapids, MI: Baker Books, 2012), passim.

26. See, for example, Duane A. Garrett, *Rethinking Genesis: The Sources and Authorship of the First Book of the Pentateuch* (Grand Rapids, MI: Baker Publishing Group, 1991); John H. Sailhamer, *The Meaning of the Pentateuch: Revelation, Composition and Interpretation* (Downers Grove, IL: Intervarsity, 2009); Gordon J. Wenham, *Word Biblical Commentary, Vol. 1: Genesis 1–15* (Nashville, TN: Thomas Nelson Publishers, 1998), xxxii–xlii; and Victor P. Hamilton, *The Book of Genesis, Chapters 1–17,* The New International Commentary on the Old Testament (Grand Rapids, MI: Wm. B. Eerdmans Publishing Co., 1990), 12–38.

27. See Gordon J. Wenham, *Word Biblical Commentary, Vol. 1: Genesis 1–15* (Nashville, TN: Thomas Nelson Publishers, 1998); an illustration of this unique chiasmus poetic meter of the Genesis Flood narrative can be found online at http://godawa.com/movies/sci-fi-fantasy/noah-facts-8-noah-vs-gilgamesh-smack/.

28. Godawa, *When Giants Were upon the Earth,* 173; citing Bill T. Arnold and David B. Weisberg, "A Centennial Review of Friedrich Delitzsch's 'Babel und Bibel' Lectures," *Journal of Biblical Literature* 121, no. 3 (Autumn 2002): 441–457; see also Godawa, *When Giants Were upon the Earth,* 172–173, citing P. J. Wiseman and D. J. Wiseman, eds., *Ancient Records and the Structure of Genesis: A Case for Literary Unity* (Nashville, TN: Thomas Nelson Publishers, 1985).

29. *Strong's Concise Bible Dictionary,* entry number H268.

30. For a recent example, see Tas Walker, "Whale Fossil Graveyard in Chile Formed Late in Noah's Flood," *Biblical Geology,* n.d., http://biblicalgeology.net/blog/whale-fossil-graveyard-chile/.

31. John C. Whitcomb, Jr. and Henry M. Morris, *The Genesis Flood: The Biblical Record and Its Scientific Implications* (Philadelphia, PA: Presbyterian and Reformed Publishing Co., 1961).

32. Henry M. Morris, Ph.D., "Why Christians Should Believe in a Global Flood," Institute for Creation Research, Acts & Facts 27, no. 8 (1998), https://www.icr.org/article/842/.

33. David R. Montgomery, "Biblical-Type Floods Are Real, and They're Absolutely Enormous," *Discover*, July-August 2012, http://discovermagazine.com/2012/jul-aug/06-biblical-type-floods-real-absolutely-enormous.

34. William Ryan and Walter Pitman, *Noah's Flood: The New Scientific Discoveries About the Event That Changed History* (New York: Simon & Schuster, 2000); and James Trefil, "Evidence for a Flood," *Smithsonian*, April 1, 2000, http://www.smithsonianmag.com/science-nature/evidence-for-a-flood-102813115/?no-ist.

35. Tim Radford, "Evidence Found of Noah's Ark Flood Victims," *Guardian*, September 14, 2000, https://www.theguardian.com/science/2000/sep/14/internationalnews.archaeology; Maria Trimarchi, "Was There Really a Great Flood?" *How Stuff Works*, n.d., http://science.howstuffworks.com/nature/climate-weather/storms/great-flood.htm.

36. Montgomery, "Biblical-Type Floods Are Real."

37. David Montgomery, *The Rocks Don't Lie: A Geologist Investigates Noah's Flood* (New York: W.W. Norton & Company, Inc., 2012).

38. Vince Stricherz, "New Book Explores Noah's Flood; Says Bible and Science Can Get Along," UWNews, University of Washington, August 14, 2012, http://www.washington.edu/news/2012/08/14/new-book-explores-noahs-flood-says-bible-and-science-can-get-along/.

39. Jenna Iacurci, "Vast Underwater Ocean Trapped Beneath Earth's Crust," *Nature World News*, June 13, 2014, http://www.natureworldnews.com/articles/7560/20140613/vast-underwater-ocean-trapped-beneath-earths-crust.htm.

40. Brandon Schmandt, Steven D. Jacobsen, Thorsten W. Becker, Zhenxian Liu, and Kenneth G. Dueker, "Dehydration Melting at the Top of the Lower Mantle," *Science* 344, no. 6189 (June 13, 2014), 1265–1268, http://science.sciencemag.org/content/344/6189/1265; see also "New Evidence for Oceans of Water Deep in the Earth," Northwestern University, press release, June 12, 2014, http://www.eurekalert.org/pub_releases/2014-06/nu-nef061114.php.

41. Iacurci, "Vast Underwater Ocean."

42. There is yet one more recent scientific theory about a Genesis-like global flood, linked to a comet that struck the earth about five thousand years ago. Bruce Masse, an environmental archaeologist at Los Alamos National Laboratory, has conjectured that the great flood may be linked to the many comets and meteors that have hit the earth throughout its history. Ever since Masse presented his idea in 2004, he has found growing support in the geological community. See Maria Trimarchi, "Was There Really a Great Flood?" *How Stuff Works*, n.d., http://science.howstuffworks.com/nature/climate-weather/storms/great-flood.htm.

43. Ryan and Pitman, *Noah's Flood: The New Scientific Discoveries*.

44. Ian Wilson, *Before the Flood: The Biblical Flood as a Real Event and How It Changed the Course of Civilization* (New York: St Martin's Griffin, 2004).

45. Harold Hunt, with Russell Grigg, "The Sixteen Grandsons of Noah," Creation Ministries International, n.d., http://creation.com/the-sixteen-grandsons-of-noah.

Chapter 3: Why the Deluge?

1. N. K. Sanders, trans., *The Epic of Gilgamesh*, Assyrian International News Agency, 20; http://www.aina.org/books/eog/eog.pdf.

2. Alfred Shuchat, *Noah, the Flood and the Failure of Man According to the Midrash Rabbah* (Jerusalem: Urim Publications, 2013), 52, 356.

3. Kevin Cathcart, Michael Maher, and Martin McNamara, eds., *The Aramaic Bible: The Targum Onqelos to Genesis*, vol. 6, trans. Bernard Grossfeld (Collegeville, MN: The Liturgical Press, 1990), 50; Michael Maher, trans., *Targum Pseudo-Jonathan: Genesis*, vol. 1 (Collegeville, MN: The Liturgical Press, 1992), 35; and Martin McNamara, trans. *Targum Neofiti 1: Genesis*, vol. 1 (Collegeville, MN: The Liturgical Press, 1992), 69.

4. Francis Brown, Samuel Rolles Driver, and Charles Augustus Briggs, *Enhanced Brown-Driver-Briggs Hebrew and English Lexicon* (Oak Harbor, WA: Logos Research Systems, 2000), 320.

5. Shuchat, *Noah, the Flood and the Failure of Man*, 158.

6. Ibid., 50.

7. Ibid., 72–77.

8. Ibid.,170–173.

9. Ibid., 361.

Chapter 4: The Forbidden Union

1. Peter Burian and Alan Shapiro, eds., *The Complete Aeschylus: Volume II: Persians and Other Plays* (Oxford: Oxford University Press: 2009), 387.

2. Brian Godawa, *When Giants Were Upon the Earth: The Watchers, the Nephilim, and the Biblical Cosmic War of the Seed* (Embedded Pictures Publishing, 2014), Kindle e-book, 156–158.

3. Robert C. Newman, "The Ancient Exegesis of Genesis 6:2, 4," *Grace Theological Journal* 5, no. 1 (1984), 13–36.

4. William Whiston, trans., *The Complete Works of Josephus* (Grand Rapids, MI: Kregel Publications, 2000), 28.

5. Godawa, *When Giants Were Upon the Earth*, 39.

6. James H. Charlesworth, *The Old Testament Pseudepigrapha*, 2 vols. (New York: Yale University Press, 1983).

7. George W. E. Nickelsburg, "1 Enoch: A Commentary on the Book of 1 Enoch," in *Hermeneia: A Critical and Historical Commentary on the Bible*, ed. Klaus Baltzer, 7 (Minneapolis, MN: Fortress Press, 2001); see also E. Isaac, "A New Translation and Introduction," in *The Old Testament Pseudepigrapha*, vol. 1, ed. James H. Charlesworth, 7 (New York, London: Yale University Press, 1983).

8. See Timothy R. Carnahan, "Book 1: Watchers," Academy for Ancient Texts, http://www.ancienttexts.org/library/ethiopian/enoch/1watchers/watchers.htm; George W. E. Nickelsburg, "1 Enoch: A Commentary on the Book of 1 Enoch," in *Hermeneia: A Critical and Historical Commentary on the Bible*, ed. Klaus Baltzer, 71–82; and Archie T. Wright, *The Origin of Evil Spirits: The Reception of Genesis 6:1–4 in Early Jewish Literature*, rev. ed. (Minneapolis, MN: Fortress Press, 2015).

9. Godawa, *When Giants Were Upon the Earth*, 13.

10. See, for example, T. E. Clontz, and J. Clontz, *The Comprehensive New Testament* (Mineral Springs, AR: Cornerstone Publications, 2009; Robert Henry Charles, ed., *Pseudepigrapha of the Old Testament*, vol. 2 (Bellingham, WA: Logos Bible Software, 2004), 178; E. Isaac, "A New Translation and Introduction," in *The Old Testament Pseudepigrapha*, vol. 1, ed. James H. Charlesworth, introduction (New York, London: Yale University Press, 1983); and George W. E. Nickelsburg, "1 Enoch: A Commentary on the Book of 1 Enoch," in *Hermeneia: A Critical and Historical Commentary on the Bible*, ed. Klaus Baltzer, 83 (Minneapolis, MN: Fortress Press, 2001).

11. Robert Henry Charles, ed., *Pseudepigrapha of the Old Testament*, vol. 2 (Bellingham, WA: Logos Bible Software, 2004), 189.

12. Godawa, *When Giants Were Upon the Earth*, 106–107. There may be another biblical connection to the traditional "gates of Hades" at Banias, as some scholars link the hairy goat-demon Pan, a pagan satyr, with the wilderness demon Azazel mentioned in the Torah's instructions in Leviticus 16 for Yom Kippur. To the Old Testament Jew, the Azazel to whom the "scapegoat" (*azazel* in Hebrew) was sent on the Day of Atonement was an analogue to, or an incarnation of, this desert goat-demon. (See Judd H. Burton, *Interview with the Giant: Ethnohistorical Notes on the Nephilim* (Burton Beyond Press, 2009), 19–20). In First Enoch, Azazel also is named as one of the leading fallen watchers who taught men to war and was bound separately in the desert for his part in the pre-Flood angelic rebellion.

13. Godawa, *When Giants Were Upon the Earth*, 28.

14. Ibid., 27–28.

15. Francis Brown, Samuel Rolles Driver, and Charles Augustus Briggs, eds., *A Hebrew and English Lexicon of the Old Testament* [based on the Hebrew lexicon of Wilhelm Gesenius as translated by Edward Robinson], 1st ed. (Oxford: Clarendon Press, 1906), 658.

16. *Strong's Exhaustive Concordance of the Bible*, entry number H5307.

17. See, for example, Richard Hess, "Nephilim" in *The Anchor Bible Dictionary*, vol. 4, ed. David Noel Freedman (New York: Doubleday, 1997); and P. W. Coxon, "Nephilim" in *Dictionary of Deities and Demons in the Bible*, rev. ed., ed. K. van der Toorn, Bob Becking, and Pieter Willem van der Horst, 619 (Wm. B. Eerdmans Publishing, 1999). One author has concluded the word means "those that cause others to fall down"; see Robert Baker Girdlestone, *Synonyms of the Old Testament* (Peabody, MA: Hendrickson Publishers, 2000).

Chapter 5: New Beginning

1. Lyrics accessed at http://bobdylan.com/songs/father-night. Copyright © 1970 by Big Sky Music; renewed 1998 by Big Sky Music.

2. Alfred Shuchat, *Noah, the Flood and the Failure of Man According to the Midrash Rabbah* (Jerusalem: Urim Publications, 2013), 123.

3. John Whitcomb and Henry Morris, *The Genesis Flood* (Phillipsburg, NJ: Presbyterian and Reformed Publishing Company, 1962), 9.

4. For more on the three-tiered cosmological view that the Bible shares with other ancient Near East cultures, see John H. Walton, *The Lost World of Genesis One: Ancient Cosmology and the Origins Debate* (Downers Grove, IL: InterVarsity Press, 2009), 23–36; Denis O. Lamoureux, *Evolutionary Creation: A Christian Approach to Evolution* (Eugene, Oregon: Wipf & Stock, 2008); and Wayne Horowitz, *Mesopotamian Cosmic Geography* (Winona Lake, IN: Eisenbrauns, 1998), xii–xiii.

5. Jenna Iacurci, "Vast Underwater Ocean Trapped Beneath Earth's Crust," *Nature World News*, June 13, 2014, http://www.natureworldnews.com/articles/7560/20140613/vast-underwater-ocean-trapped-beneath-earths-crust.htm

6. See Gordon J. Wenham, *Genesis 1–15*, vol. 1 of Word Biblical Commentary, gen. eds., David A. Hubbard and Glenn W. Barker; ed., Old Testament, John D. W. Watts, 145 (Waco, Texas: Word Inc., 1987).

7. Many of these parallels are pointed out in Allen Ross, *Creation and Blessing: A Guide to the Study and Exposition of Genesis* (Grand Rapids, MI: Baker Books, 1988), 189.

8. Peter Ward and Donald E. Brownlee, *Rare Earth: Why Complex Life Is Uncommon in the Universe* (New York: Copernicus Books, 2000).

Chapter 6: Why Again?

1. Quote accessed at https://en.wikiquote.org/wiki/George_Santayana.

2. Besides the NASB, the rendering "*days of Noah*" is adopted by the NIV, NASB (1995), and NRSV, among other English translations, and is supported by a number of Bible scholars. See, for instance, the list in footnote 41 on page 47 of Daniel R. Streett, "As It Was in the Days of Noah: The Prophets Typological Interpretation of Noah's Flood," *Criswell Theological Review* 5 (Fall 2007), 35–51, http://scholar.googleusercontent.com/scholar?q=cache:bzmMNLO5gy4J:scholar.google.com/+days+of+Noah+Hebrew+%22Isaiah+54%22&hl=en&as_sdt=0,5.

3. Daniel R. Streett, "As It Was in the Days of Noah: The Prophets Typological Interpretation of Noah's Flood," *Criswell Theological Review* 5 (Fall 2007), 39–46, http://scholar.googleusercontent.com/scholar?q=cache:bzmMNLO5gy4J:scholar.google.com/+days+of+Noah+Hebrew+%22Isaiah+54%22&hl=en&as_sdt=0,5.

4. Dennis Overbye, "Jupiter: Our Cosmic Protector?" *New York Times*, July 25, 2009, http://www.nytimes.com/2009/07/26/weekinreview/26overbye.html; and Keith Cooper, "Villain in Disguise: Jupiter's Role in Impacts on Earth," *Astrobiology*, March 12, 2012, http://www.astrobio.net/news-exclusive/villain-in-disguise-jupiters-role-in-impacts-on-earth/.

5. Ben Whitherington III with Darlene Hyatt, *Paul's Letter to the Romans: A Socio-Rhetorical Commentary* (Grand Rapids, MI: Eerdmans Publishing Co., 2004), Kindle e-book, 2.

6. J. David Pawson, *Unlocking the Bible* (London: Collins Publishing, 2007), 1020–1021.

7. Witherington, *Paul's Letter to the Romans*, 83–84.

8. R. C. Sproul, *Unseen Realities: Heaven, Hell, Angels, and Demons* (Fearn, Tain, Ross-shire, Scotland: Christian Focus Publications, 2011), part 7, "Degrees of Punishment," CBDReader e-book.

Chapter 7: The Decadence of Rome

1. From the Roman fictional work *Satyricon* by Petronius, quoted in Deborah Ruscillo, "When Gluttony Ruled!" *Archaeology* 54, no. 6 (November/December 2001), http://archive.archaeology.org/0111/abstracts/romans.html.

2. Vishal Mangalwadi, *The Book That Made Your World: How the Bible Created the Soul of Western Civilization* (Nashville, TN: Thomas Nelson, 2011), 285.

3. Eric Orlin, "Urban Religion in the Middle and Late Republic," in *A Companion to Roman Religion*, ed. Jörg Rüpke, 67–69 (Chichester, West Sussex, UK: Blackwell Publishing, 2007).

4. Mangalwadi, *The Book That Made Your World*, 305.

5. Source materials for this section include: Thomas A. J. McGinn, *The Economy of Prostitution in the Roman World* (Ann Arbor, MI: University of Michigan Press, 2004), 164; Thomas A. McGinn, *Prostitution, Sexuality, and the Law in Ancient Rome* (Oxford: Oxford University Press, 1998); Craig Williams, *Roman Homosexuality* (Oxford: Oxford University Press, 1999, 2010); Marilyn B. Skinner, *Introduction to Roman Sexualities* (Princeton, NJ: Princeton University Press, 1997); John R. Clarke, *Looking at Lovemaking: Constructions of Sexuality in Roman Art 100 B.C.–A.D. 250* (Berkeley, CA: University of California Press, 1998, 2001); Thomas K. Hubbard, *Homosexuality in Greece and Rome: A Sourcebook of Basic Documents* (Berkeley, CA: University of California Press, 2003); Rebecca Langlands, *Sexual Morality in Ancient Rome* (Cambridge: Cambridge University Press, 2006); Amy Richlin, *The Garden of Priapus: Sexuality and Aggression in Roman Humor* (Oxford: Oxford University Press, 1983, 1992), 225; and Carlin A. Barton, *The Sorrows of the Ancient Romans: The Gladiator and the Monster* (Princeton, NJ: Princeton University Press, 1993).

6. Amy Richlin, "Sexuality in the Roman Empire," in *A Companion to the Roman Empire*, ed. David S. Potter, 350 (Chichester, West Sussex, UK: Blackwell, 2006).

7. Rebecca Langlands, *Sexual Morality in Ancient Rome* (Cambridge: Cambridge University Press, 2006), 13.

8. Craig Williams, *Roman Homosexuality* (Oxford: Oxford University Press, 1999, 2010), passim; and Elizabeth Manwell, "Gender and Masculinity," in *A Companion to Catullus*, ed. Marilyn B. Skinner, 118, (Chichester, West Sussex, UK: Blackwell, 2007).

9. David J. Mattingly, *Imperialism, Power, and Identity: Experiencing the Roman Empire* (Princeton, NJ: Princeton University Press, 2011), 106; Ovid, *Tristia 2*, as cited in John R. Clarke, *Looking at Lovemaking: Constructions of Sexuality in Roman Art 100 B.C.–A.D. 250* (Berkeley, CA: University of California Press, 1998, 2001), 91–92.

10. Stephanie Lynn Budin, *The Ancient Greeks: New Perspectives* (Santa Barbara, CA: ABC-CLIO, LLC, 2004), 122–123.

11. Greg Woolf, *Ancient Civilizations: the Illustrated Guide to Belief, Mythology, and Art* (New York: Barnes & Noble, 2007), 386.

12. Jennifer Viegas, "Infanticide Common in Roman Empire," *Discovery News*, May 5, 2011, http://www.seeker.com/infanticide-common-in-roman-empire-1765237924.html#news.discovery.com.

Part Two: The Modern Rebellion

Chapter 8: *The Parallel Plunge*

1. Eli Wiesel, https://www.quotetab.com/quotes/by-elie-wiesel.

2. Source materials for this section include: *The Wannsee Conference and the Genocide of the European Jews*, trans. Dr. Caroline Pearce (Berlin: House of the Wannsee Conference Memorial and Educational Site, 2009); David Parsons, "Wannsee Revisited: Germany Grapples with the Toxic Pull of Nazi Nostalgia," *Jerusalem Post Christian Edition*, January 2012, 26–28; Birte Scholz and Estera Wieja, "Marching for Life: German Pastor Healing Wounds by Confronting Nazi Past," *Jerusalem Post Christian Edition*, January 2012, 22–25.

3. *Wannsee Conference*, 151.

4. Ibid., 204–205.

5. Anson Rabinbach and Sander L. Gilman, *The Third Reich Sourcebook* (Berkley, CA: University of California Press, 2013), 755.

6. *Wannsee Conference*, 210–211.

7. Ibid., 250–251.

8. Biographical sketches of all the Wannsee conference participants can be found in *Wannsee Conference*, 178–185.

9. Thomas Rink, "Racism and Hostility Towards Jews," *The Wannsee Conference and the Genocide of the European Jews*, trans. Dr. Caroline Pearce (Berlin: House of the Wannsee Conference Memorial and Educational Site, 2009), 21–24.

10. *The Wannsee Conference and the Genocide of the European Jews*, trans. Dr. Caroline Pearce (Berlin: House of the Wannsee Conference Memorial and Educational Site, 2009).

11. Rink, "Racism and Hostility Towards Jews," 21.

12. Source materials for this section include: Thomas Rink, "Racism and Hostility Towards Jews," *The Wannsee Conference and the Genocide of the European Jews*, trans. Dr. Caroline Pearce (Berlin: House of the Wannsee Conference Memorial and Educational Site, 2009), 21–24; Mike Hawkins, *Social Darwinism in European and American Thought, 1860–1945* (Cambridge: Cambridge University Press, 1997); Jonathan Peter Spiro, *Defending the Master Race: Conservation, Eugenics, and the Legacy of Madison Grant* (Burlington, VT: University of Vermont Press, 2009).

13. *Wannsee Conference*, 23.

14. *Wannsee Conference*, 37–39.

15. See, for example, Charles Darwin, *The Descent of Man, and Selection in Relation to Sex* (London: John Murray, 1871), 28, 125, 133–143.

16. Manfred Gerstenfeld, *The War of a Million Cuts: The Struggle Against Delegitimization of Israel and the Jews, and the Growth of New Anti-Semitism*, Jerusalem Center for Public Affairs, 2015, 56–57.

17. Ibid., 57.

18. Ibid., 57.

19. Ibid., 56–59.

Chapter 9: The Blight of Violence

1. Will Rogers, *New York Times*, December 23, 1929, http://www.notable-quotes.com/w/war_quotes_ii.html.

2. See listing at the Correlates of War Project database, http://www.correlatesofwar.org/data-sets/COW-war/cow-war-list.

3. Rudolph J. Rummel, "20th Century Democide," Powerkills website, http://www.hawaii.edu/powerkills/20TH.HTM.

4. Elihu Richter and Alex Barnea, "Tehran's Genocidal Incitement Against Israel," *Middle East Quarterly*, Summer 2009, 45–51, accessed at http://www.genocidewatch.org/images/Iran_09_SummerTehran_s_Genocidal_Incitement_Against_Israel.pdf.

5. Voice of the Islamic Republic of Iran, Tehran, "Rafsanjani's Quds Day Speech," December 14, 2001, originally broadcast in Persian, translated by BBC Worldwide Monitoring.

6. David Horovitz, "The Unfolding Farce of Obama's Deal with Iran," op-ed, *The Times of Israel*, April 8, 2015, http://www.timesofisrael.com/the-unfolding-farce-of-obamas-deal-with-iran; Lazar Berman, "Iran Militia Chief: Destroying Israel Is 'Nonnegotiable,'" *Times of Israel*, March 31, 2015, http://www.timesofisrael.com/iran-militia-chief-destroying-israel-nonnegotiable/.

7. David Parsons, "Is the Worst Over?" commentary, *Jerusalem Post Christian Edition*, November 2012, 39–41.

8. *The Wannsee Conference and the Genocide of the European Jews*, trans. Dr. Caroline Pearce (Berlin: House of the Wannsee Conference Memorial and Educational Site, 2009), 45.

Chapter 10: The Sexual Revolution

1. Rev. Billy Graham, http://www.goodreads.com/quotes/tag/morals?page=6.

2. "Marriage & Divorce," American Psychological Association, n.d., http://www.apa.org/topics/divorce/.

3. Ibid.

4. Phyllis L. Brodsky, "Where Have All the Midwives Gone?" *Journal of Perinatal Education* 17, no.4 (Fall 2008), 48–51, http://www.ncbi.nlm.nih.gov/pmc/articles/PMC2582410.

5. "Abortion: Worldwide Levels and Trends," Guttmacher Institute, for the World Health Organization, October 2009, PDF version downloaded from www.guttmacher.org.

6. "Abortion Is Not the Most Common Medical Procedure," Right to Life of Michigan, October 30, 2017, http://www.nationalrighttolifenews.org/news/2017/10/abortion-not-common-medical-procedure/#.WIPFrdKWaUl.

7. For the Gallup findings, see Jeff Jones and Lydia Saad, "Gallup Poll Social Series: Values and Beliefs—Final Topline," Gallup News (May 8–11, 2014), PDF report originally accessed at http://www.gallup.com/poll/170789/new-record-highs-moral-acceptability.aspx; Rebecca Riffkin, "New Record Highs in Moral Acceptability," Gallup News (May 30, 2014), http://www.gallup.com/poll/170789/new-record-highs-moral-acceptability.aspx.

8. "Induced Abortion Worldwide," Guttmacher Institute, for the World Health Organization, November 2015, www.guttmacher.org.

9. "Gendercide: The War on Baby Girls," *Economist*, March 4, 2010, http://www.economist.com/node/15606229.

10. "Gay Marriage Around the World," Pew Research Center, fact Sheet, June 26, 2015, http://www.pewforum.org/2015/06/26/gay-marriage-around-the-world-2013.

11. Rebecca Riffkin, "New Record Highs in Moral Acceptability," Gallup News (May 30, 2014), http://www.gallup.com/poll/170789/new-record-highs-moral-acceptability.aspx.

12. "Changing Attitudes on Gay Marriage," Pew Research Center, July 29, 2015, http://www.pewforum.org/2015/07/29/graphics-slideshow-changing-attitudes-on-gay-marriage.

13. Jay and Meridel Rawlings, filmmakers, interview with author, February 9, 2016. Their new documentary on child sex slavery in Nepal is due out in 2018 under the title "C.A.N. = Change. Action. Nepal."

14. Pat Wingert, "Priests Commit No More Abuse than Other Males," *Newsweek*, April 8, 2010, http://europe.newsweek.com/priests-commit-no-more-abuse-other-males-70625?rm=eu.

15. Pat Wingert, "Sex Abuse in the Church: Girls Also Victimized," *Newsweek*, April 14, 2010, http://www.newsweek.com/sex-abuse-church-girls-also-victimized-70741.

16. Wingert, "Priests Commit No More Abuse."

17. Shanta R. Dube, Robert F. Anda, Charles L. Whitfield, David W. Brown, Vincent J. Felitti, Maxia Dong, and Wayne H. Giles, "Long-Term Consequences of Childhood Sexual Abuse by Gender of Victim," *American Journal of Preventive Medicine* 28, no. 5 (2005), 430–438, http://www.jimhopper.com/pdfs/Dube_(2005)_Childhood_sexual_abuse_by_gender_of_victim.pdf.

18. C. May-Chahal and M. Herczog, *Child Sexual Abuse in Europe* (Strasbourg: Council of Europe Publishing, 2003).

19. Brittainy Bacon, "Stolen Innocence: Inside the Shady World of Child Sex Tourism," ABC News, July 27, 2007.

20. R. Barri Flowers, *Street Kids: The Lives of Runaway and Thrownaway Teens* (Jefferson, NC: McFarland, 2010).

21. Lawrence S. Neinstein, ed. in chief; Catherine M. Gordon, Debra K. Katzman, David S. Rosen, and Elizabeth R. Wood, assoc. eds., *Adolescent Health Care: A Practical Guide* (Philadelphia: Lippincott Williams & Wilkins, 2007), 974; J. M. Greene, S. T. Ennett, and C. L. Ringwalt, "Prevalence and Correlates of Survival Sex Among Runaway and Homeless Youth," *American Journal of Public Health* 89, no. 9 (1999), 1406–1409.

22. Sam McCormack, "Refugees Are Becoming the Face of Modern Slavery in the Middle East," Huffington Post, June 20, 2014, http://www.huffingtonpost.com/sammccormack/refugees-are-becoming-the_b_5515801.html.

23. See, for example: "PM Rejects Call to Lower Age of Consent to 15," BBC News, November 17, 2013, http://www.bbc.com/news/health-24976929; Georgia Graham, "Patricia Hewitt Called for Age of Consent to Be Lowered to Ten," *Telegraph* (London), February 28, 2014, http://www.telegraph.co.uk/news/politics/labour/10666875/Patricia-Hewitt-called-for-age-of-consent-to-be-lowered-to-ten.html; Tom de Castella and Tom Heyden, "How Did the Pro-paedophile Group PIE Exist Openly for 10 Years?" *BBC News Magazine*, February 27, 2014, http://www.bbc.com/news/magazine-26352378; Robert Booth, "Whitehall Study Wanted Age of Consent Lowered to 14 and Sentences for Sex Cut," *Guardian*, July 8, 2014, http://www.theguardian.com/uk-news/2014/jul/08/lower-age-consent-14-1979-home-office-report.

24. Rachel Moran, *Paid For: My Journey Through Prostitution* (Dublin, Ireland: Gill & MacMillan, 2013).

25. Melissa Farley and Victor Malarek, "The Myth of the Victimless Crime," *New York Times*, March 12, 2008, http://www.nytimes.com/2008/03/12/opinion/12farley.html?em&ex=1205467200&en=1fedfb27c3116307&ei=5087&_r=0&mtrref=undefined&gwh=00810C32BDB9A72922126608F161E1B9&gwt=pay&assetType=opinion.

26. "Thousands Forced into Sex Slavery to Satisfy Perverted Fantasies of the Rich," *Express Gazeta* (Kosovo), translated into English by *Pravda*, June 25, 2007, http://www.pravdareport.com/society/stories/25-06-2007/93968-sex_slavery-0/.

27. The Global Slavery Index can be accessed at http://www.globalslaveryindex.org. See also "Profits and Poverty: The Economics of Forced Labour," International Labour Organization, 2014, http://www.ilo.org/global/publications/ilo-bookstore/order-online/books/WCMS_243391/lang--en/index.htm.

28. Anna Djinn, "What Amnesty Did Wrong," The Feminista Hood, August 24, 2015, accessed through Prostitution Research and Education, http://prostitutionresearch.com/wp-content/uploads/2012/01/What-Amnesty-did-wrong.pdf.

29. "Regional Overview for the Middle East and North Africa: MENA Gender Equality Profile," United Nations Children's Fund (UNICEF) Egypt, 2011, 1, http://www.unicef. org/gender/files/REGIONAL-Gender-Eqaulity-Profile-2011.pdf; Cam McGrath, "Underage Girls Are Egypt's Summer Rentals," Inter Press Service, August 5, 2013, http://www.ipsnews.net/2013/08/underage-girls-are-egypts-summer-rentals/.

Chapter 11: Where We Went Wrong

1. Friedrich Nietzsche, *Thus Spoke Zarathustra*; trans. R. J. Hollingdale (New York: Penguin Classics Edition, 1969), 41.

2. Rodney Stark, *For the Glory of God: How Monotheism Led to Reformations, Science, Witch-Hunts, and the End of Slavery* (Princeton, NJ: Princeton University Press, 2003), 160–163, 198–199.

3. Vishal Mangalwadi, *The Book That Made Your World: How the Bible Created the Soul of Western Civilization* (Nashville, TN: Thomas Nelson, 2011), 220–245; Francis Oakley, "Christian Theology and the Newtonian Science: The Rise of the Concept of the Laws of Nature," *Church History* 30 (1961), 433–457. The American Society of Church History.

4. Peter J. Bower, "The Changing Meaning of 'Evolution,'" *Journal of the History of Ideas* 36 (1975), 95–114.

5. Brian Warner, "Charles Darwin and John Herschel," *South African Journal of Science* 105 (November/December 2009), 436, http://www.sajs.co.za/sites/default/files/publications/pdf/147-583-1-PB.pdf.

6. Andrea Wulf, *The Invention of Nature: Alexander von Humboldt's New World* (New York: Knopf, 2015).

7. John van Wyhe, "Charles Darwin: Gentleman Naturalist," 2008, *The Complete Works of Darwin Online*, John van Wyhe, ed. 2002–, http://darwin-online.org.uk/darwin.html.

8. Charles R. Darwin, *On the Origin of Species: By means of Natural Selection, or the Preservation of Favoured Races in the Struggle for Life* (London: John Murray, 1859), chapter 10.

9. Robert Chambers, *Vestiges of the Natural History of Creation* (London: John Churchill, 1844).

10. James A. Secord, *Victorian Sensation: The Extraordinary Publication, Reception, and Secret Authorship of Vestiges of the Natural History of Creation* (Chicago: University of Chicago Press, 2000), 168–169.

11. Wyhe, "Charles Darwin: Gentleman Naturalist."

12. Charles R. Darwin, *On the Origin of Species by means of Natural Selection, or the Preservation of Favoured Races in the Struggle for Life* (London: John Murray, 1859), http://darwin-online.org.uk/content/frameset?itemID=F373&viewtype=text&pageseq=1.

13. Eugene M. McCarthy, "Ape to Human Evolution: A History of the Idea," n.d., http://www.macroevolution.net/ape-to-human-evolution.html.

14. Wyhe, "Charles Darwin: Gentleman Naturalist."

15. Mike Hawkins, *Social Darwinism in European and American Thought: 1860–1945* (Cambridge: Cambridge University Press, 1997), 37.

16. Alfred Kelly, *The Descent of Darwin: The Popularization of Darwin in Germany, 1860–1914* (Chapel Hill, NC: University of North Carolina Press, 1981), 25.

17. Ernst Haeckel, *The History of Creation: Or the Development of the Earth and its Inhabitants by the Action of Natural Causes*, vol. 1 (New York: D. Appleton and Company, 1880), 6, https://www.biodiversitylibrary.org/item/22324#page/32/mode/1up.

18. Ibid.

19. Ernst Haeckel, *The History of Creation: Or the Development of the Earth and Its Inhabitants by the Action of Natural Causes*, vol. 2 (New York: D. Appleton and Company, 1880), 325, https://www.biodiversitylibrary.org/item/222835#page/361/mode/1up.

20. Haeckel, *History of Creation*, vol. 1, 256, https://www.biodiversitylibrary.org/item/22324#page/284/mode/1up.

21. Ernst Haeckel, *The Evolution of Man: A Popular Exposition of the Principal Points of Human Ontogeny and Phylogeny*, vol. 2 (London: C. K. Paul & Company, 1879), 17, http://biodiversitylibrary.org/item/59315#page/41/mode/1up.

22. Ibid., 36–37, http://biodiversitylibrary.org/item/59315#page/60/mode/1up.

23. Ibid., 169–170, https://www.biodiversitylibrary.org/item/59315#page/197/mode/1up; illustration, "Plate XIV," printed just after page 180, http://biodiversitylibrary.org/item/59315#page/209/mode/1up.

24. Ibid., 181–183, https://www.biodiversitylibrary.org/item/59315#page/211/mode/1up.

25. On this point, see Daniel Gasman, "From Haeckel to Hitler: The Anatomy of a Controversy," *eSkeptic*, n.d., http://www.skeptic.com/eskeptic/09-06-10/#feature; Daniel Gasman, *The Scientific Origins of National Socialism* (New Brunswick: Transaction Press, 2004); Stephen Jay Gould, *Ontogeny and Phylogeny* (Cambridge, MA: Belknap Press [Harvard University Press], 1985); G. J. Stein, "Biological Science and the Roots of Nazism," *American Scientist* 76 (1988), 50–58; Richard Lerner, *Final Solutions: Biology, Prejudice, and Genocide* (University Park, PA: Pennsylvania State University Press, 1982), chapter 2.

26. Kelly, *The Descent of Darwin*, 59–62.

27. Jonathan Peter Spiro, *Defending the Master Race: Conservation, Eugenics, and the Legacy of Madison Grant* (Burlington, VT: University of Vermont Press, 2009), Kindle e-book, locations 2345–2355.

28. Francis Galton, "Hereditary Talent and Character," *Macmillian's Magazine*, June and August 1865; Francis Galton, *Hereditary Genius: An Inquiry into Its Laws and Consequences* (London: Macmillan & Co., 1869); Francis Galton, *On English Men of Science: Their Nature and Nurture* (London: Macmillan & Co., 1874), 12.

29. Spiro, *Defending the Master Race*; Kindle e-book, locations 2395-2410.

30. Charles Darwin, *The Descent of Man, and Selection in Relation to Sex* (London: John Murray, 1871), 125, 141, 28.

31. Ibid., 133ff.

32. Hawkins, *Social Darwinism*, 61.

33. Ibid., 123–132, 184–215.

34. Adrian Desmond and James Moore, *Darwin's Sacred Cause: How a Hatred of Slavery Shaped Darwin's Views on Human Evolution* (Boston: Houghton Mifflin, 2009); John S. Wilkins, "Darwin," in *A Companion to the Philosophy of History and Historiography: Blackwell Companions to Philosophy*, ed. Aviezer Tucker, 408–413 (Chichester, UK: Wiley-Blackwell, 2008); Mike Hawkins, *Social Darwinism*, 36–37.

Chapter 12: The Tipping Point

1. Frederich Engels, *Dialects of Nature* (1872), quoted in Robert M. Young, *Darwin's Metaphor: Nature's Place in Victorian Culture* (Cambridge: Cambridge University Press, 1985), 52.

2. Thor Jensen, "Deisel Engine: Great Inventions that Debuted at the World's Fair," http://www.tested.com/tech/454861-inventions-debuted-worlds-fair/item/diesel-engine-1900/.

3. Jonathan Peter Spiro, *Defending the Master Race: Conservation, Eugenics, and the Legacy of Madison Grant* (Burlington, VT: University of Vermont Press, 2009), Kindle e-book, locations 2052–2069.

4. Arthur de Gobineau, *The Inequality of Human Races*, trans. Adrian Collins (New York: G. P. Putnam's Sons, 1915), 205–210.

5. Ibid., 34, 98–100, 870–872; Spiro, *Defending the Master Race*, Kindle e-book, locations 2069–2108.

6. Adolf Hitler, *Mein Kampf*, trans. James Murphy (London: Hurst and Blackett, 1939), 240–243.

7. Spiro, *Defending the Master Race*, Kindle e-book, locations 2260–2315; Mike Hawkins, *Social Darwinism in European and American Thought: 1860–1945* (Cambridge: Cambridge University Press, 1997), 191–200.

8. Georges Vacher de Lapouge, *L'Aryen: Son Rôle Social* (Paris: Albert Fontemoing, 1899), 406, 512; Spiro, *Defending the Master Race*, Kindle e-book, locations 2286–2300.

9. Mike Hawkins, *Social Darwinism in European and American Thought: 1860–1945* (Cambridge: Cambridge University Press, 1997), 194–198.

10. Lapouge, *L'Aryen*, 465–468, 474; Hawkins, *Social Darwinism*, 197; Spiro, *Defending the Master Race*, Kindle e-book, locations 2293–2308.

11. Leon Poliakov, *The Aryan Myth: A History of Racist and Nationalist Ideas in Europe*, trans. Edmund Howard (London: Sussex University Press, 1974), 270.

12. Jennifer Michael Hecht, "Vacher de Lapouge and the Rise of Nazi Science," *Journal of the History of Ideas* 61, no. 2 (2000), 285–304; Linda Clark, *Social Darwinism in France* (Tuscaloosa, AL: University of Alabama Press, 1984), 131.

13. Georges Vacher de Lapouge, "L'Anthropologie et la Science Politique," *Revue d'Anthropologie* 2 (1887), 150–151.

14. Ernst Haeckel, *The Riddle of the Universe at the Close of the Nineteenth Century*, trans. Joseph McCabe (London: Watts & Company, 1901).

15. Daniel Gasman, "From Haeckel to Hitler: The Anatomy of a Controversy," *eSkeptic*, n.d., http://www.skeptic.com/eskeptic/09-06-10/#feature.

16. Ibid.

17. John P. Jackson and Nadine M. Weidman, *Race, Racism, and Science: Social Impact and Interaction* (New Brunswick, NJ: Rutgers University Press, 2005), 87; Hawkins, *Social Darwinism*, 132–148.

18. Daniel Gasman, *The Scientific Origins of National Socialism* (New Brunswick: Transaction Press, 2004), 159.

19. Haeckel, *Riddle of the Universe*, 328.

20. R. W. M. Croughs, *Het Kind in Gezin en Samenleving* (Franeker, NL: Uitgeverij T. Wever B.V., 1979), 161–163, translated into English from the Dutch for the author by Hans Jongsma.

21. Haeckel, *Riddle of the Universe*, 9.

22. Ibid., 296.

23. Croughs, *Het Kind*, 161–163.

24. Ibid.

25. Spiro, *Defending the Master Race*, Kindle e-book, locations 2413–2430.

26. The quotes are from Houston Stewart Chamberlain, *Foundations of the Nineteenth Century*, vol. 1, trans. John Lees (New York: John Lane Company, 1912), lxxxiii, 457; the biographic notes are from: Spiro, *Defending the Master Race*, Kindle e-book, locations 2143–2263.

27. Martin Gilbert, *Israel: A History* (London: Black Swan Books, 1999), 18.

28. Leon Poliakov, *Aryan Myth*, 198; Geoffrey G. Field, *Evangelist of Race: The Germanic Vision of Houston Stewart Chamberlain* (New York: Columbia University Press, 1981), 153; Chamberlain, *Foundations*, vol. 1, 327, 331.

29. Spiro, *Defending the Master Race*; Kindle locations 2202-2219; quoting extensively from Chamberlain's *The Foundations of the Nineteenth Century*.

30. Chamberlain, *Foundations*, 328.

31. Hawkins, *Social Darwinism*, 185.

32. Geoffrey G. Field, *Evangelist of Race: The Germanic Vision of Houston Stewart Chamberlain* (New York: Columbia University Press, 1981), 2.

33. Spiro, *Defending the Master Race*, Kindle e-book, locations 2231–-2251; Kaiser's quotes from Field, *Evangelist of Race*, 250–252.

34. Roderick Stackelberg and S. A. Winkle, eds., *The Nazi Germany Sourcebook: An Anthology of Texts* (London: Routeledge, 2002), 84–85.

35. William Z. Ripley, *The Races of Europe: A Sociological Study* (New York: D. Appleton and Co., 1899).

36. Ripley, *Races of Europe*, 395–396; Spiro, *Defending the Master Race*, Kindle e-book, locations 1884-1891.

37. Ripley, *Races of Europe*, 372–373.

38. Spiro, *Defending the Master Race*, passim.

39. *The Wannsee Conference and the Genocide of the European Jews*, trans. Dr. Caroline Pearce (Berlin: House of the Wannsee Conference Memorial and Educational Site, 2009), 32.

40. Richard S. Levy, *Antisemitism: A Historical Encyclopedia of Prejudice and Persecution*, vol. 1 (Santa Barbara, CA: ABC-CLIO, 2005), 700.

41. Marvin Perry and Frederick M. Schweitzer, *Anti-Semitism: Myth and Hate from Antiquity to the Present* (Springer, 2005), ix.

42. Gilbert, *Israel: A History*, 18.

Chapter 13: Fruit of the Poison Tree

1. Anne Frank, *Anne Frank, The Diary of a Young Girl: The Definitive Edition*, ed. Otto H. Frank and Mirjam Pressler, trans. Susan Massotty (New York: Doubleday, 1995), 194, entry for Friday, April 14, 1944.

2. "ADL Blasts Christian Supremacist TV Special & Book Blaming Darwin For Hitler," Anti-Defamation League (ADL), press release, August 22, 2006, http://archive.adl. org/nr/exeres/3e0340d2-b672-45c7-8ff1-10c9eed96f42,0b1623ca-d5a4-465d-a369-df6e8679cd9e,frameless.html; "Anti-Evolution Film Misappropriates the Holocaust," Anti-Defamation League (ADL), press release, April 29, 2008, http://archive.adl. org/nr/exeres/25a3641b-c374-4f2b-9a96-c04e93960427,0b1623ca-d5a4-465d-a369-df6e8679cd9e,frameless.html.

3. See, for example: Daniel Gasman, *Haeckel's Monism and the Birth of Fascist Ideology*, book 33 of Studies in Modern European History series (New York: Peter Lang, Inc.,1998); Hannah Arendt, *Elements of Totalitarianism* (New York: Harcourt Brace Jovanovich, 1951); Ian Kershaw, *The Nazi Dictatorship: Problems and Perspectives of Interpretation*, 2nd ed. (London: Edward Arnold, 1989); Michael Burleigh and Wolfgang Wipperman, *The Racial State: Germany 1933–1945* (Cambridge: Cambridge University Press, 1991); Henry V. Dicks, *Licensed Mass Murder: A Socio-Psychological Study of Some SS Killers* (London: Heinemann, 1972); Roger Eatwell, *Fascism: A History* (London: Chatto and Windus, 1995); Ze'ev Sternhell, "Fascist Ideology," in *Fascism: A Reader's Guide*, ed. Walter Laqueur (Harmondsworth, UK: Penguin, 1976).

4. Charles Darwin, *The Descent of Man, and Selection in Relation to Sex*, 2nd rev. ed. (London: John Murray, 1896), 206.

5. Mike Hawkins, *Social Darwinism in European and American Thought: 1860–1945* (Cambridge: Cambridge University Press, 1997), 216–222; Jonathan Peter Spiro, *Defending the Master Race: Conservation, Eugenics, and the Legacy of Madison Grant* (Burlington, VT: University of Vermont Press, 2009), Kindle e-book, locations 2413–2430.

6. *Buck v. Bell*, 274 U.S. 200, 208 (1927).

7. Hawkins, *Social Darwinism*, 242–243; Allan Chase, *The Legacy of Malthus* (New York: Knopf, 1980).

8. Edwin Black, "Eugenics and the Nazis: The California Connection," *San Francisco Chronicle*, November 9, 2003, http://www.sfgate.com/opinion/article/Eugenics-and-the-Nazis-the-California-2549771.php.

9. Jonathan Peter Spiro, *Defending the Master Race: Conservation, Eugenics, and the Legacy of Madison Grant* (Burlington, VT: University of Vermont Press, 2009), Kindle e-book, locations 2742–2761.

10. Ibid., Kindle e-book, locations 2943–2945.

11. Madison Grant, *The Passing of the Great Race, or the Racial Basis of European History* (New York: Charles Scribner's Sons, 1916), 45–47.

12. Spiro, *Defending the Master Race*, Kindle e-book, locations 4583–4587.

13. Black, "Eugenics and the Nazis."

14. Thomas Rink, "Racism and Hostility Towards Jews," *The Wannsee Conference and the Genocide of the European Jews*, trans. Dr. Caroline Pearce (Berlin: House of the Wannsee Conference Memorial and Educational Site, 2009), 21–24.

15. Daniel Gasman, *The Scientific Origins of National Socialism: Social Darwinism in Ernst Haeckel and the German Monist League* (London and New York: MacDonald and American Elsevier, 1971); Gasman, *Haeckel's Monism*. See also Daniel Gasman, "From Haeckel to Hitler: The Anatomy of a Controversy," n.d., *eSkeptic*, http://www.skeptic.com/eskeptic/09-06-10/#feature.

16. Stephen Jay Gould, *Ontogeny and Phylogeny* (Cambridge, MA: Belknap Press [Harvard University Press], 1977), 77–78.

17. "Ernst Haeckel (1834–1919)," University of California Museum of Paleontology, University of California, Berkeley, 2004, http://www.ucmp.berkeley.edu/history/haeckel. html.

18. Adolf Hitler, *Hitler's Secret Book*; trans. Salvator Attanasio (New York: Grove Press, 1961), 5.

19. Hawkins, *Social Darwinism*, 273–274.

20. Adolf Hitler, *Hitler's Table Talk, 1941–1944*, trans. N. Cameron and R. H. Stevens (Oxford: Oxford University Press, 1988), 59, 84–85, 134.

21. Hawkins, *Social Darwinism*, 61–62.

22. Hitler, *Table Talk*, 28.

23. Adolf Hitler, *Mein Kampf*, trans. Ralph Manheim (London: Hutchinson, 1974), 121.

24. Hitler, *Secret Book*, 16; Hitler, *Mein Kampf*, 259.

25. Hitler, *Mein Kampf*, 348.

26. Ibid., 259.

27. Hitler, *Secret Book*, 8–9, 17–18.

28. Hawkins, *Social Darwinism*, 276.

29. Hitler, *Secret Book*, 47; see also Hitler, *Mein Kampf*, 39.

30. Hawkins, *Social Darwinism*, 279–280.

31. Black, "Eugenics and the Nazis."

32. Hitler, *Mein Kampf*, 269.

33. Hawkins, *Social Darwinism*, 283–284.

34. Heather Pringle, *The Master Plan: Himmler's Scholars and the Holocaust* (New York: Hyperion, 2006); Dominic Sandbrook, "A Nordic Civilisation on the Lost Continent of Atlantis," *Telegraph*, March 5, 2006, http://www.telegraph.co.uk/culture/books/3650719/ A-Nordic-civilisation-on-the-lost-continent-of-Atlantis.html.

35. Robert A. Pois, *National Socialism and the Religion of Nature* (London: Croom Helm, 1986), 109.

36. Stephen Jay Gould, "Darwinian Fundamentalism," *New York Review of Books* 44, no. 10 (June 12, 1997), http://www.nybooks.com/articles/1997/06/12/darwinian-fundamentalism.

37. Vishal Mangalwadi, *The Book That Made Your World: How the Bible Created the Soul of Western Civilization* (Nashville, TN: Thomas Nelson, 2011), 6–7.

38. Randy J. Guliuzza, "Darwin's Sacred Imposter: Natural Selection's Idolatrous Trap," *Acts & Facts*, 40, no. 11 (2011), 12–15, http://www.icr.org/article/darwins-sacred-imposter-natural-selections/.

Chapter 14: The Next Revolution

1. Albert Einstein, quoted in Chris Oxlade, *Nuclear Energy: Tales of Invention* (Oxford: Raintree, 2012), 12.

2. Daniel Gasman, "From Haeckel to Hitler: The Anatomy of a Controversy," *eSkeptic*, n.d., http://www.skeptic.com/eskeptic/09-06-10/#feature.

3. Francis Fukuyama, *Our Posthuman Future: Consequences of the Biotechnology Revolution* (London: Profile Books, 2003), xii.

4. Peter Dickens, "Social Darwinism," *New Dictionary of the History of Ideas, Encyclopedia. com*, http://www.encyclopedia.com/history/dictionaries-thesauruses-pictures-and-press-releases/social-darwinism.

5. "Global Trends 2030: Alternative Worlds," National Intelligence Council, December 2012, iii, 3, https://www.dni.gov/files/documents/GlobalTrends_2030.pdf.

6. "Global Trends," 83.

7. The US National Institutes of Health has very helpful background material on genetics and the Human Genome Project on their website at https://www.genome.gov/education.

8. Antonio Regalado, "Human-Animal Chimeras Are Gestating on U.S. Research Farms," *MIT Technology Review*, January 6, 2016, https://www.technologyreview.com/s/545106/human-animal-chimeras-are-gestating-on-us-research-farms/; Sara Reardon, "New Life for Pig Organs," *Nature* 527 (November 12, 2015), 152–154, http://www.nature.com/polopoly_fs/1.18768!/menu/main/topColumns/topLeftColumn/pdf/527152a.pdf.

9. Anjana Ahuja, "Petri-dish Magic Cultivates a Modern Chimera," *Financial Times*, January 17, 2016, http://www.ft.com/cms/s/0/0e5b229c-bb8a-11e5-b151-8e15c9a029fb.html#axzz40vypEqlz.

10. Claudia Joseph, "Now Scientists Create a Sheep That's 15% Human," *Daily Mail UK Online*, March 2007, http://www.dailymail.co.uk/news/article-444436/Now-scientists-create-sheep-thats-15-human.html.

11. Tracy Staedter, "Adult Human Ear Grown on a Rat," *Discovery*, January 25, 2016, http://news.discovery.com/tech/biotechnology/adult-human-ear-grown-on-a-rat-160125.htm#mkcpgn=rssnws1.

12. Sara Reardon, "New Life for Pig Organs," *Nature* 527 (November 12, 2015), 152–154; "Global Trends 2030," 13.

13. See "Comparative Genomics," National Human Genome Research Institute (last updated November 3, 2015), https://www.genome.gov/11509542; Bronwyn Herbert, "Frog Gene Map a Leap Forward for Humans," ABC Science, News in Science, Australia Broadcasting Corporation, April 30, 2010, http://www.abc.net.au/science/articles/2010/04/30/2886742.htm; "In the Footsteps of Darwin: Pigs DNA Sheds Light on Evolution and Selection," European Research Council, November 14, 2012, https://erc.europa.eu/projects-figures/stories/footsteps-darwin-pigs-dna-sheds-light-evolution-and-selection; Alison Abbott, "Pig Geneticists Go the Whole Hog," *Nature* 491 (November 15, 2012), 315–316, http://www.nature.com/news/pig-geneticists-go-the-whole-hog-1.11801; Mark Prigg, "How Animal Farm Was Right: Pigs Really Are Almost Identical to Humans, Say Scientists," *Daily Mail*, November 14, 2012, http://www.dailymail.co.uk/sciencetech/article-2232978/George-Orwell-right-Pigs-really-ARE-identical-humans.html.

14. "Diseases Treated with Stem Cells," Stem Cell Research Facts, Charlotte Lozier Institute, http://www.stemcellresearchfacts.org/treatment-list/.

15. "Stem Cell Information," National Institutes of Health, US Department of Health and Human Services, 2015, http://stemcells.nih.gov/info/basics/pages/basics4.aspx.

16. Linda K. Bevington, "An Overview of Stem Cell Research," Center for Bioethics and Human Dignity, Trinity International University (last updated August 2009), https://cbhd.org/stem-cell-research/overview.

17. For more on the ethical debate over human embryonic stem cell research, see: Bevington, "Overview of Stem Cell Research"; Sarah Chan, "The Ethics of Changing Genes in the Embryo," EuroStemCell, November 4, 2015, http://www.eurostemcell.org/commentanalysis/ethics-changing-genes-embryo; Kristina Hug, "Embryonic Stem Cell Research: An Ethical Dilemma," EuroStemCell, http://www.eurostemcell.org/factsheet/embryonic-stem-cell-research-ethical-dilemma; Thomas Baldwin, "Morality and Human Embryo Research," EMBO reports 10, no. 4 (April 2009), The European Molecular Biology Organization, 299–300, https://www.ncbi.nlm.nih.gov/pmc/articles/PMC2672902/.

18. Alice Park, "The Gene Machine: What the CRISPR Experiments Mean for Humanity," Time, July 4, 2016, 42–48.

19. Ian Sample, "GM Embryos: Time for Ethics Debate, Say Scientists," Guardian, September 2, 2015, https://www.theguardian.com/science/2015/sep/01/editing-embryo-dna-genome-major-research-funders-ethics-debate.

20. Ian Sample, "Scientists Genetically Modify Human Embryos in Controversial World First," Guardian, April 23, 2015, https://www.theguardian.com/science/2015/apr/23/scientists-genetically-modify-human-embryos-in-controversial-world-first.

21. Nina Liss-Schultz, "We Are This Close to 'Designer Babies,'" Mother Jones, February 8, 2016, http://www.motherjones.com/politics/2016/02/genome-embryo-crispr-designer-babies.

22. Robin Holliday, "The Extreme Arrogance of Anti-aging Medicine," Biogerontology 10, no. 2 (April 2009), 223–228, http://link.springer.com/article/10.1007%2Fs10522-008-9170-6.

23. Maria Konovalenko, "Third International 'Genetics of Aging and Longevity' Conference," Institute for Ethics and Emerging Technologies, May 28, 2014, http://ieet.org/index.php/IEET/more/konovalenko20140528.

24. Andrew Pollack, "A Genetic Entrepreneur Sets His Sights on Aging and Death," New York Times, March 4, 2014, http://www.nytimes.com/2014/03/05/business/in-pursuit-of-longevity-a-plan-to-harness-dna-sequencing.html; Craig Ventor, "On the Verge of Creating Synthetic Life," TED Talks video, http://ieet.org/index.php/IEET/more/konovalenko20140305; Nicholas Wade, "Researchers Say They Created a 'Synthetic Cell,'" New York Times, May 20, 2010, http://www.nytimes.com/2010/05/21/science/21cell.html.

25. "A Reimagined Research Strategy for Aging," SENS Research Foundation, n.d, http://www.sens.org/research/introduction-to-sens-research.

26. "Cloning," National Human Genome Research Institute, fact sheet, https://www.genome.gov/25020028/cloning-fact-sheet/.

27. Donald Melanson, "DoD Establishes Institute Tasked with Regrowing Body Parts," Engadget, April 22, 2008, http://www.engadget.com/2008/04/22/dod-establishes-institute-tasked-with-regrowing-body-parts/.

28. Fukuyama, Our Posthuman Future, 57.

29. "Transhumanist FAQ," h+ Magazine, http://hplusmagazine.com/transhumanist-faq/.

30. Vernor Vinge, "The Coming Technological Singularity," Whole Earth Review, Winter 1993. The URL link at http://www.ugcs.caltech.edu/~phoenix/vinge/vinge-sing.html is no longer available to the public. Vinge's original version can be accessed at https://edoras.sdsu.edu/~vinge/misc/singularity.html.

31. Nick Bostrom, "How Long Before Super-intelligence?" International Journal of Futures Studies 2 (1998).

32. Nick Bostrom, "Existential Risks: Analyzing Human Extinction Scenarios and Related Hazards," *Journal of Evolution and Technology* 9 (2002), http://www.nickbostrom.com/existential/risks.html.

33. Peter Rothman, "Biology is Technology—DARPA Is Back in the Game with a Big Vision and It Is H+" *h+ Magazine*, February 15, 2015, http://hplusmagazine.com/2015/02/15/biology-technology-darpa-back-game-big-vision-h/; "Anatomy of a Microchip That Communicates Directly Using Light," Defense Advanced Research Projects Agency (DARPA), press release, February 19, 2016, http://www.darpa.mil/news-events/2016-02-19; "Work Begins to Support Self-Healing of Body and Mind," DARPA, press release, October 5, 2015, http://www.darpa.mil/news-events/2015-10-05; Dr. Eric Van Gieson, "Electrical Prescriptions (ElectRx)," DARPA, program information, n.d, http://www.darpa.mil/program/electrical-prescriptions; "Targeted Electrical Stimulation of the Brain Shows Promise as a Memory Aid," DARPA, press release, September 11, 2015, http://www.darpa.mil/news-events/2015-09-11a.

34. Ray Kurzweil, *The Singularity Is Near: When Humans Transcend Biology* (New York: Viking Penguin, 2005).

35. Ibid., 275.

36. Matthew Bailey, "The Technological Singularity as Religious Ideology," *h+ Magazine*, April 14, 2011, http://hplusmagazine.com/2011/04/14/the-technological-singularity-as-religious-ideology/.

37. C. S. Lewis, *Mere Christianity* (Samizdat, 1952), pp. 30–31, http://samizdat.qc.ca/vc/pdfs/MereChristianity_CSL.pdf.

Chapter 15: The Righteous Remnant

1. William J. Seymour, http://www.christianquotes.info/quotes-by-author/william-j-seymour-quotes/.

2. David Parsons, "Ephraimite Theory an Unsound Doctrine," *Jerusalem Post Christian Edition*, October 2010, 29–30.

3. "The Future of World Religions: Population Growth Projections, 2010–2050," Pew Research Center, April 2, 2015, http://www.pewforum.org/2015/04/02/religious-projections-2010-2050/.

4. Tony Cauchi, "The First Great Awakening in Europe—Moravians," The Revival Library, May 2006, http://www.revival-library.org/index.php/pensketches-menu/historical-revivals/1st-great-awakening-moravians.

5. Jack Hayford, *The Charismatic Century* (New York: Warner Faith, 2000); Aaron Earls, "10 Key Trends in Global Christianity," *Facts & Trends*, LifeWay, December 12, 2016, https://factsandtrends.net/2016/12/12/10-key-trends-in-global-christianity-for-2017/; George Weigel, "World Christianity by the Numbers," February 25 2015, https://www.firstthings.com/web-exclusives/2015/02/world-christianity-by-the-numbers.

6. Philip Jenkins, *The Next Christendom: The Coming of Global Christianity*, 3rd ed. (Oxford: Oxford University Press, 2011).

7. Todd M. Johnson, PhD, and Brian J. Grimm, PhD, eds., World Religion Database, Brill Publishing and The Institute on Culture, Religion, and World Affairs (CURA), Boston University, http://www.worldreligiondatabase.org/wrd_default.asp.

8. Todd Nettleton, *Iran: Desperate for God* (Bartlesville, OK: Voice of the Martyrs, and Bartlesville, OK: Living Sacrifice Book Company, 2011); Jürgen Bühler, "Revival Springs from Arab Winter," *Jerusalem Post Christian Edition*, February 2012, 38–41.

9. Johnson and Grimm, World Religion Database.

10. Ibid.; "America's Changing Religious Landscape," Pew Research Center, May 12, 2015, http://www.pewforum.org/2015/05/12/americas-changing-religious-landscape/; "The Future of World Religions: Population Growth Projections, 2010–2050," Pew Research Center, April 2, 2015, http://www.pewforum.org/2015/04/02/religious-projections-2010-2050/.

11. "2015 Sees Sharp Rise in Post-Christian Population," Barna Research Group, August 12, 2015, https://www.barna.org/barna-update/culture/728-america-more-post-christian-than-two-years-ago#.VsIQbrR96Uk.

12. "Changing Attitudes on Gay Marriage," Pew Research Center, July 29, 2015, http://www.pewforum.org/2015/07/29/graphics-slideshow-changing-attitudes-on-gay-marriage/.

13. "Abortion Viewed in Moral Terms," Pew Research Center, August 15, 2013, http://www.pewforum.org/2013/08/15/abortion-viewed-in-moral-terms/.

14. "Religion in Latin America," Pew Research Center, 2015, http://www.pewforum.org/2014/11/13/religion-in-latin-america/.

Chapter 16: The Building Up of Zion

1. Israel's founding prime minister, David Ben-Gurion, in an interview with CBS, October 5, 1956, http://virtualjerusalem.com/culture.php?Itemid=12793.

2. *Strong's Concise Bible Dictionary*, entry number H314.

3. *Strong's Concise Bible Dictionary*, entry number H6725; see its usage, for example, as "signposts" in Jeremiah 31:21.

4. The still-existing Palestine Exploration Fund has a website at http://www.pef.org.uk/history/.

5. Michael B. Oren, *Power, Faith and Fantasy: America in the Middle East, 1776 to the Present* (New York: W. W. Norton & Company, 2007), 122–148; John Black, "The Humble Origins of Israel's Amazing 'Green Thumb': The Saga of the Christians Who Taught Jews How to Farm Again," *Jerusalem Post Christian Edition*, June 2012, 26–29; Jerry Klinger, "Lt. Col. John Henry Patterson: The Christian Godfather of the Israeli Army," Jewish American Society for Historic Preservation, n.d., http://www.jewish-american-society-for-historic-preservation.org/images/Patterson_-_JASHP-1.pdf; Aaron Hecht, "The Legend Behind the Wingate Institute," *Jerusalem Post Christian Edition*, June 2008.

Chapter 17: Reason and Revelation

1. John C. Sanford, *Genetic Entropy and the Mystery of the Genome* (Lima, NY: Elim Publishing, 2005), v.

2. Francis S. Collins, *The Language of God: A Scientist Presents Evidence for Belief* (New York: Simon & Schuster, 2006).

3. Francis S. Collins, "Why This Scientist Believes in God," CNN, commentary, April 6, 2007, http://edition.cnn.com/2007/US/04/03/collins.commentary/index.html?eref=rss_tops.

4. Stephen C. Meyer, "Pro-Darwin Consensus Doesn't Rule Out Intelligent Design," CNN, commentary, November 24, 2009, http://edition.cnn.com/2009/OPINION/11/23/meyer.intelligent.design/.

5. "Evolution, Creationism, Intelligent Design," Gallup News, May 2014, http://www.gallup.com/poll/21814/evolution-creationism-intelligent-design.aspx.

6. "Timeline: From Darwin and Mendel to the Human Genome Project," National Human Genome Research Institute, https://www.genome.gov/25019887/online-education-kit-timeline-from-darwin-and-mendel-to-the-human-genome-project/; Stephanie Pappas, "Unraveling the Human Genome: 6 Molecular Milestones," *Live Science*, September 5, 2012, http://www.livescience.com/22956-human-genome-milestones.html.

7. Daniel James Devine, "Debunking junk," *World*, October 6, 2012, http://www.worldmag.com/2012/09/debunking_junk.

8. Gina Kolata, "Bits of Mystery DNA, Far from 'Junk,' Play Crucial Role," *New York Times*, September 5, 2012, http://www.nytimes.com/2012/09/06/science/far-from-junk-dna-dark-matter-proves-crucial-to-health.html?_r=0; Casey Luskin, "Junk No More: ENCODE Project Nature Paper Finds 'Biochemical Functions' for 80% of the Genome," *Evolution News*, September 5, 2012, http://www.evolutionnews.org/2012/09/junk_no_more_en_1064001.html.

9. Nicholas Wade, "Long-Held Beliefs Are Challenged by New Human Genome Analysis," *New York Times*, February 12, 2001, http://www.nytimes.com/2001/02/12/us/long-held-beliefs-are-challenged-by-new-human-genome-analysis.html.

10. Stephen C. Meyer, *Signature in the Cell: DNA and the Evidence for Intelligent Design* (San Francisco, CA: HarperOne, 2009); see http://www.signatureinthecell.com/.

11. John C. Sanford, *Genetic Entropy and the Mystery of the Genome* (Lima, NY: Elim Publishing, 2005).

12. Ibid., v–viii, 1–4, 15–27, 33–41, 45–64, 115–120.

13. Michael J. Behe, *Darwin's Black Box: The Biochemical Challenge to Evolution* (New York: Free Press, 2006); Michael J. Behe, *The Search for the Limits of Darwinism* (New York: Free Press, 2008).

14. Charles Darwin, *On the Origin of Species by Means of Natural Selection, or the Preservation of Favoured Races in the Struggle for Life*, 1st ed. (London: John Murray, 1859), 189.

15. Ann Gibbons, "Calibrating the Mitochondrial Clock," *Science* 279, no. 5347 (January 2, 1998), 28–29; Thomas J. Parsons, David S. Muniec, Kevin Sullivan, Nicola Woodyatt, Rosemary Alliston-Greiner, Mark R. Wilson, Dianna L. Berry, et. al, "A High Observed Substitution Rate in the Human Mitochondrial DNA Control Eegion," *Nature Genetics* 15 (1997), 363–368, http://www.nature.com/ng/journal/v15/n4/abs/ng0497-363.html; Brian Thomas, "Mother of All Humans Lived 6,000 Years Ago," Institute for Creation Research, September 7, 2010, https://www.icr.org/article/5657/; Bert Thompson and Brad Harrub, "How Many Times Does 'Mitochondrial Eve' Have to Die?" Apologetics Press, In the News, n.d., http://espanol.apologeticspress.org/articles/2332.

16. Ewen Callaway, "Genetic Adam and Eve Did Not Live Too Far Apart in Time: Studies Re-date 'Y-Chromosome Adam' and 'Mitochondrial Eve,'" *Nature*, August 6, 2013, http://www.nature.com/news/genetic-adam-and-eve-did-not-live-too-far-apart-in-time-1.13478.

17. Douglas L. T. Rohde, Steve Olson, and Joseph T. Chang, "Modelling the Recent Common Ancestry of All Living Humans," *Nature* 431, no, 7008 (2004), 562–566.

18. Jerry Bergman and Jeffrey Tomkins, "The Chasm Between the Human and Chimpanzee Genomes: A Review of the Evolutionary Literature," in *Proceedings of the Seventh International Conference on Creationism*, ed. M. Horstemeyer, Pittsburgh, PA, 2013, Creation Science Fellowship, Institute for Creation Research, http://www.icr.org/i/pdf/technical/Chasm-Between-Human-Chimp-Genomes.pdf; Jeffrey P. Tomkins, "New Research Evaluating Similarities Between Human and Chimpanzee DNA," Institute for Creation Research, n.d., http://www.icr.org/i/pdf/technical/Research-Evaluating-Similarities-Human-Chimp-DNA.pdf; "Comparative Genomics," National Human Genome Research Institute (last updated November 3, 2015), https://www.genome.gov/11509542/.

19. Alasdair Wilkins, "How Mitochondrial Eve Connected All Humanity and Rewrote Human Evolution," *io9 Backgrounder*, January 24, 2012, http://io9.gizmodo.com/5878996/how-mitochondrial-eve-connected-all-humanity-and-rewrote-human-evolution.

20. *Strong's Concise Bible Dictionary*, entry numbers H1254 and H3335.

21. Eric Metaxas, "Science Increasingly Makes the Case for God," *Wall Street Journal*, December 25, 2014, http://www.wsj.com/articles/eric-metaxas-science-increasingly-makes-the-case-for-god-1419544568.

22. Ibid.

Conclusion

1. Carl C. Gaither and Alma E. Cavazos-Gaither, eds., *Gaither's Dictionary of Scientific Quotations* (Berlin, Germany: Springer Science & Business Media, 2008), 1035.

BIBLIOGRAPHY

Newspapers, Journals and Other Media Sources

ABC News

Archaeology

Associated Press

Assyrian International News Agency

Atlantic

Australian Broadcasting Corporation

British Broadcasting Corporation

Bloomberg

Catholic Herald (UK)

Catholic News Service

CBS News

Charisma

Christianity Today

CNN

Daily Mail (UK)

[Daily] *Telegraph* (UK)

Discover

Discovery

Der Spiegel

Economist

Financial Times

Fox News

Guardian (UK)

h+ Magazine

Haaretz

Huffington Post

Jewish Telegraphic Agency

Jerusalem Post

Jerusalem Post Christian Edition

Los Angeles Times

National Geographic

Nature

NBC News

New York Review of Books

New York Times

Newsweek

New Zealand Herald

Philadelphia Inquirer

Religion News Service

Reuters

San Francisco Chronicle

Science

Scientific American

Smithsonian

Telegraph (London)

Time

Times of Israel

USA Today

Wall Street Journal

Washington Post

World

World Net Daily

Books

Arendt, Hannah. *Elements of Totalitarianism*, New York: Harcourt Brace Jovanovich, 1951.

———. *The Origins of Totalitarianism*, London: Andre Deutsch, 1986.

Baltzer, Klaus, ed. *Hermeneia—A Critical and Historical Commentary on the Bible*. Minneapolis, MN: Fortress, 2001.

Barlow, Nora, ed. *The Autobiography of Charles Darwin 1809–1882*. London: Collins, 1958.

Barton, Carlin A. *The Sorrows of the Ancient Romans: The Gladiator and the Monster*. Princeton University Press, 1993.

Behe, Michael J. *Darwin's Black Box: The Biochemical Challenge to Evolution*. New York: Free Press, 2006.

———. *The Search for the Limits of Darwinism*, New York: Free Press, 2008.

Bellamy, H.S. *Moons, Myths and Man. A Reinterpretation*. London: Faber & Faber, 1936.

Bittner, Jobst. *Breaking the Veil of Silence*, Tübingen, Germany: TOS Publishing, 2013.

Boggess, Steve. *The Search for Noah's Ark*, Mustang, OK: Tate Publishing and Enterprises, 2009. https://books.google.co.il/books?id=KTTPtlWrSdsC&printsec=frontcover&source.

Brown, Francis, Samuel Rolles Driver, and Charles Augustus Briggs. *Enhanced Brown-Driver-Briggs Hebrew and English Lexicon*. Oak Harbor, WA: Logos Research Systems, 2000.

———, eds. *A Hebrew and English Lexicon of the Old Testament* [based on the Hebrew lexicon of Wilhelm Gesenius as translated by Edward Robinson], 1ˢᵗ ed. Oxford: Clarendon Press, 1906.

Budin, Stephanie Lynn. *The Ancient Greeks: New Perspectives*. Santa Barbara, CA: ABC-CLIO, LLC, 2004.

Burian, Peter, and Alan Shapiro, eds. *The Complete Aeschylus: Volume II: Persians and Other Plays*. Oxford: Oxford University Press, 2009.

Burleigh, Michael, and Wolfgang Wipperman. *The Racial State: Germany 1933–1945*. Cambridge University Press, 1991.

Burton, Judd H. *Interview with the Giant: Ethnohistorical Notes on the Nephilim*. Burton Beyond Press, 2009.

Cathcart, Kevin, Michael Maher, and Martin McNamara, eds. *The Aramaic Bible: The Targum Onqelos to Genesis*. Vol. 6. Translated by Bernard Grossfeld. Collegeville, MN: The Liturgical Press, 1990.

Chamberlain, Houston Stewart. *Foundations of the Nineteenth Century, Foundations of the Nineteenth Century*, vol. 1. Translated by John Lees. New York: John Lane Company, 1912.

Chambers, Robert. *Vestiges of the Natural History of Creation*. London: John Churchill, 1844.

Charles, Robert Henry, ed., *Pseudepigrapha of the Old Testament*, vol. 2. Bellingham, WA: Logos Bible Software, 2004.

Charlesworth, James H. *The Old Testament Pseudepigrapha*. 2 vols. New York: Yale University Press, 1983.

Chase, Allan. *The Legacy of Malthus*. New York: Knopf, 1980.

Clark, Linda. *Social Darwinism in France*. Tuscaloosa, AL: University of Alabama Press, 1984.

Clarke, John R. *Looking at Lovemaking: Constructions of Sexuality in Roman Art 100 B.C.–A.D. 250*. Berkeley, CA: University of California Press, 1998, 2001.

Clontz, T. E. and J. Clontz. *The Comprehensive New Testament*. Mineral Springs, AR: Cornerstone Publications, 2009.

Collins, Francis S. *The Language of God: A Scientist Presents Evidence for Belief*. New York: Simon & Schuster, 2006.

Croughs, R. W. M. *Het Kind in Gezin en Samenleving* (Franeker, NL: Uitgeverij T. Wever B.V., 1979). Translated into English from the Dutch for the author by Hans Jongsma.

Darwin, Charles R. *On the Origin of Species: By means of Natural Selection, or the Preservation of Favoured Races in the Struggle for Life*. London: John Murray, 1859.

Darwin, Charles. *The Descent of Man, and Selection in Relation to Sex*. London: John Murray, 1871.

———. *The Descent of Man, and Selection in Relation to Sex*, 2nd rev. ed. London: John Murray, 1896.

———. *The Voyage of the Beagle*. Hayes Barton Press, 1950.

Darwin, Francis, ed. *The Life and Letters of Charles Darwin*, vol. 2. London: John Murray, 1887.

Desmond, Adrian, and James Moore. *Darwin's Sacred Cause: How a Hatred of Slavery Shaped Darwin's Views on Human Evolution*. Boston: Houghton Mifflin, 2009.

Dicks, Henry V. *Licensed Mass Murder: A Socio-Psychological Study of Some SS Killers*. London: Heinemann, 1972.

Eatwell, Roger. *Fascism: A History*. London: Chatto and Windus, 1995.

Enns, Peter. *The Evolution of Adam: What the Bible Does and Doesn't Say about Human Origins*. Grand Rapids, MI: Baker Books, 2012.

Frank, Anne. *Anne Frank, The Diary of a Young Girl: The Definitive Edition*. Edited by Otto H. Frank and Mirjam Pressler, translated by Susan Massotty. New York: Doubleday, 1995.

Freedman, David Noel, ed. *The Anchor Bible Dictionary*. New York: Doubleday, 1997.

Field, Geoffrey G. *Evangelist of Race: The Germanic Vision of Houston Stewart Chamberlain*. New York: Columbia University Press, 1981.

Flowers, R. Barri. *Street Kids: The Lives of Runaway and Thrownaway Teens*. Jefferson, NC: McFarland, 2010.

Fukuyama, Francis. *Our Posthuman Future: Consequences of the Biotechnology Revolution*. London: Profile Books, 2002.

Gaither, Carl C., Alma E. Cavazos-Gaither, eds. *Gaither's Dictionary of Scientific Quotations*. Berlin, Germany: Springer Science & Business Media, 2008.

Galton, Francis. *Hereditary Genius: An Inquiry into Its Laws and Consequences*. London: Macmillan & Co., 1869.

———. *On English Men of Science: Their Nature and Nurture*. London: Macmillan & Co., 1874.

Garrett, Duane A. *Rethinking Genesis: The Sources and Authorship of the First Book of the Pentateuch*, Grand Rapids, MI: Baker Publishing Group, 1991.

Gasman, Daniel. *Haeckel's Monism and the Birth of Fascist Ideology*. Book 33 of Studies in Modern European History series. New York: Peter Lang, Inc.,1998.

———. *The Scientific Origins of National Socialism: Social Darwinism in Ernst Haeckel and the German Monist League*. London and New York: MacDonald and American Elsevier, 1971.

———. *The Scientific Origins of National Socialism*. New Brunswick: Transaction Press, 2004.

Gerstenfeld, Manfred. *The War of a Million Cuts: The Struggle Against Delegitimization of Israel and the Jews, and the Growth of New Anti-Semitism*. Jerusalem Center for Public Affairs, 2015.

Gesenius, Friedrich Wilhelm. *Hebrew-Chaldee Lexicon of the Old Testament Scriptures*. London: Samuel Bagster and Sons, 1846.

Gilbert, Martin. *Israel: A History*. London: Black Swan Books, 1999.

Girdlestone, Robert Baker. *Synonyms of the Old Testament*. Peabody, MA: Hendrickson Publishers, 2000.

Gobineau, Arthur de. *The Inequality of Human Races*. Translated by Adrian Collins. New York: G.P. Putnam's Sons, 1915.

Godawa, Brian. *When Giants Were Upon the Earth: The Watchers, the Nephilim, and the Biblical Cosmic War of the Seed*. Embedded Pictures Publishing, Kindle e-book, 2014.

Gold, Dore. *The Fight for Jerusalem: Radical Islam, the West, and the Future of the Holy City*. Washington, D.C.: Regnery Publishing, 2009.

Gould, Stephen J. *Ontogeny and Phylogeny*. Cambridge, MA: Belknap Press [Harvard University Press], 1977, 1985.

Grant, Madison. *The Passing of the Great Race, or the Racial Basis of European History*. New York: Charles Scribner's Sons, 1916.

Gulston, Charles. *Jerusalem: The Tragedy and the Triumph*, Grand Rapids, MI: Zondervan Publishing House, 1978.

Haeckel, Ernst. *Freedom in Science and Teaching*. London: C. Kegan Paul & Co., 1879.

———. *The Evolution of Man: A Popular Exposition of the Principal Points of Human Ontogeny and Phylogeny*. 2 vols. London: C. K. Paul & Company, 1879. http://biodiversitylibrary.org/item/59315#page/41/mode/1up.

———. *The History of Creation: Or the Development of the Earth and Its Inhabitants by the Action of Natural Causes*. 2 vols. New York: D. Appleton, 1880, https://www.biodiversitylibrary.org

———. *The Riddle of the Universe at the Close of the Nineteenth Century*. Translated by Joseph McCabe. London: Watts & Company, 1901.

Hamilton, Victor P. *The Book of Genesis, Chapters 1—17*. The New International Commentary on the Old Testament. Grand Rapids, MI: Wm. B. Eerdmans Publishing Co., 1990.

Hawkins, Mike. *Social Darwinism in European and American Thought, 1860–1945*. Cambridge: Cambridge University Press, 1997.

Hayford, Jack. *The Charismatic Century*, New York: Warner Faith, 2000.

Hedding, Malcolm. *Understanding Revelation*, Nashville, TN: Intend Publishing, 2013.

Herzl, Theodor. *The Jewish State*, New York: Dover Publications, Inc., 2008 (Based on the English translation published by the American Zionist Emergency Council, 1946.)

Hitler, Adolf. *Hitler's Secret Book*. Translated by Salvator Attanasio. New York: Grove Press, 1961.

―――. *Hitler's Table Talk, 1941–1944*. Translated by N. Cameron and R. H. Stevens. Oxford: Oxford University Press, 1988.

―――. *Mein Kampf*. Translated by James Murphy. London: Hurst and Blackett, 1939.

―――. *Mein Kampf*. Translated by Ralph Manheim. London: Hutchinson, 1974.

Horowitz, Wayne. *Mesopotamian Cosmic Geography*. Winona Lake, IN: Eisenbrauns, 1998.

Hubbard, Thomas K. *Homosexuality in Greece and Rome: A Sourcebook of Basic Documents*. Berkeley, CA: University of California Press, 2003.

Irwin, Mary. *The Unsolved Mystery of Noah's Ark*. Bloomington, IN: WestBow Press, 2012.

Jackson, John P., and Nadine M. Weidman. *Race, Racism, and Science: Social Impact and Interaction*. New Brunswick, NJ: Rutgers University Press, 2005.

Jenkins, Philip. *The Next Christendom: The Coming of Global Christianity*, 3rd ed. Oxford: Oxford University Press, 2011.

Kang, C. H., and Ethel R. Nelson. *The Discovery of Genesis*. St. Louis: Concordia Publishing House, 1979.

Katz, Shmuel. *Battleground: Fact and Fantasy in Palestine*. New York: Bantam, 1977.

Kelly, Alfred. *The Descent of Darwin: The Popularization of Darwin in Germany, 1860–1914.* Chapel Hill, NC: University of North Carolina Press, 1981.

Kershaw, Ian. *The Nazi Dictatorship: Problems and Perspectives of Interpretation,* 2nd ed. London: Edward Arnold, 1989.

Kirby, Peter, ed. Early Jewish Writings: Wisdom of Solomon, 2017. www.earlyjewishwritings.com.

Küntzel, Matthias. *Germany and Iran: From the Aryan Axis to the Nuclear Threshold.* Translated by Colin Meade. Candor, NY: Telos Press Publishing, 2014.

Kurzweil, Ray. *The Age of Spiritual Machines: When Computers Exceed Human Intelligence.* New York: Viking Penguin, 1999.

———. *The Singularity Is Near: When Humans Transcend Biology.* New York: Viking Penguin, 2005.

Lamoureux, Denis O. *Evolutionary Creation: A Christian Approach to Evolution.* Eugene, Oregon: Wipf & Stock, 2008.

Langlands, Rebecca. *Sexual Morality in Ancient Rome.* Cambridge: Cambridge University Press, 2006.

Lapouge, Georges Vacher de. *L'Aryen: Son Rôle Social.* Paris: Albert Fontemoing, 1899.

Laqueur, Walter, ed. *Fascism: A Reader's Guide.* Harmondsworth, UK: Penguin, 1976.

Lerner, Richard. *Final Solutions: Biology Prejudice and Genocide.* University Park, PA: Pennsylvania State University Press, 1982.

Levy, Richard S. *Antisemitism: A Historical Encyclopedia of Prejudice and Persecution.* Vol. 1. Santa Barbara, CA: ABC-CLIO, 2005.

Lewis, C.S. *Mere Christianity.* Quebec, Canada: Samizdat, 2014.

Lewis, C. S. *Mere Christianity.* Quebec, Canada Samizdat, 1952. http://samizdat.qc.ca/vc/pdfs/MereChristianity_CSL.pdf.

Maher, Michael, trans. *Targum Pseudo-Jonathan: Genesis.* Vol. 1. Collegeville, MN: The Liturgical Press, 1992.

Mangalwadi, Vishal. *The Book That Made Your World: How the Bible Created the Soul of Western Civilization*. Nashville, TN: Thomas Nelson, 2011.

Marshall, Paul, Lela Gilbert and Nina Shea. *Persecuted: The Global Assault on Christians*. Nashville, TN: Thomas Nelson, 2013.

Mattingly, David J. *Imperialism, Power, and Identity: Experiencing the Roman Empire*. Princeton, NJ: Princeton University Press, 2011.

May-Chahal, C., and M. Herczog. *Child Sexual Abuse in Europe*. Strasbourg, France: Council of Europe Publishing, 2003.

McGinn, Thomas A. *Prostitution, Sexuality and the Law in Ancient Rome*. Oxford: Oxford University Press, 1998.

——. *The Economy of Prostitution in the Roman World*. Ann Arbor, MI: University of Michigan Press, 2004.

McNamara, Martin, trans. *Targum Neofiti 1: Genesis*. Vol. 1. Collegeville, MN: The Liturgical Press, 1992.

Meyer, Stephen C. *Signature in the Cell: DNA and the Evidence for Intelligent Design*. San Francisco, CA: HarperOne, 2009.

Montgomery, David. *The Rocks Don't Lie: A Geologist Investigates Noah's Flood*. New York: W.W. Norton & Company, Inc., 2012.

Moran, Rachel. *Paid For: My Journey Through Prostitution*. Dublin, Ireland: Gill & MacMillan, 2013.

Neinstein, Lawrence S., ed. in chief; Catherine M. Gordon, Debra K. Katzman, David S. Rosen, and Elizabeth R. Wood, assoc. eds., *Adolescent Health Care: A Practical Guide*. Philadelphia: Lippincott Williams & Wilkins, 2007.

Nettleton, Todd. *Iran: Desperate for God*. Voice of the Martyrs and Living Sacrifice Book Company, 2011.

Nissen, Henri. *Noah's Ark: Ancient Accounts and New Discoveries*. Translated (from Danish) by Tracy Jay Skondin, et al. Copenhagen: Scandinavian Publishing House, 2012. https://books.google.co.il/books?id=ygFrBgAAQBAJ&printsec=frontcover&source.

Nietzsche, Friedrich. *Thus Spoke Zarathustra*. Translated by R. J. Hollingdale. New York: Penguin Classics Edition, 1969.

Oren, Michael B. *Power, Faith and Fantasy: America in the Middle East, 1776 to the Present*. New York: W. W. Norton & Company, Inc., 2007.

Oxlade, Chris. *Nuclear Energy: Tales of Invention*. Oxford: Raintree, 2012.

Parrot, Friedrich. *Journey to Ararat*. New York: Harper and Bros., 1846.

Pawson, J. David. *Unlocking the Bible*. London: HarperCollins Publishing, 2007.

Perry, Marvin, and Frederick M. Schweitzer. *Anti-Semitism: Myth and Hate from Antiquity to the Present*. Springer, 2005.

Pois, Robert A. *National Socialism and the Religion of Nature*. London: Croom Helm, 1986.

Poliakov, Leon. *The Aryan Myth: A History of Racist and Nationalist Ideas in Europe*. Translated by Edmund Howard. London: Sussex University Press, 1974.

Potter, David S., ed. *A Companion to the Roman Empire*. Chichester, West Sussex, UK: Blackwell, 2006.

Pringle, Heather. *The Master Plan: Himmler's Scholars and the Holocaust*. New York: Hyperion, 2006.

Rabinbach, Anson, and Sander L. Gilman. *The Third Reich Sourcebook*. Berkley, CA: University of California Press, 2013.

Richards, Robert J. *The Tragic Sense of Life: Ernst Haeckel and the Struggle Over Evolutionary Thought*. Chicago, IL: University Of Chicago Press, 2009.

Richlin, Amy. *The Garden of Priapus: Sexuality and Aggression in Roman Humor*. Oxford: Oxford University Press, 1983, 1992.

Ripley, William Z. *The Races of Europe: A Sociological Study*. New York: D. Appleton and Co., 1899.

Ross, Allen. *Creation & Blessing: A Guide to the Study and Exposition Of Genesis.* Grand Rapids, MI: Baker Books, 1988.

Rüpke, Jörg, ed. *A Companion to Roman Religion.* Chichester, West Sussex, UK: Blackwell Publishing, 2007.

Ryan, William, and Walter Pitman. *Noah's Flood: The New Scientific Discoveries About the Event That Changed History.* New York: Simon & Schuster, 2000.

Sailhamer, John H. *The Meaning of the Pentateuch: Revelation, Composition and Interpretation.* Downers Grove, IL: Intervarsity, 2009.

Sanford, John C. *Genetic Entropy and the Mystery of the Genome.* Lima, NY: Elim Publishing, 2005.

Secord, James A. *Victorian Sensation: The Extraordinary Publication, Reception, and Secret Authorship of Vestiges of the Natural History of Creation.* Chicago, University of Chicago Press, 2000.

Shuchat, Alfred. *Noah, the Flood and the Failure of Man According to the Midrash Rabbah,* Jerusalem: Urim Publications, 2013.

Skinner, Marilyn B., ed. *A Companion to Catullus.* Chichester, West Sussex, UK: Blackwell, 2007.

———. *Introduction to Roman Sexualities.* Princeton, NJ: Princeton University Press, 1997.

Spiro, Jonathan Peter. *Defending the Master Race: Conservation, Eugenics, and the Legacy of Madison Grant.* Burlington, VT: University of Vermont Press, 2009.

Sproul, R.C. *Unseen Realities: Heaven, Hell, Angels, and Demons.* Fearn, Tain, Ross-shire, Scotland: Christian Focus Publications, 2011, CBDReader e-book.

Stackelberg, Roderick, and S. A. Winkle, eds. *The Nazi Germany Sourcebook: An Anthology of Texts,* London: Routeledge, 2002.

Stark, Rodney. *For the Glory of God: How Monotheism Led to Reformations, Science, Witch-Hunts and the End of Slavery.* Princeton, NJ: Princeton University Press, 2003.

Strong, James. *The New Strong's Exhaustive Concordance of the Bible*. Nashville: Thomas Nelson Publishers, 1996.

———. *The New Strong's Concise Dictionary of the Words in the Greek Testament and the Hebrew Bible*. Oak Harbor, WA: Logos Research Systems, Inc., 2009.

Tucker, Aviezer, ed. *A Companion to the Philosophy of History and Historiography: Blackwell Companions to Philosophy*. Chichester, UK: Wiley-Blackwell, 2008.

Toorn, K. van der, Bob Becking, and Pieter Willem van der Horst, eds. *Dictionary of Deities and Demons in the Bible*, rev. ed. Grand Rapids, MI: Wm. B. Eerdmans Publishing, 1999.

US Supreme Court. *Buck v. Bell*, 274 U.S. 200, 208 (1927).

Walton, John H. *The Lost World of Genesis One: Ancient Cosmology and the Origins Debate*. Downers Grove, IL: InterVarsity Press, 2009.

Wannsee Conference and the Genocide of the European Jews. Translated by Dr. Caroline Pearce. Berlin: House of the Wannsee Conference Memorial and Educational Site, 2009.

Ward, Peter, and Donald E. Brownlee. *Rare Earth: Why Complex Life Is Uncommon in the Universe*. New York: Copernicus Books, 2000.

Wells, Jonathan. *The Myth of Junk DNA*. Seattle, WA: Discovery Institute Press, 2011.

Wenham, Gordon J. *Genesis 1–15*, vol. 1 of Word Biblical Commentary, gen. eds., David A. Hubbard and Glenn W. Barker; ed., Old Testament, John D. W. Watts. Waco, Texas: Word Inc., 1987.

———. *Word Biblical Commentary, Vol. 1: Genesis 1–15*. Nashville, TN: Thomas Nelson Publishers, 1998.

Whiston, William, trans. *The Complete Works of Josephus*. Grand Rapids, MI: Kregel Publishing, 1981.

Whiston, William, trans. *The Complete Works of Josephus*. Grand Rapids, MI: Kregel Publications, 2000.

Whitcomb, Jr., John C., and Henry M. Morris. *The Genesis Flood: The Biblical Record and Its Scientific Implications*. Philadelphia, PA: Presbyterian and Reformed Publishing Co., 1961.

Whitherington III, Ben, with Darlene Hyatt. *Paul's Letter to the Romans: A Socio-Rhetorical Commentary*. Grand Rapids: Eerdmans Publishing Co, 2004, Kindle e-book.

Widlanski, Michael. *Battle for Our Minds: Western Elites and the Terror Threat*. New York, NY: Threshold Editions, 2012.

Williams, Craig. *Roman Homosexuality*. Oxford: Oxford University Press, 1999, 2010.

Wilson, Ian. *Before the Flood: The Biblical Flood as a Real Event and How It Changed the Course of Civilization*. New York: St Martin's Griffin, 2004.

Wiseman, P. J., and D. J. Wiseman, eds. *Ancient Records and the Structure of Genesis: A Case for Literary Unity*. Nashville, TN: Thomas Nelson Publishers, 1985.

Woolf, Greg. *Ancient Civilizations: the Illustrated Guide to Belief, Mythology, and Art*. New York: Barnes & Noble, 2007.

Wright, Archie T. *The Origin of Evil Spirits: The Reception of Genesis 6:1–4 in Early Jewish Literature*, rev. ed. Minneapolis, MN: Fortress Press, 2015.

Wulf, Andrea. *The Invention of Nature: Alexander von Humboldt's New World*. New York: Knopf, 2015.

Young, Robert M. *Darwin's Metaphor: Nature's Place in Victorian Culture*. Cambridge: Cambridge University Press, 1985.

Zangwill, Israel. *The Melting Pot: Drama in Four Acts*. New York: Macmillan Company, 1920.

Articles, Essays and Published Documents

Abbott, Alison. "Pig Geneticists Go the Whole Hog," *Nature* 491 (November 15, 2012).

Ahuja, Anjana. "Petri-dish Magic Cultivates a Modern Chimera." *Financial Times*, January 17, 2016.

American Psychological Association. "APA Resolution Opposing Child Sexual Abuse," adopted May 1999, in Frank V. York and Robert H. Knight, "Homosexual Behavior & Pedophilia." Family Research Council, 2000.

———. "Marriage & Divorce," American Psychological Association, n.d. http://www.apa.org/topics/divorce/.

Amnesty International, "Global Movement Votes to Adopt Policy to Protect Human Rights of Sex Workers." Amnesty International, press release, August 11, 2015.

Anti-Defamation League. "ADL Blasts Christian Supremacist TV Special and Book Blaming Darwin for Hitler." Anti-Defamation League, press release, August 22, 2006.

———. "Anti-Evolution Film Misappropriates the Holocaust." Anti-Defamation League, press release, April 29, 2008.

Arnold, Bill T., and David B. Weisberg. "A Centennial Review of Friedrich Delitzsch's 'Babel und Bibel' Lectures." *Journal of Biblical Literature* 121, no. 3 (Autumn, 2002).

Bacon, Brittainy. "Stolen Innocence: Inside the Shady World of Child Sex Tourism." ABC News, July 27, 2007.

Bailey, Matthew. "The Technological Singularity as Religious Ideology." *h+ Magazine*, April 14, 2011. http://hplusmagazine. com/2011/04/14/the-technological-singularity-as-religious-ideology/.

Baldwin, Steve. "Child Molestation and the Homosexual Movement." *Regent University Law Review* 14 (2001–2002).

Baldwin, Thomas. "Morality and Human Embryo Research." *EMBO reports* 10, no. 4 (April 2009), The European Molecular Biology Organization. https://www.ncbi.nlm.nih.gov/pmc/articles/ PMC2672902/.

Barna Research Group. "2015 Sees Sharp Rise in Post-Christian Population." Barna Research Group, August 12, 2015. https://www.barna.org/barna-update/culture/728-america-more-post-christian-than-two-years-ago#.VsIQbrR96Uk.

———. "Year in Review: Barna's Top 10 Findings in 2015." Barna Research Group, December 16, 2015. https://www.barna.com/research/year-in-review-barnas-top-10-findings-in-2015/.

Barry, Rebecca Rego. "Charles Darwin Letter Repudiating the Bible Heads to Auction." *Guardian* (US edition), September 16, 2015. https://www.theguardian.com/books/2015/sep/15/charles-darwin-letter-auction-religion-bible-creationism.

Bergman, Jerry, and Jeffrey Tomkins. "The Chasm Between the Human and Chimpanzee Genomes: A Review of the Evolutionary Literature." In *Proceedings of the Seventh International Conference on Creationism*, edited by M. Horstemeyer, Pittsburgh, PA, 2013, Creation Science Fellowship, Institute for Creation Research. http://www.icr.org/i/pdf/technical/Chasm-Between-Human-Chimp-Genomes.pdf.

Ben-Gurion, David. Interview with CBS News, October 5, 1956. Accessed at http://virtualjerusalem.com.

Berman, Lazar. "Iran Militia Chief: Destroying Israel Is 'Nonnegotiable'." *Times of Israel*, March 31, 2015. http://www.timesofisrael.com/iran-militia-chief-destroying-israel-nonnegotiable/.

Bevington, Linda K. "An Overview of Stem Cell Research." Center for Bioethics and Human Dignity, Trinity International University, last updated August 2009. https://cbhd.org/stem-cell-research/overview.

Black, Edwin. "Eugenics and the Nazis: The California Connection." *San Francisco Chronicle*, November 9, 2003. http://www.sfgate.com/opinion/article/Eugenics-and-the-Nazis-the-California-2549771.php.

Black, John. "The Humble Origins of Israel's Amazing 'Green Thumb': The Saga of the Christians Who Taught Jews How to Farm Again." *Jerusalem Post Christian Edition*, June 2012.

Blankley, Bethany. "What US Pastors Can Expect Soon: It's Going to Get Ugly." *Charisma News*, February 10, 2016.

Bono, Agostino. "John Jay Study Reveals Extent of Abuse Problem." Catholic News Service, n.d.

Booth, Robert. "Whitehall Study Wanted Age of Consent lowered to 14 and Sentences for Sex Cut." *Guardian*, July 8, 2014. http://www.theguardian.com/uk-news/2014/jul/08/lower-age-consent-14-1979-home-office-report.

Bostrom, Nick. "Existential Risks: Analyzing Human Extinction Scenarios and Related Hazards." *Journal of Evolution and Technology* 9 (2002). http://www.nickbostrom.com/existential/risks.html.

———. "How Long Before Super-intelligence?" *International Journal of Futures Studies* 2 (1998).

Bower, Peter J. "The Changing Meaning of 'Evolution'." *Journal of the History of Ideas* 36 (1975).

Boyle, Alan. "Noah's Ark Found? Not So Fast." NBC News, April 27, 2010. http://www.nbcnews.com/science/noahs-ark-found-not-so-fast-6C10404024.

British Broadcasting Corporation. "PM Rejects Call to Lower Age of Consent to 15." *BBC News*, November 17, 2013. http://www.bbc.com/news/health-24976929.

Brodsky, Phyllis L. "Where Have All the Midwives Gone?" *Journal of Perinatal Education* 17, no.4 (Fall 2008). http://www.ncbi.nlm.nih.gov/pmc/articles/PMC2582410.

Bühler, Jürgen. "Revival Springs from Arab Winter." *Jerusalem Post Christian Edition*, February 2012.

Callaway, Ewen. "Genetic Adam and Eve Did Not Live Too Far Apart in Time: Studies Re-date 'Y-Chromosome Adam' and 'Mitochondrial Eve.'" *Nature*, August 6, 2013. http://www.nature.com/news/genetic-adam-and-eve-did-not-live-too-far-apart-in-time-1.13478.

Castella, Tom de, and Tom Heyden, "How Did the Pro-paedophile Group PIE Exist Openly for 10 Years?" *BBC News Magazine*, February 27, 2014. http://www.bbc.com/news/magazine-26352378.

Carnahan, Timothy R. "Book 1: Watchers." Academy for Ancient Texts. http://www.ancienttexts.org/library/ethiopian/enoch/1watchers/watchers.htm.

Cauchi, Tony. "The First Great Awakening in Europe—Moravians." The Revival Library, May 2006. http://www.revival-library.org/index.php/pensketches-menu/historical-revivals/1st-great-awakening-moravians.

Chan, Sarah. "The Ethics of Changing Genes in the Embryo." EuroStemCell, November 4, 2015. http://www.eurostemcell.org/commentanalysis/ethics-changing-genes-embryo.

Charlotte Lozier Institute. "Diseases Treated with Stem Cells." Stem Cell Research Facts, Charlotte Lozier Institute. http://www.stemcell-researchfacts.org/treatment-list/.

"Child Abuse." *The Canadian Encyclopedia*. www.thecanadianencyclopedia.ca.

Collins, Francis S. "Why This Scientist Believes in God." CNN, commentary, April 6, 2007. http://edition.cnn.com/2007/US/04/03/collins.commentary/index.html?eref=rss_tops_____.

Cooper, Keith, "Villain in Disguise: Jupiter's Role in Impacts on Earth," *Astrobiology*, March 12, 2012. http://www.astrobio.net/news-exclusive/villain-in-disguise-jupiters-role-in-impacts-on-earth/.

Coxon, P. W. "Nephilim." In *Dictionary of Deities and Demons in the Bible*, rev. ed., edited by K. van der Toorn, Bob Becking, and Pieter Willem van der Horst. Grand Rapids, MI: Wm. B. Eerdmans Publishing, 1999.

Crimmins, Carmel. "Biden Urges U.S. Business in Davos to Lean on Anti-gay States." Reuters News Agency, January 20, 2016.

Crouse, Bill. "Ron Wyatt: Are His Claims Bonafide?" *noahsarksearch.com*, no. 17 (May–June 1988).

Defense Advanced Research Projects Agency (DARPA). "Anatomy of a Microchip that Communicates Directly Using Light." DARPA, press release, February 19, 2016. http://www.darpa.mil/news-events/2016-02-1.

———. "Targeted Electrical Stimulation of the Brain Shows Promise as a Memory Aid." DARPA, press release, September 11, 2015. http://www.darpa.mil/news-events/2015-09-11a.

———. "Work Begins to Support Self-Healing of Body and Mind." DARPA, press release, October 5, 2015. http://www.darpa.mil/news-events/2015-10-0.

Devine, Daniel James. "Debunking Junk." *World*, October 6, 2012. http://www.worldmag.com/2012/09/debunking_junk.Dickens, Charles. *A Tale of Two Cities*, London: Chapman & Hall, 1859.

Dickens, Peter. "Social Darwinism." In *New Dictionary of the History of Ideas. Encyclopedia.com.* http://www.encyclopedia.com/history/dictionaries-thesauruses-pictures-and-press-releases/social-darwinism.

Djinn, Anna. "What Amnesty Did Wrong." The Feminista Hood, August 24, 2015, accessed through Prostitution Research and Education. http://prostitutionresearch.com/wp-content/uploads/2012/01/What-Amnesty-did-wrong.pdf.

Dube, Shanta R., Robert F. Anda, Charles L. Whitfield, David W. Brown, Vincent J. Felitti, Maxia Dong, and Wayne H. Giles. "Long-Term Consequences of Childhood Sexual Abuse by Gender of Victim." *American Journal of Preventive Medicine* 28, no. 5 (2005). http://www.jimhopper.com/pdfs/Dube_(2005)_Childhood_sexual_abuse_by_gender_of_victim.pdf.

"Ernst Haeckel (1834–1919)." University of California Museum of Paleontology, University of California, Berkeley, 2004. http://www.ucmp.berkeley.edu/history/haeckel.html.

European Research Council. "In the Footsteps of Darwin: Pigs DNA Sheds Light on Evolution and Selection." European Research Council, November 14, 2012.

https://erc.europa.eu/projects-figures/stories/
footsteps-darwin-pigs-dna-sheds-light-evolution-and-selection.

Fagan, Patrick F. "The Effects of Pornography on Individuals, Marriage, Family and Community." Family Research Council, n.d.

Farley, Melissa, and Victor Malarek. "The Myth of the Victimless Crime." *New York Times*, March 12, 2008. http://www.nytimes.com/2008/03/12/opinion/12farley.html.

Freeman, R. B. "Journal of Researches." The Complete Works of Darwin Online, 1977, http://darwin-online.org.uk/EditorialIntroductions/Freeman_JournalofResearches.html.

Fukuyama, Francis. "The End of History?" *National Interest*, Summer 1989. https://www.embl.de/aboutus/science_society/discussion/discussion_2006/ref1-22june06.pdf.

———. "Second Thoughts: The Last Man in a Bottle." *National Interest* 56 (Summer 1999). https://www.embl.de/aboutus/science_society/discussion/discussion_2006/ref2-22june06.pdf.

Gallup News, "Evolution, Creationism, Intelligent Design," Gallup News, May 2014. http://www.gallup.com/poll/21814/evolution-creationism-intelligent-design.aspx.

Galton, Francis. "Hereditary Talent and Character." *Macmillian's Magazine*, June and August 1865.

———. "Letter to the Editor." *Times* (London), June 5, 1873.

Gasman, Daniel. "From Haeckel to Hitler: The Anatomy of a Controversy." *eSkeptic*, n.d. http://www.skeptic.com/eskeptic/09-06-10/#feature.

"Gendercide: The War on Baby Girls." *Economist*, March 4, 2010. http://www.economist.com/node/15606229.

Gibbons, Ann. "Calibrating the Mitochondrial Clock." *Science* 279, no. 5347 (January 2, 1998).

Gibson, Owen. "Migrant Workers Suffer 'Appalling Treatment' in Qatar World Cup Stadiums, Says Amnesty." *Guardian*, March 31, 2016.

Gieson, Dr. Eric Van. "Electrical Prescriptions (ElectRx)," DARPA, program information, n.d. http://www.darpa.mil/program/electrical-prescriptions.

Gorman, Christine. "Tissue Mash-up: A Q&A with Juan Carlos Izpisua Belmonte." *Scientific American*, January 25, 2016.

Gould, Stephen Jay. "Darwinian Fundamentalism." *New York Review of Books* 44, no. 10 (June 12, 1997). http://www.nybooks.com/articles/1997/06/12/darwinian-fundamentalism.

Graham, Georgia. "Patricia Hewitt Called for Age of Consent to Be Lowered to Ten." *Telegraph* (London), February 28, 2014. http://www.telegraph.co.uk/news/politics/labour/10666875/Patricia-Hewitt-called-for-age-of-consent-to-be-lowered-to-ten.html.

Gray, Richard. "Growing Human Organs in Pigs and Sheep Takes a Step Closer: New Guidelines Will Allow Research on Human-animal Hybrids." *Daily Mail*, February 11, 2016.

Greene, J. M., S. T. Ennett, and C. L. Ringwalt. "Prevalence and Correlates of Survival Sex Among Runaway and Homeless Youth." *American Journal of Public Health* 89, no. 9 (1999).

Greenwald, Edwin B. "Turk Reports 'Ship' Atop Mt. Ararat." Associated Press, November 13, 1948. http://www.noahsarksearch.com/reshit.htm.

Guliuzza, Randy J. "Darwin's Sacred Imposter: Natural Selection's Idolatrous Trap." *Acts & Facts* 40, no.11 (2011). http://www.icr.org/article/darwins-sacred-imposter-natural-selections/.

Guttmacher Institute. "Abortion: Worldwide Levels and Trends." Guttmacher Institute, for the World Health Organization, October 2009. PDF version downloaded from www.guttmacher.org.

———. "Induced Abortion Worldwide." Guttmacher Institute, for the World Health Organization, November 2015. www.guttmacher.org.

Hecht, Aaron. "The Legend Behind the Wingate Institute." *Jerusalem Post Christian Edition*, June 2008.

Hecht, Jennifer Michael. "Vacher de Lapouge and the Rise of Nazi Science." *Journal of the History of Ideas* 61, no. 2 (2000).

Hedding, Malcolm. "Christian Zionism in Balance." *Jerusalem Post Christian Edition*, June 2011.

Heller, Steven. "The 20th Century Was for Kids." *Atlantic*, July 19, 2012.

Herbert, Bob. "Today's Hidden Slave Trade." *New York Times*, October 27, 2007.

Herbert, Bronwyn. "Frog Gene Map a Leap Forward for Humans." ABC Science, News in Science, Australia Broadcasting Corporation, April 30, 2010. http://www.abc.net.au/science/articles/2010/04/30/2886742.htm.

Hess, Richard. "Nephilim." In *The Anchor Bible Dictionary*, vol. 4. Edited by David Noel Freedman. New York: Doubleday, 1997.

Holliday, Robin. "The Extreme Arrogance of Anti-aging Medicine." *Biogerontology* 10, no. 2 (April 2009). http://link.springer.com/article/10.1007%2Fs10522-008-9170-6.

Hopper, Jim. "Child Abuse Statistics." www.jimhopper.com (updated 2016).

Horovitz, David, "The Unfolding Farce of Obama's Deal with Iran," op-ed. *The Times of Israel*, April 8, 2015. http://www.timesofisrael.com/the-unfolding-farce-of-obamas-deal-with-iran.

Hug, Kristina. "Embryonic Stem Cell Research: An Ethical Dilemma." EuroStemCell. http://www.eurostemcell.org/factsheet/embryonic-stem-cell-research-ethical-dilemma.

Hunt, Harold, with Russell Grigg. "The Sixteen Grandsons of Noah." Creation Ministries International, n.d. http://creation.com/the-sixteen-grandsons-of-noah.

Iacurci, Jenna. "Vast Underwater Ocean Trapped Beneath Earth's Crust." *Nature World News*, June 13, 2014. http://www.natureworldnews.com/articles/7560/20140613/vast-underwater-ocean-trapped-beneath-earths-crust.htm.

Isaac, E. "A New Translation and Introduction." In *The Old Testament Pseudepigrapha*. Vol. 1. Edited by James H. Charlesworth. New York, London: Yale University Press, 1983.

Jensen, Thor. "Deisel Engine: Great Inventions That Debuted at the World's Fair." http://www.tested.com/tech/454861-inventions-debuted-worlds-fair/item/diesel-engine-1900/.

Jewish Telegraphic Agency. "August Rohling Upholder of Ritual Murder Charge Against Jews Dies Aged 92." Jewish Telegraphic Agency, January 28, 1931.

Johnson, Todd M., and Brian J. Grim, eds. World Religion Database, Brill Publishing and The Institute on Culture, Religion, and World Affairs (CURA), Boston University. http://www.worldreligiondatabase.org/wrd_default.asp.

Jones, Jeff, and Lydia Saad. "Gallup Poll Social Series: Values and Beliefs: Final Topline." Gallup News Service (May 8–11, 2014). http://www.gallup.com/file/poll/170798/Moral_Acceptability_140530.pdf.

Joseph, Claudia. "Now Scientists Create a Sheep That's 15% Human." *Daily Mail UK Online*, March 2007. http://www.dailymail.co.uk/news/article-444436/Now-scientists-create-sheep-thats-15-human.html.

Klinger, Jerry. "Lt. Col. John Henry Patterson: The Christian Godfather of the Israeli Army," n.d. Jewish American Society for Historic Preservation. http://www.jewish-american-society-for-historic-preservation.org/images/Patterson_-_JASHP-1.pdf.

Kolata, Gina. "Bits of Mystery DNA, Far from 'Junk,' Play Crucial Role." *New York Times*, September 5, 2012. http://www.nytimes.com/2012/09/06/science/far-from-junk-dna-dark-matter-proves-crucial-to-health.html.

Konovalenko, Maria. "Third International 'Genetics of Aging and Longevity' Conference." Institute for Ethics and Emerging Technologies, May 28, 2014. http://ieet.org/index.php/IEET/more/konovalenko20140528.

Kraft, Dina. "Israelis Pioneer Stem-cell Research." Jewish Telegraphic Agency, June 15, 2005. https://www.jta.org/2005/06/15/life-religion/features/israelis-pioneer-stem-cell-research.

Lapouge, Georges Vacher de. "L'Anthropologie et la Science Politique." *Revue d'Anthropologie* 2 (1887).

Lalor, Kevin, and Rosaleen McElvaney. "Overview of the Nature and Extent of Child Sexual Abuse in Europe." School of Social Sciences and Law, Dublin Institute of Technology, n.d.

Leonard, Thomas C. "Mistaking Eugenics for Social Darwinism: Why Eugenics Is Missing from the History of American Economics." Supplement to *History of Political Economy* 37 (2005).

Lewis, Aidan. "Looking Behind the Catholic Sex Abuse Scandal." BBC News, May 4, 2010. http://news.bbc.co.uk/2/hi/8654789.stm.

Lewis, Bernard. "The Periodization of History—Excerpts." Gatestone Institute, International Policy Council, February 16, 2009. https://www.gatestoneinstitute.org/323/the-periodization-of-history---excerpts.

Lewontin, Richard. "Billions and Billions of Demons." Review of *The Demon-Haunted World: Science as a Candle in the Dark* by Carl Sagan. *New York Review*, January 9, 1997.

Liss-Schultz, Nina. "We Are This Close to 'Designer Babies.'" *Mother Jones*, February 8, 2016. http://www.motherjones.com/politics/2016/02/genome-embryo-crispr-designer-babies.

Lovgren, Stefan. "Noah's Ark Quest Dead in Water—Was It a Stunt?" *National Geographic News*, September 20, 2004. http://news.nationalgeographic.com/news/2004/09/0920_040920_noahs_ark.html.

Lugo, Luis. "Spirit and Power—A 10-Country Survey of Pentecostals." Pew Research Center, October 5, 2006.

Luskin, Casey. "Junk No More: ENCODE Project Nature Paper Finds 'Biochemical Functions' for 80% of the Genome." *Evolution News* September 5, 2012. http://www.evolutionnews.org/2012/09/junk_no_more_en_1064001.html.

Manwell, Elizabeth. "Gender and Masculinity." In *A Companion to Catullus*, edited by Marilyn B. Skinner. Chichester, West Sussex, UK: Blackwell, 2007.

Mayell, Hillary. "Noah's Ark Found? Turkey Expedition Planned for Summer." *National Geographic News*, April 27, 2004. http://news.nationalgeographic.com/news/2004/04/0427_040427_noahsark.html.

McCarthy, Eugene M. "Ape to Human Evolution: A History of the Idea," n.d. http://www.macroevolution.net/ape-to-human-evolution.html.

McCormack, Sam. "Refugees Are Becoming the Face of Modern Slavery in the Middle East." Huffington Post, June 20, 2014. http://www.huffingtonpost.com/sammccormack/refugees-are-becoming-the_b_5515801.html.

McGrath, Cam. "Underage Girls Are Egypt's Summer Rentals." Inter Press Service, August 5, 2013. http://www.ipsnews.net/2013/08/underage-girls-are-egypts-summer-rentals/.

Melanson, Donald. "DoD Establishes Institute Tasked with Regrowing Body Parts." *Engadget*, April 22, 2008. http://www.engadget.com/2008/04/22/dod-establishes-institute-tasked-with-regrowing-body-parts/.

Metaxas, Eric. "Science Increasingly Makes the Case for God." *Wall Street Journal*, December 25, 2014. http://www.wsj.com/articles/eric-metaxas-science-increasingly-makes-the-case-for-god-1419544568.

Meyer, Cordula, Conny Neumann, Filelius Schmid, Petra Truckendanner, and Steffen Winter. "Unprotected: How Legalizing Prostitution Has Failed." Translated by Christopher Sultan. *Der Spiegel*, May 30, 2013. http://www.spiegel.de/international/germany/human-trafficking-persists-despite-legality-of-prostitution-in-germany-a-902533-5.html.

Meyer, Stephen C. "Pro-Darwin Consensus Doesn't Rule Out Intelligent Design." CNN, commentary, November 24, 2009. http://edition.cnn.com/2009/OPINION/11/23/meyer.intelligent.design/.

Miller, Emily McFarlan. "Methodist General Conference to Discuss LGBT issues—Again." Religion News Service, May 6, 2016. http://religionnews.com/2016/05/06/methodist-general-conference-to-discuss-lgbt-issues-again/.

Minor, Jack. "'Gay' Laws Set Stage for Pedophilia 'Rights.'" *World Net Daily*, July 18, 2013.

Mitchell, Andre. "Experts to Present New evidence on Noah's Ark on Oct. 15 in Special Christian eEvent." *Christianity Today*, October 11, 2015. http://www.christiantoday.com/article/experts.to.present.new.evidence.on.noahs.ark.on.oct.15.in.special.christian.event/67195.htm.

Montgomery, David R. "Biblical-Type Floods Are Real, and They're Absolutely Enormous." *Discover*, July–August 2012. http://discovermagazine.com/2012/jul-aug/06-biblical-type-floods-real-absolutely-enormous.

Morris, Henry M. "Why Christians Should Believe in a Global Flood." Institute for Creation Research, Acts & Facts 27, no. 8 (1998). https://www.icr.org/article/842/.

"Mount Ararat Photo Album." noahsarksearch.com, n.d. http://www.noahsarksearch.com/LeeElfred/LeeElfred.htm.

National Human Genome Research Institute. "Cloning." National Human Genome Research Institute, fact sheet. https://www.genome.gov/25020028/cloning-fact-sheet/.

———. "Comparative Genomics." National Human Genome Research Institute (last updated November 3, 2015). https://www.genome.gov/11509542

———. "Timeline: From Darwin and Mendel to the Human Genome Project," National Human Genome Research Institute. https://www.genome.gov/25019887/online-education-kit-timeline-from-darwin-and-mendel-to-the-human-genome-project/.

National Intelligence Council. "Global Trends 2030: Alternative Worlds." National Intelligence Council, December 2012. https://www.dni.gov/files/documents/GlobalTrends_2030.pdf.

"New Evidence for Oceans of Water Deep in the Earth." Northwestern University, press release, June 12, 2014. http://www.eurekalert.org/pub_releases/2014-06/nu-nef061114.php.

Newman, Robert C. "The Ancient Exegesis of Genesis 6:2, 4." *Grace Theological Journal* 5, no. 1 (1984).

Northwest Creation Network. "Flood Legends from Around the World." Northwest Creation Network. http://nwcreation.net/noahlegends.html.

Nickelsburg, George W. E. "1 Enoch: A Commentary on the Book of 1 Enoch." In *Hermeneia: A Critical and Historical Commentary on the Bible*, edited by Klaus Baltzer. Minneapolis, MN: Fortress Press, 2001.

United States Department of State. "Office to Monitor and Combat Trafficking in Persons, Trafficking in Persons Report: Russia Country Narrative." United States Department of State, 2014.

Oakley, Francis. "Christian Theology and the Newtonian Science: The Rise of the Concept of the Laws of Nature." *Church History* 30 (1961). The American Society of Church History.

O'Malley, J. P. "World Must Confront Jihadism's Roots in Islamic Doctrine, Says Author." *The Times of Israel*, May 30, 2015.

Orlin, Eric. "Urban Religion in the Middle and Late Republic." In *A Companion to Roman Religion*, edited by Jörg Rüpke. Chichester, West Sussex, UK: Blackwell Publishing, 2007.

Overbye, Dennis. "Jupiter: Our Cosmic Protector?" *New York Times*, July 25, 2009. http://www.nytimes.com/2009/07/26/weekinreview/26overbye.html.

Pappas, Stephanie. "Unraveling the Human Genome: 6 Molecular Milestones." *Live Science*, September 5, 2012. http://www.livescience.com/22956-human-genome-milestones.html.

Park, Alice. "The Gene Machine: What the CRISPR Experiments Mean for Humanity." *Time*, July 4, 2016.

Parsons, David. "Covering for Islamic Cruelty: MECC Conference Downplays Muslim Persecution of Christians, Blames Region's Ills on Israel." *Jerusalem Post Christian Edition*, July 2013.

———. "The Cross-pollination of Jew Hatred." *Jerusalem Post Christian Edition*, May 2012.

———. "Ephraimite Theory an Unsound Doctrine." *Jerusalem Post Christian Edition*, October 2010.

———. "From Munich to Mushroom Clouds: Is It Really 1938 Again?" *Charisma News*, April 28, 2015.

———. "Hooray for the Golden Agers!" *Jerusalem Post Christian Edition*, December 2102.

———. "Is the Worst Over?" *Jerusalem Post Christian Edition*, November 2012.

———. "Under Siege: The Sad Plight of Middle East Christians." *Jerusalem Post Christian Edition*, February 2011.

———. "Unmasking the Real Obama Doctrine." *Jerusalem Post*, April 12, 2015.

———. "Wannsee Revisited: Germany Grapples with the Toxic Pull of Nazi Nostalgia." *Jerusalem Post Christian Edition*, January 2012.

Parsons, Thomas J., David S. Muniec, Kevin Sullivan, Nicola Woodyatt, Rosemary Alliston-Greiner, Mark R. Wilson, Dianna L. Berry, et. al. "A High Observed Substitution Rate in the Human Mitochondrial DNA Control Region." *Nature Genetics* 15 (1997). http://www.nature.com/ng/journal/v15/n4/abs/ng0497-363.html.

Pew Research Center. "Abortion Viewed in Moral Terms." Pew Research Center, August 15, 2013. http://www.pewforum.org/2013/08/15/abortion-viewed-in-moral-terms/.

———. "America's Changing Religious Landscape." Pew Research Center, May 12, 2015. http://www.pewforum.org/2015/05/12/americas-changing-religious-landscape/.

———. "Changing Attitudes on Gay Marriage." Pew Research Center, July 29, 2015. http://www.pewforum.org/2015/07/29/graphics-slideshow-changing-attitudes-on-gay-marriage.

———. "The Future of World Religions: Population Growth Projections, 2010–2050." Pew Research Center, April 2, 2015. http://www.pewforum.org/2015/04/02/religious-projections-2010-2050/.

———. "Gay Marriage Around the World." Pew Research Center, fact sheet, June 26, 2015. http://www.pewforum.org/2015/06/26/gay-marriage-around-the-world-2013.

———. "Religion in Latin America." Pew Research Center, 2015. http://www.pewforum.org/2014/11/13/religion-in-latin-america.

Pollack, Andrew. "A Genetic Entrepreneur Sets His Sights on Aging and Death." *New York Times*, March 4, 2014. http://www.nytimes.com/2014/03/05/business/in-pursuit-of-longevity-a-plan-to-harness-dna-sequencing.html.

Prigg, Mark. "How Animal Farm Was Right: Pigs Really Are Almost Identical to Humans, Say Scientists." *Daily Mail*, November 14, 2012. http://www.dailymail.co.uk/sciencetech/article-2232978/George-Orwell-right-Pigs-really-ARE-identical-humans.html.

"Profits and Poverty: The Economics of Forced Labour." International Labour Organization, 2014. http://www.ilo.org/global/publications/ilo-bookstore/order-online/books/WCMS_243391/lang--en/index.htm.

Radford, Tim. "Evidence Found of Noah's Ark Flood Victims." *Guardian*, September 14, 2000. https://www.theguardian.com/science/2000/sep/14/internationalnews.archaeology.

Reardon, Sara. "New Life for Pig Organs." *Nature* 527, November 12, 2015. http://www.nature.com/polopoly_fs/1.18768!/menu/main/topColumns/topLeftColumn/pdf/527152a.pdf.

Regalado, Antonio. "Human-Animal Chimeras Are Gestating on U.S. Research Farms." *MIT Technology Review*, January 6, 2016. https://www.technologyreview.com/s/545106/human-animal-chimeras-are-gestating-on-us-research-farms.

"Regional Overview for the Middle East, and North Africa: MENA Gender Equality Profile." United Nations Children's Fund (UNICEF) Egypt, 2011. http://www.unicef.org/gender/files/REGIONAL-Gender-Eqaulity-Profile-2011.pdf

"Regulation of Stem cell research in Europe." EuroStemCell, n.d. https://www.eurostemcell.org/regulation-stem-cell-research-europe.

"A Reimagined Research Strategy for Aging." SENS Research Foundation, n.d. http://www.sens.org/research/introduction-to-sens-research.

Richlin, Amy. "Sexuality in the Roman Empire." In *A Companion to the Roman Empire*, edited by David S. Potter. Chichester, West Sussex, UK: Blackwell, 2006.

Richter, Elihu, and Alex Barnea. "Tehran's Genocidal Incitement Against Israel." *Middle East Quarterly*, Summer 2009. Accessed at http://www.genocidewatch.org/images/Iran_09_SummerTehran_s_Genocidal_Incitement_Against_Israel.pdf.

Rohde, Douglas L. T., Steve Olson, and Joseph T. Chang. "Modelling the Recent Common Ancestry of All Living Humans." *Nature* 431, no, 7008 (2004).

Riffkin, Rebecca. "New Record Highs in Moral Acceptability." Gallup News (May 30, 2014). http://www.gallup.com/poll/170789/new-record-highs-moral-acceptability.aspx.

Right to Life of Michigan. "Abortion Is Not the Most Common Medical Procedure." Right to Life of Michigan, October 30, 2017. http://www.nationalrighttolifenews.org/news/2017/10/abortion-not-common-medical-procedure/.

Rothman, Peter. "Biology is Technology—DARPA Is Back in the Game with a Big Vision and It Is H+." *h+ Magazine*, February 15, 2015. http://hplusmagazine.com/2015/02/15/biology-technology-darpa-back-game-big-vision-h/.

Rummel, Rudolph J. "20th Century Democide." Powerkills website. http://www.hawaii.edu/powerkills/20TH.HTM.

Ruscillo, Deborah. "When Gluttony Ruled!" *Archaeology* 54, no. 6 (November/December 2001). http://archive.archaeology.org/0111/abstracts/romans.html.

"Russia, China Continue to Allow Human Trafficking." *Washington Post*, June 23, 2013.

Sample, Ian. "GM Embryos: Time for Ethics Debate, Say Scientists." *Guardian*, September 2, 2015. https://www.theguardian.com/science/2015/sep/01/editing-embryo-dna-genome-major-research-funders-ethics-debate.

———. "Scientists Genetically Modify Human Embryos in Controversial World First." *Guardian*, April 23, 2015. https://www.theguardian.com/science/2015/apr/23/scientists-genetically-modify-human-embryos-in-controversial-world-first.

Sandbrook, Dominic. "A Nordic Civilisation on the Lost Continent of Atlantis." *Telegraph*, March 5, 2006. http://www.telegraph.co.uk/culture/books/3650719/A-Nordic-civilisation-on-the-lost-continent-of-Atlantis.html.

Sanders, N. K., trans. *The Epic of Gilgamesh*. Assyrian International News Agency. http://www.aina.org/books/eog/eog.pdf.

Schaffer, Michael D. "Sex-abuse Crisis Is a Watershed in the Roman Catholic Church's History in America." *Philadelphia Inquirer*, June 25, 2012.

Schmandt, Brandon, Steven D. Jacobsen, Thorsten W. Becker, Zhenxian Liu, and Kenneth G. Dueker. "Dehydration Melting at the Top of the Lower Mantle." *Science* 344, no. 6189 (June 13, 2014). http://science.sciencemag.org/content/344/6189/1265.

Scholz, Birte, and Estera Wieja. "Marching for Life: German Pastor Healing Wounds by Confronting Nazi Past." *Jerusalem Post Christian Edition*, January 2012.

Snelling, Andrew A. "Coal Beds and Noah's Flood." *Answers in Genesis*, June 1, 1986.

———. "Geologic Evidences for the Genesis Flood." *Answers in Genesis*, September 18, 2007.

Spoerl, Joseph S. "Review of 'Matthias Küntzel, Germany and Iran: From the Aryan Axis to the Nuclear Threshold'." *Jerusalem Center for Public Affairs*, May 24, 2016.

Staedter, Tracy. "Adult Human Ear Grown on a Rat." *Discovery*, January 25, 2016. http://news.discovery.com/tech/biotechnology/adult-human-ear-grown-on-a-rat-160125.htm#mkcpgn=rssnws1.

Stein, G. J. "Biological Science and the Roots of Nazism." *American Scientist*, 76 (1988).

"Stem Cell Information." National Institutes of Health, US Department of Health and Human Services, 2015. http://stemcells.nih.gov/info/basics/pages/basics4.aspx.

Sternhell, Ze'ev. "Fascist Ideology." In *Fascism: A Reader's Guide*, edited by Walter Laqueur. Harmondsworth, UK: Penguin, 1976.

Streett, Daniel R. "As It Was in the Days of Noah: The Prophets Typological Interpretation of Noah's Flood." *Criswell Theological Review* 5 (Fall 2007). http://scholar.googleusercontent.com/scholar?q=cache:bzmMNLO5gy4J:scholar.google.com/+days+of+Noah+Hebrew+%22Isaiah+54%22&hl.

Stricherz, Vince. "Vince Stricherz, "New Book Explores Noah's Flood; Says Bible and Science Can Get Along." UWNews, University of Washington, August 14, 2012. http://www.washington.edu/news/2012/08/14/new-book-explores-noahs-flood-says-bible-and-science-can-get-along/.

Thomas, Brian. "Mother of All Humans Lived 6,000 Years Ago," Institute for Creation Research, September 7, 2010. https://www.icr.org/article/5657/.

Thompson, Bert, and Brad Harrub. "How Many Times Does 'Mitochondrial Eve' Have to Die?" Apologetics Press, In the News, n,d. http://espanol.apologeticspress.org/articles/2332.

"Thousands Forced into Sex Slavery to Satisfy Perverted Fantasies of the Rich." *Express Gazeta* (Kosovo). Translated into English by *Pravda*, June 25, 2007. http://www.pravdareport.com/society/stories/25-06-2007/93968-sex_slavery-0/.

Tigay, Chanan. "Ex-Colleague: Expedition Faked Noah's Ark Find," AOL News, April 29, 2010.

Titova, Nadya, and Frank Brown. "Stem Cell Rip-Off." *Newsweek*, November 8, 2004.

Tomkins, Jeffrey P. "New Research Evaluating Similarities Between Human and Chimpanzee DNA." Institute for Creation Research, n.d. http://www.icr.org/i/pdf/technical/Research-Evaluating-Similarities-Human-Chimp-DNA.pdf.

"Transhumanist FAQ," *h+ Magazine*. http://hplusmagazine.com/transhumanist-faq/.

Trefil, James. "Evidence for a Flood," *Smithsonian*, April 1, 2000. http://www.smithsonianmag.com/science-nature/evidence-for-a-flood-102813115/.

Trimarchi, Maria. Maria Trimarchi, "Was There Really a Great Flood?" *How Stuff Works*, n.d. http://science.howstuffworks.com/nature/climate-weather/storms/great-flood.htm.

United Nations. "World Report on Violence Against Children." United Nations, 2006.

US Department of State, Office to Monitor and Combat Trafficking in Persons. "The Facts About Child Sex Tourism, February 29, 2008.

Viegas, Jennifer. "Infanticide Common in Roman Empire," *Discovery News*, May 5, 2011. http://www.seeker.com/infanticide-common-in-roman-empire-1765237924.html#news.discovery.com.

Vinge, Vernor. "The Coming Technological Singularity." *Whole Earth Review*, Winter 1993. See https://edoras.sdsu.edu/~vinge/misc/singularity.html3.

Voice of the Islamic Republic of Iran. "Rafsanjani's Quds Day Speech." Voice of the Islamic Republic of Iran, Tehran, December 14, 2001. Translated by BBC Worldwide Monitoring.

Volokh, Eugene. "Statutory Rape Laws and Ages of Consent in the U.S." *Washington Post*, May 1, 2015.

Wade, Nicholas. Long-Held Beliefs Are Challenged by New Human Genome Analysis," *New York Times*, February 12, 2001. http://www. nytimes.com/2001/02/12/us/long-held-beliefs-are-challenged-by-new-human-genome-analysis.html.

———. "Researchers Say They Created a 'Synthetic Cell'." *New York Times*, May 20, 2010. http://www.nytimes.com/2010/05/21/science/21cell.html.

Warner, Brian. "Charles Darwin and John Herschel," *South African Journal of Science* 105 (November/December 2009). http://www.sajs. co.za/sites/default/files/publications/pdf/147-583-1-PB.pdf.

Walker, Tas. "Whale Fossil Graveyard in Chile Formed Late in Noah's Flood," *Biblical Geology*, n.d. http://biblicalgeology.net/blog/whale-fossil-graveyard-chile/.

Weber, Jeremy, and Ted Olsen. "Wheaton College, Larycia Hawkins to 'Part Ways'." *Christianity Today*, February 6, 2016.

Wyhe, John van. "Charles Darwin: Gentleman Naturalist," 2008, *The Complete Works of Darwin Online*, John van Wyhe, ed. 2002–. http://darwin-online.org.uk/darwin.html.

Wilkins, Alasdair. "How Mitochondrial Eve Connected All Humanity and Rewrote Human Evolution." *io9 Backgrounder*, January 24, 2012. http://io9.gizmodo.com/5878996/how-mitochondrial-eve-connected-all-humanity-and-rewrote-human-evolution.

Wilkins, John S. "Darwin." In *A Companion to the Philosophy of History and Historiography: Blackwell Companions to Philosophy*, edited by Aviezer Tucker. Chichester, UK: Wiley-Blackwell, 2008.

Wingert, Pat. "Priests Commit No More Abuse than Other Males." *Newsweek*, April 8, 2010. http://europe.newsweek.com/priests-commit-no-more-abuse-other-males-70625?rm=eu.

———. "Sex Abuse in the Church: Girls Also Victimized." *Newsweek*, April 14, 2010. http://www.newsweek.com/sex-abuse-church-girls-also-victimized-70741.

Zoll, Rachel. "Letters: Catholic Bishops Warned in '50s of Abusive Priests." Associated Press. Published in *USA Today*, March 31, 2009.

Zylstra, Sarah Eekhoff. "John Kerry: ISIS Is Responsible for Genocide Against Christians." *Christianity Today*, March 17, 2016.

Speeches

Kennedy, John F. "Inaugural Address," Washington, D.C., January 20, 1961.

Videos and TV Reports

Ashford, Janet, prod. *The Timeless Way: A History of Birth from Ancient to Modern Times*. Injoy Videos, 1998.

British Broadcasting Corporation. "Irish Church Knew Abuse 'Endemic.'" BBC News. May 20, 2009. http://news.bbc.co.uk/2/hi/europe/8059826.stm.

———. "Sex Crimes and the Vatican." *Panorama*, BBC, January 6, 2006. Transcript available at http://news.bbc.co.uk/2/hi/programmes/panorama/5402928.stm.

Fox News. "Does New Evidence Point to Noah's Ark?" Fox News, October 16, 2015. http://video.foxnews.com/v/4561729115001/does-new-evidence-point-to-noahs-ark/?#sp=show-clips.

TED Talks. "Cynthia Kenyon Experiments That Hint of Longer Lives." Ted Talks, July 2011. Video and transcript available at www.ted.com/.

———. "Dan Buettner: How to Live to Be 100." Ted Talks, September 2009. Video and transcript available at www.ted.com/.

———. "On the Verge of Creating Synthetic Life." Ted Talks, n.d. Accessed at http://ieet.org/.

Websites

http://archive.adl.org (Anti-Defamation League)

http://archive.archaeology.org (*Archaeology* online archive: Archaeological Institute of America)

http://articles.philly.com (*Philadelphia Inquirer* online archive) http://aspe.hhs.gov (US Department of Health and Human Services, ASPE Office)

http://avalon.law.yale.edu (Avalon Project online archive, Yale Law School library)

http://bobdylan.com (Bob Dylan official site: Sony Music Entertainment)

http://biblicalgeology.net (Tas Walker's Biblical Geology)

http://biodiversitylibrary.org (Biodiversity Heritage Library)

http://chartsbin.com (ChartsBin)

http://creation.com (Creation Ministries International)

http://darwin-online.org.uk (The Complete Works of Charles Darwin Online, John van Wyhe, editor).

http://discovermagazine.com (*Discover* magazine)

http://edition.cnn.com (Cable News Network, CNN)

http://espanol.apologeticspress.org (Apologetics Press)

http://etc.usf.edu (Educational Technology Clearinghouse, University of South Florida)

http://europe.newsweek.com (*Newsweek*, European edition)

http://galton.org (Sir Francis Galton online archive, Gavan Tredoux, editor)

http://genome.cshlp.org (Genome Research, Cold Spring Harbor Laboratory Press)

http://godawa.com (Official site of author Brian Godawa)

http://hplusmagazine.com (*h+* magazine, Humanity Plus)

http://ieet.org (Institute for Ethics and Emerging Technologies)

http://io9.gizmodo.com (Gizmodo blog)

http://jcpa.org (Jerusalem Center for Public Affairs)

http://journals.plos.org (PLOS Biology)

http://link.springer.com (Springer International Publishing)

http://news.bbc.co.uk (News site of British Broadcasting Corporation) http://news.discovery.com (News site of Discovery Communications)

http://news.nationalgeographic.com (News site of National Geographic Society)

http://ngm.nationalgeographic.com (*National Geographic* magazine)

http://noahsarksearch.com (Noah's Ark Search, B. J. Corbin, editor)

http://nwcreation.net (Northwest Creation Network)

http://penelope.uchicago.edu (University of Chicago libraries, James Eason, editor)

http://peterennsonline.com (Peter Enns site)

http://prostitutionresearch.com (Prostitution Research & Education)

http://reasonandmeaning.com (Reason and Meaning blog, John G. Messerly, editor)

http://religionnews.com (Religion News Service)

http://samizdat.qc.ca (Samizdat blog)

http://scholar.googleusercontent.com (Google Scholar online library)

http://science.howstuffworks.com (How Stuff Works site, InfoSpace Holdings LLC.)

http://science.sciencemag.org (*Science*, American Association for the Advancement of Science.

http://stemcells.nih.gov (National Institutes of Health, US Department of Health and Human Services)

http://us2000.org (US2000 blog)

https://answersingenesis.org (Answers in Genesis)

https://archive.org (Internet Archive online library)

https://bookmate.com (Bookmate e-book service)

https://books.google.co.il (Google Books online library)

https://cbdreader.christianbook.com (Christian Book e-Reader service)

https://cbhd.org (The Center for Bioethics & Human Dignity, Trinity International University) https://docs.google.com (Google Docs online library)

https://en.wikiquote.org (WikiQuote online library)

https://erc.europa.eu (European Research Council)

https://etherwave.wordpress.com (Ether Wave Propaganda blog)

www.abc.net.au (Australian Broadcasting Corporation)

www.abrahamlincolnonline.org (Abraham Lincoln Online archive)

www.aina.org (Assyrian International News Agency)

www.americancatholic.org (Franciscan Media site)

www.amnesty.org (Amnesty International)

www.ancient.eu (Ancient History Encyclopedia)

www.ancienttexts.org (Academy for Ancient Texts)

www.apa.org (American Psychological Association)

www.archives.gov (The U.S. National Archives and Records Administration)

www.arlingtoncemetery.net (Arlington National Cemetery site)

www.astrobio.net (*Astrobiology Magazine*)

www.barna.org (Barna Research Group)

www.baseinstitute.org (Bible Archaeology, Search & Exploration Institute)

www.biography.com (*Biography* site, A&E Television Networks)

www.britannica.com (*Encyclopedia Britannica*)

www.catholicherald.co.uk (*Catholic Herald* [UK])

www.charismanews.com (*Charisma* news site)

www.christianitytoday.com (*Christianity Today*)

www.christianquotes.info (Christian Quotes site, Telling Ministries)

www.coe.int (Council of Europe)

www.correlatesofwar.org (The Correlates of War Project, Plone Foundation) www.dailymail.co.uk (*Daily Mail* Online)

www.darpa.mil (Defense Advanced Research Projects Agency)

www.dni.gov (Office of the Director of National Intelligence)

www.earlyjewishwritings.com (Early Jewish Writings, Peter Kirby, editor)

www.economist.com (*Economist*)

www.embl.de (European Molecular Biology Laboratory)

www.encyclopedia.com (Encyclopedia.com)

www.engadget.com (Engadget tech site)

www.eurekalert.org (Eurekalert, American Association for the Advancement of Science)

www.eurostemcell.org (EuroStemCell)

www.evolutionnews.org (Evolution News and Views)

www.foxnews.com (Fox News)

www.ft.com (*Financial Times*)

www.gallup.com (Gallup polling firm)

www.gatestoneinstitute.org (Gatestone Institute International Policy Council)

www.genocidewatch.org (Genocide Watch, International Alliance to End Genocide)

www.genome.gov (National Human Genome Research Institute)

www.globalslaveryindex.org (The Global Slavery Index)

www.goodreads.com (Goodreads online community)

www.guttmacher.org (Guttmacher Institute)

www.hawaii.edu (University of Hawaii system)

www.heritage-history.com (Heritage History Academy electronic library)

www.history.com (History Channel, A&E Television Networks)

www.huffingtonpost.com (Huffington Post)

www.icr.org (Institute for Creation Research)

www.ilo.org (International Labour Organization)

www.ipsnews.net (Inter Press Service News Agency)

www.jewish-american-society-for-historic-preservation.org (JASHP)

www.jewishvirtuallibrary.org (Jewish Virtual Library, American-Israeli Cooperative Enterprise)

www.jimhopper.com (Jim Hopper blog)

www.jpost.com (*Jerusalem Post*)

www.jta.org (Jewish Telegraphic Agency)

www.livescience.com (Live Science, Purch [Tech Media Network])

www.macroevolution.net (Macroevolution.net, Gene McCarthy, editor)

www.motherjones.com (*Mother Jones*, Foundation for National Progress)

www.nature.com (*Nature*, Nature Research)

www.natureworldnews.com (Nature World News)

www.nbcnews.com (NBC News)

www.ncbi.nlm.nih.gov (U.S. National Institutes of Health)

www.news.discovery.com (Discovery Communications, division of Group Nine Media)

www.nickbostrom.com (Nick Bostrom blog)

www.notable-quotes.com (Notable Quotes)

www.nybooks.com (*New York Review of Books*)

www.nytimes.com (*New York Times*)

www.palwatch.org (Palestinian Media Watch)

www.pef.org.uk (The Palestine Exploration Fund)

www.pewforum.org (Pew Research Center)

www.pravdareport.com (Pravda.Ru)

www.presidency.ucsb.edu (The American Presidency Project, University of California, Santa Barbara) www.protectionproject.org (The Protection Project)

www.psychwww.com (Psych Web, Russell A. Dewey, editor)

www.quotetab.com (Quote Tab)

www.regent.edu (Regent University)

www.reuters.com (Reuters News Agency, Thomson Reuters)

www.revival-library.org (The Revival Library, Tony Cauchi, editor)

www.roman-emperors.org (*De Imperatoribus Romanis*: An Online Encyclopedia of Roman Rulers and Their Families)

www.roman-empire.net (Illustrated History of the Roman Empire)

www.sacred-texts.com (Internet Sacred Text Archive)

www.sajs.co.za (South African Journal of Science, Academy of Science of South Africa.

www.sciencedaily.com (ScienceDaily, Dan Hogan, editor)

www.scientificamerican.com (*Scientific American*, Springer Nature)

www.sens.org (SENS Research Foundation)

www.sfgate.com (*San Francisco Chronicle*)

www.signatureinthecell.com (*Signature in the Cell* book blog, Stephen C. Meyer, author)

www.skeptic.com (eSkeptic, the Skeptics Society)

www.smithsonianmag.com (*Smithsonian*, Smithsonian Institution)

www.spiegel.de (*Der Spiegel* Online)

www.state.gov (US Department of State)

www.stemcellresearchfacts.org (Stem Cell Research Facts)

www.technologyreview.com (*MIT Technology Review*)

www.ted.com (TED Institute Talks: Technology, Entertainment and Design)

www.telegraph.co.uk (*Telegraph* [UK])

www.tested.com (*Tested* TV series, Whalerock Industries)

www.theatlantic.com (*Atlantic* magazine, The Atlantic Monthly Group)

www.thecanadianencyclopedia.ca (*The Canadian Encyclopedia* online, Historica Foundation)

www.theguardian.com (*Guardian* [UK])

www.timesofisrael.com (*Times of Israel*)

www.ucmp.berkeley.edu (University of California Museum of Paleontology)

ww.ugcs.caltech.edu (UnderGraduate Computer Science, California Institute of Technology)

www.unicef.org (United Nations International Children's Emergency Fund)

www.unviolencestudy.org (United Nations Secretary-General's Study on Violence Against Children)

www.usatoday.com (*USA Today*)

www.ussc.gov (U.S. Sentencing Commission)

www.washingtonpost.com (*Washington Post*)

www.washington.edu (University of Washington)

www.webroot.com (Webroot Cybersecurity)

www.wnd.com (*World Net Daily*)

www.worldmag.com (*World* magazine)

www.worldreligiondatabase.org (World Religion Database, Todd M. Johnson and Brian J. Grim, editors)

www.wsj.com (*Wall Street Journal*)

www.wyattmuseum.com (Wyatt Archaeological Research)

www.youtube.com (YouTube)

ABOUT THE AUTHOR

D avid R. Parsons is an author, attorney, journalist, ordained minister, and Middle East specialist who serves as Vice President and Senior Spokesman for the International Christian Embassy Jerusalem. Based in Jerusalem for the past twenty years, Parsons has been responsible for the Christian Embassy's public relations and media contacts with the Israeli and foreign press corps, as well as for managing and editing its various publications, among other duties.

Parsons earned a BA in History (1981) and a Juris Doctorate degree (1986) from Wake Forest University. After practicing law in his home state of North Carolina for five years, he served from 1991 to 1995 in Washington, DC, as General Counsel and a registered pro-Israel lobbyist for the Christians' Israel Public Action Campaign.

Parsons first began serving with the International Christian Embassy in Jerusalem in 1995. Since becoming the ICEJ media spokesman in 1997, he has conducted interviews with hundreds of print and broadcast journalists from around the world. His commentaries and other writings also have been published in newspapers and journals worldwide.

Parsons served for eight years as coeditor of the monthly magazine *The Jerusalem Post Christian Edition*. He also spent ten years producing and co-hosting *Front Page Jerusalem*, the premier Christian radio talk show out of Israel.

In December 2008, he received an honorary ordination from the Liberty Christian Fellowship ministerial association out of Dallas, Texas.

Originally from the Outer Banks of North Carolina, Parsons lives in Jerusalem with his wife, Josepha, and son, Yonathan Amos.

Floodgates Blog

For more information on *Floodgates*, please visit: www.floodgatesblog.com.
There you will find:
Updates and commentaries from the author
Photos and illustrations related to the book
Reviews by peers
Endorsements by Christian leaders
Reactions from other readers
Videos about the author and the inspiration behind *Floodgates*

Donations

If you would like to join in the "building up of Zion,"
please donate on-line at: www.icej.org/buildupzion

Or direct your donations to:
International Christian Embassy Jerusalem
PO Box 1192
Jerusalem 91010-02 Israel

To support the teaching ministry of David Parsons,
please direct your donations to:
Dayspring Farms
PO Box 163
Kill Devil Hills, NC 27948
USA